The Elements of
Logical Analysis and Inference

The Elements of

Logical Analysis and Inference

MAX HOCUTT / *The University of Alabama*

Winthrop Publishers, Inc.   **Cambridge, Massachusetts**

© 1979 by Winthrop Publishers, Inc.
17 Dunster Street, Cambridge, Massachusetts

10 9 8 7 6 5 4 3 2 1

Text and Cover Design by Amato Prudente

Library of Congress Cataloging in Publication Data

Hocutt, Max
    The elements of logical analysis and inference.
    Includes index.
    1. Logic.   I. Title.
BC50.H62   160   78-27190
ISBN 0-87626-220-5

For
JIMMY
and
SANDRA

Contents

vii

Contents

UNIT III | Arguments

ix

Contents

Contents

Preface

There is at least one x such that x is a logic textbook, but there is room for another if it is different in ways that make it better. I am not the one to judge whether this book is better, but I may say how it is different.

First, it differs in organization. I have designed it with pedagogy in mind. Instead of being composed of a few long chapters, it has forty-one short ones, one for each day of the typical semester course. Each unit attempts to teach one well-defined lesson and is followed by exercises designed to reinforce the lesson. This should make the book extremely easy to use. Just begin at the beginning and cover a chapter a day until the book is finished.

The forty-one chapters comprise a reasonably complete introduction to logic, both deductive and inductive, in both its semantic and its formal aspects. If you think your students are not up to covering this much material, omit Chapters 36–41 on statistics or Chapters 29–35 on quantification, and adjust your schedule accordingly. I think you will find, though, that the book is already written at a low enough level and paced slowly enough so that it can easily be mastered by lower level undergraduates in state universities. Students will find the course not half so demanding or difficult as freshman algebra.

The chapters are arranged so that there is a grading of difficulty and continuous progress from beginning to end, simple topics coming before complex ones and later lessons building on earlier lessons. For example, on the premise that analyzing and appraising arguments in natural English should be the end of a logic course, not the beginning, I start with single statements and truth conditions and do not mention groupings of statements or validity until much later, when the student is better equipped to deal with them. When I do introduce arguments, they are artificially simple. I do not ask the student to schematize difficult examples before I have taught him to evaluate easy ones. In short, I reverse the standard order of proceeding, which requires students to fathom

Preface

some very sophisticated pieces of argumentative discourse before teaching them the logical alphabet.

The forty-one chapters also constitute an integrated whole. Rightly understood, logic is all of a piece, but most textbooks make it seem otherwise. The standard text has a section on informal logic, another on formal deductive logic, and still another on inductive logic. It treats these as if they have nothing to do with one another. By contrast, I make the formal logic of truth functions grow out of truth value semantics and I connect induction with deduction by showing how to substitute numbers for truth values so as to get probabilities, and by showing how modus tollens and probability combine to yield experimental reasoning. The result should be both a broader view of the whole and a deeper insight into the parts.

My book not only differs in outline, but also in content, both in what it includes and in what it omits. Most importantly, all the logic that I introduce is truth functional, even the quantification and the statistics. Put another way, I limit coverage to the simplest parts of logic, omitting such complexities as multivariate quantification altogether. I do this because the simplest parts of logic are also the most useful and the easiest to understand and because truth functional logic has the great advantage that decision procedures are available and easily inculcated.

I have done all that I can to make logic easy, but I have resisted the temptation to make it easy by replacing it by something else. The mistaken notion that formal logic is dull and useless has led many teachers and writers of logic texts to spend more time on "informal logic." Few have paused to reflect that "informal logic" is a contradiction in terms—logic is formal, by definition. "Informal logic" is really rhetoric and although rhetoric is an important and fascinating study, it is better taught by the speech department than by logicians. People think dealing with words easier and more practical than having to use abstract symbols, but this is the reverse of the truth. Nothing is more complicated than propaganda, nothing is simpler than modus ponens, and I don't see how a person who can't spot a fallacy of affirming the consequent will be able to spot the far more subtle sin of appealing to one's unconscious aversions and desires. Logic, being basic to everything else, is the simplest and most useful study there is. So this is unapologetically a book of real—that is to say, formal—logic.

Since this *is* a book of logic, it does not contain a section on "informal fallacies," but many of that odd collection of sophisms, confusions, and errors find places elsewhere.* Equivocation and the various sorts of ambiguity that can cause it

---

* For a thorough scholarly and analytical critique of the notion of "informal fallacy," see C. L. Hamblin's excellent book, *Fallacies*, Methuen and Co. Ltd., London, 1970.

are discussed at length in the section on semantics, as are definitions, the means of resolving ambiguities. Hasty generalization is considered in connection with reasoning from samples. Division and composition come in when I treat 'some' and 'all'. And so on. Only "fallacies of relevance," that is, appeals to emotion, are omitted altogether; but, given that nobody knows how to define relevance, that is just as well. What we cannot define, we cannot teach. Of course, we can teach '*ad hominem*' and the like, but so can the speech department.

What I have done to make logic easier is to resist asking the student to deal with formulas of a complexity greater than those he is likely to encounter in daily life: nothing in nineteen variables when two will make the point just as well. What I have done to make logic more interesting and more useful to more people is to emphasize applications rather than theory. An example will illustrate what I mean: When most books take up proof construction they provide a short and economical list of elementary rules, and they set a high standard of rigor. By contrast, I give a long and redundant set of rules, and am somewhat casual about rigor. Doing so has two pronounced advantages. First, it makes constructing proofs easy, even for less ingenious students. Second, it familiarizes the student with a very large number of elementary argument forms. By including in my list a rule allowing transformation of statements in accordance with definitions, I facilitate application of the formal rules to natural languages.

I reserve no section for categorical syllogisms, but they are here. They have just been absorbed into a broader discussion of quantificational inference and treated as a special case. Because I see no clear sense in which the predicate of a particular negative is distributed, I teach Venn diagrams instead of the traditional rules of distribution. Incidentally, I offer a novel, truth functional treatment of the traditional square of opposition and of other immediate inferences.

I put a great deal more emphasis than is usual upon the metalogical concepts of consistency, implication, and equivalence. Since people use these every day, I think it important that they understand them, but my emphasis, as always, is upon grasping the concepts, not on dealing with difficult cases.

Perhaps the most novel feature of the book is its inclusion of a section on statistical inference. This replaces the usual section on "inductive" logic. In place of Mill's methods, I offer the sign test and coefficients of correlation, which are far superior. In place of loose talk about reasoning by analogy (unless you can tell someone how to identify and count "respects," it does no good to explain that an analogy is better if the things are alike in more respects), I offer a reasonably exact, but simple, discussion of reasoning from samples. The passing of induction will be mourned by some, but I am not among them. I believe the logic of scientific inference to be hypothetico-deductive, not inductive after Mill's fashion. In fact, I don't believe there is any such thing as inductive logic. Logic is deductive; reasoning is valid, or it is invalid. This applies, as my own treatment illustrates, even to probability inference, which is strictly deductive in form. "Induction" is better thought of as guesswork, the formation of hypotheses to be tested in accordance with strict canons of reasoning. If this is right, a treatment like mine is long overdue.

I have egoistically and egotistically called this "my book," but many people helped to make it. Everyone who knows Willard Quine's writings will discover immediately where I learned most of what I have put into the book.

Readers for the publisher, Donald Marquis and Robert Kimball, made many helpful suggestions and saved me from many egregious errors. Especially useful was the long and detailed critique done by Hugh McCann. My colleague, Kathleen Johnson Wu, helped me with the section on quantification and my friend, James Mclean, checked out the section on statistics. My wife, Lois Etheredge Hocutt, typed most of the manuscript and helped in many small ways to make it a better one. Winthrop's copy editor, Janice Bolster, found countless bugs in what I had smugly thought to be first rate copy, and suggested several useful additions. Winthrop's production editor, Herbert Nolan, is responsible for the handsome format of the text. I wish I could think of somebody as responsible for the vices of the book as these people are for its virtues, but I can't. I am grateful to them all, as I am to Winthrop's editor, Paul O'Connell, who would not let the conversation stop at "You must be kidding! Another logic text?" If this book has sufficient merit to justify its existence, these people deserve much of the credit.

Max Hocutt

The Elements of
Logical Analysis and Inference

UNIT I

Semantics

I / True Statements and False Statements

Statements

Biologists study cells; geologists study rocks; mathematicians study numbers; logicians study statements. Biologists tell us how to distinguish live cells from dead; mathematicians tell us how to distinguish even numbers from odd; geologists tell us how to distinguish igneous rocks from sedimentary; logicians tell us how to distinguish true statements from false.* Since it is very important to be able to distinguish true statements from false ones, logic is very important.

What is a *statement*? We shall here use the word to mean anything that is true or false, anything that has *truth value*. For example, it is true that $2 + 2 = 4$ and false that all rocks are igneous. So "$2 + 2 = 4$" and "All rocks are igneous" count as statements.

Statements are normally made by *using* (that is, uttering, inscribing, and so on) declarative sentences, as questions are asked by using interrogative sentences and commands are given by using imperative sentences. Questions and commands don't have truth value. "Is the door closed?" has an answer but no truth value. "Close the door!" can be obeyed or disobeyed, but it is not either true or false, and it cannot be affirmed or denied. Truth and falsity, then, are properties of the use (the utterance, inscription, and so on) of certain declarative sentences on certain occasions

---

* These informal remarks are not intended as definitions. Their function is solely to introduce the topic.

3

to say what is so or is not so. The use of such a sentence on such an occasion constitutes the making of a statement, which statement is either true or false.

To the remark that only statements have truth value, you might object that other things besides statements can be true and false—for example, beliefs. This is a reasonable objection, but beliefs can be stated, and the statement is what is true or false. In fact, you can't say what a belief is without stating it: to identify the belief that granite is an igneous rock, you have to mention the statement "Granite is an igneous rock." So beliefs are not exceptions to the rule that only statements are true or false.

Nor is love an exception. "True love" would be better described as "genuine love" or perhaps as "steadfast love." "False love" is not, truly speaking, love at all. It would be better described as an imitation, or pretense, of love. What are true or false in the literal senses of these words are statements that someone loves someone or declarations of love, like "I love you." By contrast, a false statement is just as truly a statement, if not just as true a statement, as a true one.

We have remarked that only statements have truth value, that anything either true or false is a statement. We should now observe that all statements have truth value, that every statement is either true or false. It doesn't matter that we don't know which. No one knows whether Betelgeuse has planets, but the statement "Betelgeuse has planets" is either true or false, and it can't be both.

"Nonsensical statements" may seem to be exceptions to this rule. For example, "Doobles are dabbles" is neither true nor false. This, however, doesn't prove that some statements lack truth value. It isn't a statement; it is just babble. Nonsensical statements are not statements any more than false love is love or sawhorses are horses. A statement makes sense; what doesn't isn't a statement.

The same goes for "incomplete statements." "Toilet Liquid is better" is not true or false unless we are told what Toilet Liquid is better than. The "statement" needs to be completed before it will be a statement. It is not yet a statement. It is a statement in the making, a partial statement; that is, it is part of a statement. Only whole statements have truth value.

What applies to nonsensical statements and incomplete statements also applies to "vague statements," "statements" that have no clear truth value, such as the politician's "I am opposed to unnecessary spending" or "I will vote against excessive taxation and immorality in government." Unnecessary for what? Excessive by what standard? What counts as

4

immorality? Without further interpretation, such "statements" have no truth value. They are therefore not statements in the present strict sense of the word.

As we noted before, statements are made by using sentences. Strictly speaking, it is the sentences used, not the statements made by using them, that are nonsensical, incomplete, or vague. A person may utter a sentence without thereby making a clear, complete, or sensible statement. That is, a person may utter an unclear, incomplete, or nonsensical sentence and fail thereby to say anything that is clearly true or false. Such utterances are called "statements" only by courtesy. It is somewhat like calling a piece of doggerel "bad poetry": "bad poetry" is not poetry at all but an attempt at it that failed. Similarly, the use of a sentence may be an attempt at making a statement that results only in an unclear, incomplete, or nonsensical "statement" and therefore results in no statement.

To our earlier observation that every statement is either true or false, we should add that no statement is both. Again, the exceptions are only apparent. "Ambiguous statements" seem to be exceptions, but they are not. Consider the sentence "All laws are human-made." This is true if said about civil laws, like the law against double-parking, but false if laws of nature, like the law of gravity, are included. Nonetheless, someone who used this sentence would not be making a statement that was both true and false. Whether his "statement" was true or false would depend on what he used the sentence to mean. If by 'laws' he meant civil laws, his statement would be true; if he meant natural laws, it would be false; if he meant both, it would still be false. Nothing he could say would be both true and false.

Obviously, a certain amount of idealization is involved in thus speaking. You might protest that, according to our definition, there are no such things as statements, there being no sentence that is free from ambiguity or vagueness, no sentence that does not admit of further interpretation. Logicians' talk of statements is, however, like physicists' talk of vacuums or geometers' talk of squares. One might as well protest that nothing perfectly suits the definitions of these things, there being no absolutely empty spaces or squares that don't deviate in some minute particular from absolute squarehood. Imperfection, though real, doesn't make talk of perfect vacuums, squares, or statements pointless! No space is absolutely empty, but some spaces come closer than others, and many come close enough for the purposes at hand. No square is without defect if inspected closely enough, but some squares are devoid of imperfection by operating standards. No sentence has completely precise and unequivocal meaning, but some are definite and unequivocal enough to suit.* Just as a space counts as a vacuum if it is empty enough for our purposes, so the use of a sentence will count as a statement if it is clear and complete enough for our purposes.

Truth

We have said that some statements are true, some false. If you have a philosophical temperament or are Pontius Pilate, you will ask, "What is *truth*?" That is usually thought to be a difficult question, and in some ways it is; but you already know the answer. Consider the statement "There is milk in the refrigerator." What is required for that statement to be true? Just that there be milk in the refrigerator. As Aristotle pointed out, if you say what is, your statement is true; if you say what isn't, it is false. Take any statement you like: for example, "The door is closed." That statement is true if the door is closed and false if it isn't. Similarly, the statement "The earth is round" is true if the earth is round and false otherwise.

Hence, there is really not much room for mystification about the question "What is truth?" You already have a fairly good idea. You know what it means to say "It is true that there are eggs in the basket": it means much the same thing as to say "There are eggs in the basket." You understand what it means to call a given statement true if you understand the statement, and you understand the statement if you know what would have to be the case for it to be true. Indeed, that is what it means to *understand* a statement: it means to know what would have to be so if the statement were true. You understand the statement "Yo tengo un dolor de cabeza" if you know that it is true if and only if the speaker has a headache; otherwise, you do not understand it.

Isn't truth relative? A matter of opinion? Some people who think so advance the following argument. They say: "Flat-earthers think the earth to be flat. So it is flat to them. We think the earth to be round. So it is round to us. Hence, the earth is both flat and round, flat to some, round to others." Such people are very confused. Saying that the earth is flat to flat-earthers and round to us doesn't mean that the earth's

---

* Hence, by distinguishing sentences from statements, I don't mean to imply that some statements are not sentences.

shape varies with our opinions. "The earth is flat to flat-earthers" just means that flat-earthers believe that the earth is flat. That doesn't show that the earth is flat. Flat-earthers are wrong; their belief is false.

How do we know? Well, suppose we don't know. Suppose we are wrong. Suppose the earth is flat, as the flat-earthers believe. That still won't prove that truth is relative. Opinions are relative, but truth is not. If the earth is flat, then you and I are wrong to believe it round; the flat-earthers are right. It isn't a question of opinion; it is a question of fact. A statement is true if it states a fact; otherwise, it is false. So "The earth is round" is true if the earth is round, false if the earth is flat.

You will notice that we did not here appeal to the majority opinion. The statement "The earth is round" is not true because it expresses the majority opinion, but because the earth is in fact round, whatever the majority opinion. The earth was not flat when most people thought it flat, and if most people still thought so, it still wouldn't be flat.

Knowledge

In order to make the point that truth doesn't depend on our opinion, or anybody else's, we just pretended that we do not know that the earth is, as we believe, round, but of course we do know. Our opinion is not just an opinion. It is true opinion, genuine knowledge.

How do we know that? In brief, we know it because we can prove it. Demonstrating that the earth is round are the observations that the prow of an outgoing vessel disappears below the horizon before its sails do, that the eclipse of the sun by the earth casts a curved shadow on the moon, and that people have sailed around the earth. The most recent proof is pictures of the earth taken from outer space. Moreover, these are just a few of the facts showing that our opinion is not just a prejudice but well-founded knowledge.

You now understand what it is for a statement to be true, at least insofar as you understand the statement itself. To put it briefly and circularly, a statement is true if it is a fact. You also understand what is required for knowledge that a statement is true: ability to adduce facts that show it to be true; ability to prove it. Later, we shall learn somewhat more fully what is involved in proving something to be true.

7

Exercises

A. Which of the following are, or describe, statements?

    1. 'Twas brillig, and the slithy toves did gyre and gimble in the wabe.

    2. Are you going to town?

    3. X is green.

    4. The earth is a ball.

    5. $9 > 11$

    6. anything that has truth value

    7. Please bring me some water.

    8. interrogative sentences

    9. nonsensical statements

    10. commands

B. Which of the following are true, which false, and which neither?

    1. false teeth

    2. exclamations

    3. Incomplete statements are statements.

    4. 'Twas brillig, and the slithy toves did gyre and gimble in the wabe.

    5. If S is true, S is a statement.

    6. Ambiguous statements may be both true and false.

    7. All laws are human-made.

    8. Truth and falsity are truth values.

    9. "The earth is flat" is true if everybody believes it.

    10. Ambiguous sentences may be used to make statements that are true and statements that are false.

    11. If it has truth value, it is a statement.

    12. Bank statements are statements.

    13. No statement can be both true and false.

    14. Every statement is true or false.

    15. We use sentences to make statements.

16. We may use the same sentence to make different statements.

17. Sentences may be used to produce statements that have no truth value.

18. A sentence can be vague; a statement cannot.

19. Statements are ideals, like perfect vacuums.

20. Truth is majority opinion.

2 / *Ambiguous Sentences*

Causes and Cures of Ambiguity

Sam says, "Dorothy is dumb." As it happens, Dorothy is intelligent but mute. Is Sam's statement true, or is it false? Obviously, it depends on what Sam meant. If he meant that she is speechless, it is true; if he meant that she is stupid, it is false. Our problem is that Sam's words can be taken either way. He made what is usually called an "ambiguous statement." As we have already noted, however, it would be a mistake to declare Sam's statement both true and false, or neither. We should say, rather, that the sentence Sam uttered can be used to make either of two very different statements, one true and the other false. We can't tell from that sentence alone which statement, if either, Sam used it to make. In short, it is the sentence Sam used that is ambiguous, not the statement he used it to make.

The distinguishing mark of an *ambiguous sentence*, then, is that it can be used to make, or can be understood as making, either of two different statements, one true, the other false. Another example of an ambiguous sentence is "George is a big man." No truth value can be assigned to this sentence until we know whether the speaker means to credit George with large size, high social position, or magnanimity. Is he saying that George's volume is considerable, that George's status is high, or that George's character is praiseworthy? Questions of truth must be deferred until we know.

How are we to know? There are two ways. If the speaker is at hand, we can ask him what he meant. We can invite him to restate his point by using

10

a sentence that is less subject to diverse interpretations. Pointing out the ambiguity in the way he bespoke himself, we can encourage him to *resolve* that ambiguity by finding an unambiguous way to express his thought. Thus, we can ask, "Sam, did you mean to say that Dorothy has a low IQ, or that she can't talk?" Similarly, we can ask, "Are you talking about George's height, social standing, or what?" If we are fortunate, the new sentence will be such that we can reasonably interpret it in only one way, and it will be either clearly true or clearly false.

If we must resolve the ambiguity ourselves, the best way to do so is by looking at the context. If Sam was engaged in trying to explain some social gaffe of which Dorothy was guilty, then he was casting aspersions on her intelligence. On the other hand, if he made his remark after having just observed Dorothy make use of sign-language, it records his discovery that she can't speak.

Notice that the word 'context' here refers to both the verbal and the nonverbal surroundings. "Dorothy is dumb" means "Dorothy is stupid" either in association with the words "Dorothy just made the most unbelievable *faux pas*" or in association with the *faux pas* itself. Likewise, if 6′ 3″ George is in your presence, or if you have just been told that George is 6′ 3″, you know that "George is a big man" means that he is tall.

Relevant context can also include more than what occurs at the time of the statement. The remark might have a history, and the speaker certainly will have one, some of it known to the listener, who will find that history useful in interpreting what was said. For example, suppose you know that Sam never uses the word 'dumb' to describe people who can't talk, finding that usage insensitive and offensive. Then you can be reasonably sure that he is not doing so in the present case. Or suppose you know that the person who said "George is a big man" does not regard others as large unless they are over 6′ 6″. That knowledge will enable you to rule out one interpretation in favor of others.

The importance of context cannot be overemphasized. It determines what statement is being made. The use of an ambiguous sentence in one context makes one statement, and use of the same sentence in another context makes a quite different statement. Said in one context, "Dorothy is dumb" means something true; said in another, it means something false. It is the same sentence in both cases, but quite different statements. That is why we earlier defined a statement as a sentence used in a particular context. The context makes the sentence the statement it is. So the context is part of what we are talking about when we talk about the statement made.

11

The sentences we have so far examined are ambiguous by virtue of containing the ambiguous adjectives 'big' and 'dumb'. Sentences may also contain ambiguous names. If we say "Jane Smith went to the party," which Jane Smith do we mean, and which party? There are many, and our sentence will be true of some of them but not of all. If someone asks whether we believe in God, or advises us to do the will of God, which God is meant? We may believe in Allah but not Zeus, in Jehovah but not Osiris. Following the will of one may entail disobeying the will of others.

If names are ambiguous, pronouns are doubly so, for we use pronouns as surrogates for names. When someone says, "She kissed him," which she and which him are meant? "I went shopping" is true or false depending on who is speaking. "You shouldn't take penicillin" is true or false depending on who is listening. "It won't work" is true or false depending on what you mean to denote by 'it' and by 'work'.

Indeed, any part of speech can be ambiguous, including, as the latter example illustrates, verbs. What does the speaker count as 'working'? Was Khrushchev's "We will bury you" threat or prophecy? Is "Our mothers bore us" in the past tense or the present?

Simple ambiguities can be thus blamed on a single word, but other ambiguities must be attributed to word groupings, there being words that have different grammatical functions in different combinations. Think of the expression 'sea horse'. If you didn't know better, you might think it has a grammar similar to 'gray horse', which designates a kind of horse; but a gray horse is both gray and a horse, whereas a sea horse is neither a sea nor even a horse. In 'gray horse' both terms have *attributive* use, each being true of that of which the compound of the two is true. By contrast, in 'sea horse' both terms have *syncategorematic* use, neither alone describing what the two together describe. Unlike 'gray horse', 'sea horse' is an indissoluble unit, better thought of as one word than the two it appears to be. Perhaps a hyphen between the words, to indicate their essential unity, would be in order. Of course, you would never be tempted to think of a sea horse as being a horse. The expression is not ambiguous to you, but we encountered an expression in the first chapter that was ambiguous because of syncategorematic use. We spoke there of "false love," which we decided is neither false nor love but a pretense of love, or perhaps a false declaration of love—something that it would be false to describe as love. 'False' and 'statement' are used attributively in 'false statement', but 'false' and 'love' are used syncategorematically in 'false love'.

Another construction in which words play a different grammatical role than may seem on the surface to be the case is illustrated by Robert Ingersoll's account of creation. He reports that, in the beginning, God made things *ex nihilo*, out of nothing. "Then," he says, "God ran out of nothing and had to borrow a rib from Adam." Here Ingersoll treats the word 'nothing' as if it were a name of the stuff God made things out of, when the point is rather that there is no such stuff. The same joke is repeated with a variation in the remark about the rich man who started from scratch, the scratch his rich father provided him. Lewis Carroll has fun with this ambiguity when he has the king in *Through The Looking Glass* ask Alice whom she can see on the road. When she answers, "Nobody," he replies fretfully, "I only wish *I* had such eyes! To be able to see Nobody! And at that distance too! Why, it's as much as *I* can do to see real people, by this light!" When the messenger comes along the same road, the king asks him whom he has passed. When he, too, replies, "Nobody," the King says, "Quite right, this young lady saw him too. So of course Nobody walks slower than you." When the messenger sullenly responds, "I do my best. I'm sure nobody walks much faster than I do," the King retorts, witheringly, "He can't do that, or else he'd have been here first."

There is no generic name for such ambiguities unless they may be called *amphibolies*, these being defined as ambiguities caused by looseness, inadequacy or uncertainty of grammatical construction. Perhaps, however, better examples of amphiboly are such ambiguous prepositional constructions as "To Mary John is kind." Does this mean that John treats Mary kindly, or that Mary believes John to be kind? On the first interpretation, the sentence is about John; on the second, it is about Mary. "For me, smoking is good" is even more amphibolous. Does it mean that smoking does the speaker good, that he likes to smoke, or that he approves of smoking? The grammar is so loose that we cannot tell.

Another example of amphiboly is "I saw a horse looking out the window," which suggests that the horse was looking out the window at the speaker, rather than the other way around. An example of amphiboly given by Aristotle is "I wish that you the enemy may capture," which leaves in doubt whether the speaker wants his auditor to be capturer or captured. Sometimes also classified as amphiboly is ambiguity of pronominal cross-reference, as in "Mary was talking to George and Sam when, suddenly, she kissed him," but there is perhaps just as good reason to count this as simple ambiguity of the pronoun 'him'.

Ambiguity caused not so much by looseness of grammatical structure as by insufficiency thereof is illustrated by a sign that used to be common along Alabama roadsides,

Slow Men at Work.

Meant as a command to check one's speed, it was often gleefully taken as caustic comment on the pace of the roadside laborers.

We have seen that simple ambiguities can be resolved by replacing one word or phrase by another. Resolving a grammatical ambiguity requires a more radical measure—restructuring the entire sentence. Thus, "I saw a horse looking out the window" gives way to "Looking out the window, I saw a horse." Similarly, "I see nothing" gives way to "I do not see something." "Slow Men at Work" resolves to "Slow down; men are at work," rather than to "There are slow men at work"; and "I wish that you the enemy may capture" is rephrased as either "I wish that the enemy may capture you" or "I wish that you may capture the enemy."

A source of ambiguity peculiar to writing is punctuation. Is '4 × 9 + 3' to be taken as equal to '39' or as equal to '48'? Parentheses will resolve the matter, yielding either '(4 × 9) + 3' or '4 × (9 + 3)'. If we intend the statement "Give me the man Jones" to be addressed to Jones rather than to be about Jones, we should insert a comma, thus: "Give me the man, Jones."

Written ambiguities may often be resolved in speech by putting the emphasis upon different words, or by letting pauses punctuate, but this process can be more easily illustrated aloud than on paper.

Equivocation

Why worry so much about the causes and cures of ambiguity? Because ambiguity can cause a great deal of trouble. In argument it often causes the fallacy of *equivocation*, which occurs when the same expression is used in two different ways in the same context. An example of equivocal reasoning is: "Mary is mute, therefore dumb. Dumb people are stupid. So Mary is stupid." Here a false conclusion is inferred from a true one by means of an equivocation on the word 'dumb'. The danger of such equivocation is one reason for not calling deaf mutes "dumb."

Equivocation resulting from ambiguous prepositional construction produces the false doctrine that truth is relative. We criticized this reasoning in the first chapter, but it won't hurt to do so again. The argument is that what is true for one person is not true for another, so that truth is relative

14

to persons. Saying that something is "true for Sue" is, however, just a misleading way of saying that Sue believes it to be true. What Sue believes Harry may not. Hence, opinion is relative, but it doesn't follow that truth is. "The earth is flat for flat-earthers" is not about the earth; it is about flat-earthers. It does not say what shape the earth is, but only what shape flat-earthers think it is. Only its amphibolous construction makes one think otherwise.

Not all the troubles caused by ambiguity are so esoteric or so implausible. I once knew of a professor who was fired because someone noticed his name on the list of those regarded by the House Unamerican Activities Committee as "sympathetic to communism." No one noticed until too late that HUAC had a different person by the same name in mind. Such is the harm ambiguity of a name can do. The harm amphiboly can cause is illustrated by the classical example of Croesus, the king of Lydia. The Oracle of Delphi informed him that if he attacked Persia, he would "destroy a great kingdom." He did: his own. Any lawyer will tell you how much money can be cost by some unnoticed ambiguity of syntax, vocabulary, or punctuation in a carelessly written will, contract, or law. It pays to be alert to possible ambiguities.

This is not to say that ambiguity has no uses. It is obvious that the Oracle of Delphi found a use for amphiboly. The syncategorematic expression 'picnic ham' is useful to the grocer, who needn't tell you that pork shoulder isn't suitable for a picnic. There is advantage in being able to phrase lies in a way that may seem true. Nor are all uses of ambiguities pernicious. Puns are often funny. Think of the child's "The moron drowned because he was smoking a cigarette and threw the wrong butt in the river" or of Groucho Marx's "I shot an elephant in my pajamas; what he was doing in my pajamas I'll never know" (I didn't say they were very funny). Poetry has greater meaning precisely because it admits of diverse interpretations. "Full many a flower is born to blush unseen" is rich because it can be read as providing consolation to unappreciated people; when taken as a literal remark about flowers, it is platitudinous, trite. Ambiguity is bad only when you need the literal truth and don't need it admixed with, or obscured by, falsehood.

Vagueness

Ambiguity should not be confused with vagueness. A sentence is ambiguous if it can be taken in a way that is clearly true and also in a way that is clearly false. It is *vague* if neither clearly true nor clearly false. Hence "Barry Goldwater is square" is ambiguous, being true if interpreted to mean that the senator is conservative but false if taken to mean that he is four-cornered and equal-sided. On the other hand, "Barry Goldwater is rich" and "Barry Goldwater is tall" are neither clearly true nor clearly false, Goldwater being of middling wealth and height. Similarly, "Smith is cold" may be true if it means that she is unfriendly and false if the claim is that her temperature is low, but "Smith is intelligent" will be neither clearly true nor clearly false if her IQ is around 100.

In these cases, vagueness is a matter of indeterminacy of boundary. How much wealth is necessary to constitute one a rich person? How high does an IQ have to be to justify describing its possessor as intelligent? Here the vagueness is like that emphasized by the question whether one's middling-sized place of origin counts as a large town or a small city. How large an area or how big a population is required to make a town into a city? Such vagueness will occasion indeterminacy of count. How many continents there are depends on whether the large landmass Eurasia counts as one continent or two. How many poor people there are depends on where you draw the poverty line.

The politician's opposition to "excessive spending" may also illustrate vagueness about boundaries (how much is excessive?), but his opposition to "unnecessary spending" illustrates something else, although it too is usually called "vagueness." So do "George is a nice boy" and "The supreme being exists." In these cases, lack of clarity about truth value is not the product of twilight zones or gray regions. It is explained, rather, by the nature of the words 'unnecessary', 'nice', and 'supreme', which admit of such a variety of diverse interpretations that one has no good idea what might be intended by them. What spending is unnecessary?—domestic spending, military spending? What counts as a nice boy?—a rich one, a well-mannered one, a considerate one, a hard-working one? People have different ideas of supremacy. What is the speaker's? Is the supreme being a person or something impersonal, the universe or the creator of the universe?

Vagueness of whichever variety has both advantage and disadvantage. The advantage is that a vague sentence is less likely to provoke disagreement. That is why, as Jerry Brown has said, "In politics, a little vagueness goes a long way." Opposing domestic spending will alienate welfare advocates; opposing military spending will alienate hawks; opposing unnecessary spending will alienate nobody and may get both hawk and welfare statist on your side. Believing in Allah will please only Muslims;

believing in Jehovah will please only Jews; believing in God will please everybody.

For this advantage a price is paid: the vaguer the sentence, the less it says. The politician who opposes "excessive and unnecessary spending" opposes nothing. He reveals none of his fiscal priorities or plans. The theist who believes only in something vaguely described as a "supreme being" has no definite theological conviction. The person who describes Jack as a "nice" boy tells you nothing at all about Jack. The vague sentence thus gains immunity from falsifiability only by being empty, only by saying practically nothing. A sentence that says something definite and clear runs a definite and clear risk of being shown false. That is why John Stuart Mill was paid a compliment by whoever said, "He wrote so clearly he could be found out."

A fertile source of both vagueness and ambiguity is abstract names, like 'man'. This word is not only ambiguous in denoting both 'male' and 'male plus female'; it is also ambiguous in denoting both the species and its members ("Man has been on earth for fifty million years" is about the species, not about each member of the species). Furthermore, even when a remark is about the members of the species, one cannot always be sure which members it is about. Aristotle said, "Man is a rational animal." Which men was he discussing?—surely not all. I once heard psychologist Bruno Bettleheim say, "Man has a problem of excess leisure." He wasn't talking about me, and I had no idea whom he meant until he complained about wasting time watching television. Then I guessed that he meant working-class people in industrialized societies. Much obscure philosophy is marked by vaporous discourse about that abstraction 'man', and not a little is infected by equally vapid talk about 'woman'.

Vagueness has, like ambiguity, both good uses and bad. It is bad when the exact truth is needed, but it is essential to, for example, diplomacy and polite conversation. Consider "The president and the prime minister had productive talks." That report contributes more to world peace than "They shouted at each other for two hours." How much better it is to say "That was an interesting performance" than "It wasn't too good," or "That's a colorful dress" than "What a loud dress!" while leaving it up to your hearer to interpret your remark in a favorable way.

Minimizing Guesswork

We have noted several causes of ambiguity in sentences: words, grammatical constructions, punctuation, and the possibility of different oral emphasis. We have also noted the cures: asking the speaker what he meant and looking at the context. But what if the speaker can't or won't say what he meant, and what if the context is insufficient to resolve the ambiguity? In that case, you must guess.

Good writers and good speakers of didactic prose try to minimize guesswork and the work of examining context. They want you to know exactly what they mean, and they take measures to see that you have a minimum of difficulty in discovering it. By taking this trouble they cut down their readers' labor. When they introduce a pronoun, they make sure it refers back to something or somebody that has recently been less ambiguously identified. They don't start telling you what "he" did without telling you which he they have in mind. When they wish to praise a book, they don't use all-purpose words like 'good' or 'super'. They choose the right adjective for the specific purpose and call the book "informative," "entertaining," or "gracefully written." Like other skills, however, the skill of precise and unambiguous speech is acquired only through hard work, as is the valuable skill of detecting imprecise and ambiguous speech.

Exercises

A. Classify the following as simple ambiguities, amphibolies, or ambiguities of punctuation. Then resolve them.

1. I read a book going home.

2. *A:* "It is cold today."
   B: "Well, warm it up by the fire."

3. Mary and Sue were talking. She insulted her.

4. Mary is a real Christian, but she doesn't believe in God.

5. We held a meeting to deal with the problem in 1968. (Source: TV news)

6. State Tech hopes to recover from Monday night's loss against State University at home tonight. (Source: Sports page of local paper)

7. According to our textbook, I don't think the existence of God can be proved. (Source: Student exam)

8. $2 + 3 \times 4 = 20$.

9. John ran to see Mary crying.

10. John will go if Mary is there and Susan is there.

18

11. I entered the cafe, expecting Pierre. In his chair was not Pierre, but nothing. I encountered the absence of Pierre. Life is filled with such encounters with nonbeing.

12. I like you best next to me.

13. Professor Jones is a poor teacher.

14. Ford: Chevrolet cars are smaller than they were. Chevrolet: Our cars are bigger than the old models.

15. Alfred is an accused murderer.

16. Job cursed the day he was born. (Source: Unknown)

17. Shirts must be worn to be fed. (Sign in restaurant)

B. Point out the equivocations in the following; indicate the sorts of ambiguity involved.

1. Laws are human-made. So the law of gravity is human-made.

2. There are two men in the room: the real man and the man in the mirror.

3. I can't stick my finger through this table top; so it is solid. There are spaces between the molecules that make up this table top; so it is not solid. So it is both solid and not solid.

4. You look at Mary and see a devil; I look at her and see an angel. Therefore, we look at the same person, but we do not see the same person.

5. A person dies every five minutes. So you will die every five minutes.

6. Man is mortal. So one day the human species must die out.

C. In which is the word 'horses' syncategorematic; in which attributive?

1. picture horses

2. charley horses

3. straw horses

4. horses in the mind

5. horses in the pasture

6. horses that are ridden

7. horses that are imagined

8. mythical horses

9. real horses (as opposed to unreal horses)

19

10. genuine horses

D. Replace the vague words by more exact ones.

1. That is a good horse.

2. Mary is a good girl.

3. This tastes bad.

4. I want a large house.

5. Extremity in politics is reprehensible.

6. There is something in the room.

7. Smith's behavior is abnormal.

8. Jones is mentally ill.

3 / *Ambiguity Again*

In the preceding chapter you were warned against confusing two different things that might be meant by one word. Here I want to warn you against confusing the word with the thing. As difficult as doing that may seem, people often manage it. Let us begin with a silly example, the child's pun

(1)   The chair has four legs and five letters.

This, of course, is nonsense. The truth is rather that the chair has four legs and the word 'chair' has five letters. The example fuses the word with the thing.

For another example, consider the following two statements:

(2)   Mark Twain was a writer;

(3)   Mark Twain was a pseudonym.

Which, if either, is true? If you say, "Both," do you mean to say,

(4)   Mark Twain was a writer and a pseudonym?

If so, you have confused Mark Twain with his name. (4) is false. Mark Twain had a pseudonym, but he wasn't his pseudonym.

The cause of this puzzle is the ambiguous sentence (3), which is false if about the person Mark Twain and true only if about the name 'Mark Twain'. Mark Twain was a writer whose pseudonym was 'Mark Twain', but the writer Mark Twain was no more a pseudonym than the pseudonym 'Mark Twain' was a writer. To resolve its ambiguity, we should rewrite (3) as

(5)   The name 'Mark Twain' was a pseudonym,

putting the name of the writer in single quotation marks to form a name of his name. We may also write (5) more briefly as

(6)   'Mark Twain' was a pseudonym.

(6) is unambiguously true. So is

(7)   Mark Twain was a writer, and 'Mark Twain' was his pseudonym.

Notice that (7), unlike (4), embodies no thing-word ambiguity.

Use-Mention Confusion

Thing-word confusion is more commonly called *use-mention confusion*. You *use* a word to speak about the thing. When you want to speak about the word itself, you *mention* the word. Once my two-year old said, "Damn!" I admonished, "Jimmy, you shouldn't say 'damn'." A bright child, and an impertinent one, he replied, "You just said it." He was wrong: he said it; I mentioned it.

When writing, we indicate the distinction by putting single quotation marks around words we are mentioning and by leaving these words unquoted when we are using them. Thus, if I say,

Love is wonderful,

I am using the word 'love' to speak of the wonderful thing love. By contrast, if I say,

'Love' is a four-letter word,

I am mentioning the word 'love', not using it. (I am, however, using the name of the word 'love' to mention the word. To form a name of a word, phrase, or sentence, we enclose it in single quotation marks.) There is ambiguity in

Love is a four-letter word.

If that statement is meant to be about love, it is false.

Thinking such pedantic distinctions superfluous, you may protest, "Surely no one ever confuses the thing with its name." Would that you were right! Unhappily, such confusion is all too common, especially when the thing named is an abstract object, such as a number. Consider the statement

There are 9 Supreme Court justices.

Does the number 9 occur here? If you answered affirmatively, you confused the number 9 with the numeral '9'. What occurs here is the numeral '9', the name of the number. The number itself does not occur. You cannot write down the number 9 any more than you can write down the person Mark Twain. You can only write down the numeral '9', as you can write down the name 'Mark Twain'.

Not convinced? Well, look at the following three inscriptions:

9   IX   nine

Which is the number? The answer is "None." The first inscription is the arabic numeral; the second is the roman numeral; the third is an English word. All name the number 9, but none is the number 9. All of them can be written down or pronounced. None of them can be divided by 3 or multiplied by 6.

Something essentially like use-mention confusion occurs when people confuse the thing with a concept, or idea, of the thing. Again, the best illustrations are abstract entities, like freedom. A student of mine once insisted mightily that freedom is "just a concept." (Another said "God is an idea.") Now people fight for freedom, but who would knowingly fight for a concept? We have a concept of freedom, as we have a concept of a horse. But freedom is no more a concept than is a horse. Surely, people in prison have a concept of freedom, even if they have no freedom. (As to whether God is an idea, ideas are things in your head, but God, I presume is not.) One might as well say that freedom (or God) is just a name as say it is just a concept (or idea).

It may be that what the student meant by saying "Freedom is just a concept" is "Freedom does not exist; just the concept of freedom does." If so, he was wrong, but at least he was making sense. He just chose a very ambiguous and misleading way of saying what he meant. Similarly, a better way to say "God is just an idea" is to say "People have ideas of God, but nothing corresponds to those ideas; there is no God." If God exists, that is also false, but at least it makes sense, as the original did not.

It is a mistake to confuse a thing with its name (or with the idea or concept of the thing), even when the thing does not exist. Unicorns don't exist, but someone would have to be muddled to declare "Unicorns are just a word (or just an idea, or just a concept)." Unicorns have legs and a horn but contain no letters. The word 'unicorn' contains letters but has no legs or horn. A unicorn is not identical with the word 'unicorn'. Instead of saying that it is, we would do better to declare that nothing answers to the word 'unicorn'. The word exists but not the unicorn.

23

(Similarly, we have an idea of unicorns, but there is nothing corresponding to our idea, nothing it is an idea of, just as there are no unicorns for pictures of unicorns to picture.)

Definitions: nominal and real

Use-mention confusion also plagues discussion of definitions. Although there is a persistent conviction that definitions of things are the only "real definitions," definitions of words being denigrated as mere "nominal definitions," you can't define a thing; definition is always definition of a word—or rather, as we shall shortly see, of a use of the word.

To be sure, you can describe the thing, and describing the thing is defining the word. For defining a word is saying what it means, and the best way to tell someone what a word means is to tell him what sorts of things it is used to mean. So you can define the word 'chair' by describing chairs. Notice, however, that it is the word 'chair' that you thus define, as it is the chairs that you describe. You don't thereby define the chairs, any more than you describe the word. You can't define a chair, any more than you can spell one. You can only define, as you can only spell, the word 'chair'.

The tendency to think otherwise is just the product of loose talk. We casually say things like

Define chair,

meaning

Tell me what the word 'chair' means.

Then we forget that the first statement of the pair is nonsense unless it means the second. An excellent illustration of the result is theological confusion caused by the request to define 'God'. When asked to do so, many theists react as if they had been asked to do something impious. They protest, "You can't define God. God is infinite, and man is finite, and the finite cannot define the infinite." This response confuses God with his name, which really is a serious impiety. When people ask you to define the word 'God', they are just asking you to tell them what you are talking about when you use the word. They are not asking you to do something obscene to God. Defining is setting limits, but they are not asking you to put limits upon what has no limits, to make the infinite finite. They are just asking you to put limits upon your use of the word, asking you to distinguish what you call "God" from what you do not call "God".

24

Ironically, you do that in a sense when you say that God is infinite. By saying so, you indicate that you exclude finite things, like this book, from the denotation of the word 'God'.

Verbal Disputes and Agreements

An especially interesting and common sort of thing-word confusion occurs when there are *verbal agreements* or *disagreements*—that is, when people agree or disagree in words but not in fact, because they use the same words but mean different things. We and the Russians both believe in "democracy," but they mean communism while we mean capitalism. Our agreement is purely verbal. To suppose that we really agree on the best form of government would be to confuse the word 'democracy' with democracy. Verbal disagreement is as common as verbal agreement and has the same cause. Suppose we and some Russians got into a dispute about whether their form of government or ours is "really a democracy." That would be a purely verbal dispute, a disagreement over words, not over forms of government. The question would just be whether to call their system or ours "democracy."

Some of the best illustrations of verbal agreement and disagreement occur in theological discussion. When you ask, nearly everybody believes in "God." We therefore conclude that nearly everybody is a theist. On close examination, however, we find that one believer's god is Jehovah, another's is Osiris. One person believes that the universe was created and calls its creator "God," while another believes that the universe was uncreated and calls the universe itself "God." And so on. In short, we find that there is agreement on the word 'God' but disagreement on what the word means. Therefore, concluding that we are all theists is as laughable as the reply of Bertrand Russell's jailor to the information that Russell was an agnostic: "Well, I guess we all believe in the same God." If we don't mean the same thing by the word, that isn't so. That each of us believes in some one thing he calls "God" does not mean that there is some one thing that we all call "God" and believe in. That each of us believes in "God" in some sense of the word does not mean that we all believe in God.

When, in the next chapter, we come to discuss definitions more fully, we shall want to avoid thus confusing the word with the thing. We shall want to recognize that we define only words, even when we do so by describing the things. For now, let us turn to other matters.

Quotations and Assertions

A special form of use-mention confusion is *quotation-assertion confusion.* A reporter recently polled our community on its attitude towards the local blue laws. She duly and accurately reported that the majority of citizens oppose the ordinances, only to receive mountains of indignant mail from irate citizens who support them. Her correspondents were guilty of confusing quotation with assertion, as were those ancient rulers who executed bearers of bad tidings.

Suppose I declare, "Jones says that Smith is a crook." I do not thereby declare that Smith is a crook. I only declare that Jones declares it. The distinction is elementary but frequently neglected. It is so common to confuse quotation with assertion that if you don't add an explicit disclaimer, you are liable to be taken as affirming what you are merely quoting. When you say, "Jones says that Smith is a crook," you must add, "but I don't believe it." Otherwise, you are liable to be accused of slandering Smith.

Advertisers frequently exploit this confusion. The grocer announces

"Fresh" fish and orange "juice,"

with the intent of making you think the frozen fish is fresh and the orange drink is juice. All the grocer is saying, however, is that somebody might mistake the frozen fish for fresh fish and the orange drink for orange juice— that somebody might (mistakenly) declare the fish "fresh" and the beverage "juice."

Should you be taken in, blame yourself. The grocer met the requirements of the law when he put *scare quotes* around the words 'fresh' and 'juice'. These nullify the force of the words they enclose, making those words syncategorematic rather than attributive. Quotation marks function like the expression 'so-called'. A so-called intellectual may be no intellectual, but only somebody who calls himself, or is called, an "intellectual." Hence, there was no contradiction in our remark in earlier chapters that ambiguous "statements" were not really statements. It is simply tempting to call them "statements," because they otherwise resemble statements.

Normally, enclosing statements (or sentences) in quotation marks indicates that they are being mentioned rather than used, quoted rather than asserted. Another device for achieving the same effect is also used in this book: isolating the statement or sentence on a single line, as when we write

John is tall.

Sentences thus isolated are not being asserted. We are just focusing on them so that we can assert things about them.

Quoted expressions are normally being mentioned rather than used, but the rule is not inflexible. Sometimes a quoted expression is doing double duty. Consider

"Mark Twain" was a writer.

Is that about the person or about his name? If it is elliptical for

The person called "Mark Twain" was a writer,

the answer is "Both." Much the same duality is displayed by "The 'boy most likely to succeed' is not likely to succeed," in which the expression 'boy most likely to succeed' is quoted (and therefore mentioned) but also used to refer to the boy who was so described.

Similarly, by adding an endorsement we may assert a statement we are quoting. Hence, the words 'is true' in

"Mark Twain was a writer" is true

have the effect of erasing the quotation marks, leaving us asserting

Mark Twain was a writer.

Notice, however, that we don't erase the quotation marks when we add the words "true for" to a quoted statement.

"The earth is flat" was true for the people in the Middle Ages

does not assert

The earth was flat in the Middle Ages.

Most people are careless about quotation marks, but as the preceding example illustrates, there is often good reason for care. Confusing a thing with its name is one of the most primitive, pervasive, and pernicious of fallacies. It accounts not only for confused philosophical ideas, like the belief that truth is relative, but also for the superstition that knowing a person's name is having power over him, for the silly notion that words are dirty if the things they denote are, and for countless other equally ridiculous but harmful beliefs and attitudes.

Exercises

A. In which of the following is the word 'flat' being mentioned, in which used?

1. The people in the Middle Ages said that the earth was flat.

2. The people in the Middle Ages believed that the earth was flat.

3. The earth was flat to people in the Middle Ages.

4. That the earth is flat was widely believed in the Middle Ages.

5. According to flat-earthers, the earth is flat.

6. The earth is flat.

7. The earth is said to be flat.

8. It is no longer universally believed that the earth is flat.

9. The earth is flat to some, round to others.

10. The earth is flat, I believe.

B. Resolve the ambiguity of any of the following that are ambiguous.

1. Sex is a dirty word.

2. "Sex" is dirty.

3. Sex is fun.

4. These books are full of sex.

5. These books are sexy.

6. Define sex.

7. Describe 'sex'.

8. Describe sex.

9. Sex contains three letters.

10. Describe the word sex.

C. In which of the following is the name 'Socrates' mentioned, in which used?

1. "Socrates was the wisest and justest and best man that I ever knew."

2. Socrates was said by Plato to be wise, just, and good.

3. Plato portrayed Socrates as wise, just, and good.

4. Socrates was wise, just, and good.

5. Plato believed that Socrates was wise, just, and good.

D. Avoid the conclusion by resolving the ambiguities.

Mary was the woman who did it, said Sara.
Mary did not do it.
So Sara said that the woman who did not do it did it.

E. Which of the following asserts, and which quotes, "God is good"?

1. It is said that God is good.

2. I believe that God is good.

3. It is said that God is good, and the saying is true.

4. "God is good."

5. Many people believe that God is good.

4 / Stipulations and Defective Definitions

Stipulations

We are sometimes asked to resolve an ambiguous expression by defining it, but the verb 'to define' is itself ambiguous. One defines a word by saying what it means, but a word may mean one thing to you, something else to others. Therefore, when you define it, you may do either of two different things: (1) you may indicate how you yourself use the word; or (2) you may indicate how others use it. To do the first is to define the word by *stipulating* a meaning for it. To do the second is to state its *lexical*, or dictionary, definition. An example of a stipulation is

(1)   When I say 'snarf' I mean breakfast.

Examples of lexical definition are

(2)   When speakers of English use the word 'breakfast', they mean the first meal of the day

and

(3)   When psychologists use the word 'reinforcer', they mean anything that increases the frequency or strength of behavior.

A stipulation, then, is a statement of one's own idiolect. Lexical definitions are reports on the usage of some linguistic group, reports of the existence of an established verbal convention.

Stipulations may also take the form of commands or invitations. For example, we may say, "Let us use the word 'snarf' to mean breakfast" or "We shall use the word 'snarf' to mean breakfast." Lexical definitions are usually phrased without explicit mention of the group whose usage is being reported.   Instead of (2) we are more likely to say merely, "The word 'breakfast' means the first meal of the day," leaving it understood that this is a remark about speakers of English.   Or we may say, "A reinforcer is anything that increases the frequency or strength of behavior," by way of ellipsis for (3).   Don't let these variations obscure the fact that saying how you use a word is one thing; indicating how the word is customarily used by others is another.   Keep these two things separate, and know which you are doing and which someone else is doing.

Humpty Dumptyism

There is a widespread but pernicious conviction that one may stipulate any meaning one wishes for a word and use it accordingly.   The paradigm case is Humpty Dumpty, who used the word 'glory' to mean 'nice knock-down argument'.   When Alice rebuked him for misusing the word, he replied that he would use words as he saw fit and talk as he pleased, as though he had a perfect right to do so.   He didn't.   Why not?   Because talking in unaccustomed ways creates ambiguity and causes confusion.   It misleads people who are expecting you to use words as others do.

Don't suppose Humpty Dumptyism occurs only in books.   It is a common, if objectionable, practice.   There is a legend that a state legislator once undertook to simplify his son's homework by introducing a bill to fix the value of 'π' at a nice round 3.25.   What the poor, ignorant gentleman overlooked was that π is the ratio of the circumference of the circle to its diameter, which is 3.1416 and which cannot be made to come out as 3.25 by act of the legislature.   Less laughably, advertisers show Humpty Dumpty's attitude when they advertise wieners with 40 percent meat in them as "pure beef," meaning, as Ralph Nader has said, only that all the meat that is used is beef.   Calling light bread "100 percent wheat" when it isn't whole wheat illustrates a similarly dishonest disregard for conventional usage.

Such perversity is even more objectionable when there are questions of social or institutional policy at stake, and somebody obscures the issues or begs the questions by Humpty Dumptyish use of words.   Recently I heard a dispute between two experts on teacher evaluation.   One claimed that good teaching was satisfying your pupils, whom he thought of as "consumers."   On the basis of this definition and the maxim that the customer is always right, he advocated evaluating faculty by polling their students.

The other replied that you shouldn't call something "good teaching" unless it results in learning, and added that there is no proof that student ratings reflect what students learn. He wanted to appraise teachers by examining their students and finding out how much had been learned. The first disputant replied, "Well, that may be your definition; mine is different." That reply annoyed the second disputant almost as much as Humpty Dumpty annoyed Alice, who was infuriated, and rightly so. According to *Webster's*, to teach is to make to learn. From this it follows that to teach well is to make to learn well. So the second disputant was using the words in the standard, and therefore in the correct, way.

It may seem as if the first disputant was also using the words in a standard way. For students do often describe X as a "good teacher" when they only mean to say that X is likable. So the problem may seem to be that existing usage of the word 'good' is ambiguous. It isn't: no doubt, what counts as "good" for some people does not count as "good" for others, but the word 'good' is not ambiguous when paired with the name of a profession. In such a context, 'good' means 'skilled', not 'likable'. A good carpenter knows how to carpenter; he may or may not also be personable. A good physician is skilled at curing; he may or may not also be agreeable. Given that this is the standard grammatical pattern, it would be misleading to recommend someone as a "good lawyer" when you meant only that he is a pleasant chap, hearty and well met. Just so, it is misleading to call someone a "good teacher" when all you mean is that students like him.

The error of trying to prove one's point of view by declaring it true by one's own definition was exposed by Abraham Lincoln, who pointed out that you can't give a dog an extra leg by defining 'dog' as 'five-legged animal'. Our first disputant was arguing, "Good teachers are teachers whom students rate highly, because I mean by 'good teacher' one whom students rate highly." One might as well reason, "The earth is flat, because it is shaped like a ball, and that is the shape I call 'flat.'" Nevertheless, many people do reason in this way. I have heard it urged that the United States is full of impoverished people, because many are below the government's official poverty level. The statistic is correct but misleading in such a context. I have also heard it argued that there are no atheists, "because everybody believes in something," as if theism consisted in believing in anything you pleased, including money or sex.

There is a morality for talk as there is for other behavior, and that morality requires us to use words as other people use them, lest we mislead and confuse one another. Public words are public property, to do with as the public sees fit. They don't belong to you and me to appropriate for our private advantage.

Why fight over the rights to a word? Because, as one politician wisely said, "Words are the substance of politics." Indeed, they are the substance of human affairs. A rose is a rose by any name, but call poison oak a "rose" and somebody is sure to plant it. Call slavery "freedom" and somebody is sure to advocate it (indeed, it has happened too often). Call strychnine "water" and somebody will drink it. You do much harm when you don't use the right names for things. Imagine the havoc the legislator would have caused if he had had his way with 'π'. Imagine what will happen to learning if those who equate good teaching with popularity prevail.

I have been protesting Humpty Dumptyism, the practice of defining common words in uncommon or idiosyncratic ways, substituting one's idiolect for majority usage. My objection has been that this practice creates ambiguity, which can cause much confusion. It does less harm if one is open and forthright about it: announcing beforehand that you call circles "squares" is better than proceeding to do so without prior warning; that warning might prevent somebody from ordering six thousand square pegs for drilled round holes. The practice is not to be recommended, however, even when it is preceded by explicit announcement. It complicates life unnecessarily, and complication can also cause confusion. In matters of word usage, if not in matters of opinion, the majority should prevail.

The Uses of Stipulations

When, then, is a stipulation in order? Are there never any occasions on which one may declare one's intent to use a word in some unaccustomed way? Of course. Most notably, you may use a word as you please if it is one that you invented. Suppose I observe a new species of bird, a three-toed warbler with a pink head, a chartreuse tail, and polka-dot wings. I coin a neologism 'tarbler' and stipulate that, henceforth, that will be the bird's common name. I have a right to do that. The bird was my discovery, and the word was my invention. The bird needs a name and the name I chose has, to my knowledge at least, no other established use. So, if I wish, I may call the bird what I please and invite others to do the same.

Stipulation is also legitimate when the expression, although an old one, lacks clear or unambiguous meaning. In such a case, one may legitimately choose among its many meanings. We earlier found reason to abandon the practice of calling deaf mutes "dumb," and there may be equally good reason to foreswear the venerable tradition of using the word 'men' to mean both men alone and men plus women. We need, but don't have, a good substitute. Any stipulation that reduces ambiguity is insofar good. Our objection is to stipulations that increase ambiguity.

Stipulation is even urgent when the expression in question is so hopelessly ambiguous as to admit of practically no clear interpretation. Consider the words 'liberal' and 'conservative'. Once clear in meaning and names of compatible things (a liberal being one who believed in liberty and a conservative one who believed in conserving liberty), they have been so abused and misused that they no longer mean anything clear and definite, except that each is the opposite of the other (nowadays a 'liberal' is likely to be one who puts welfare above liberty; such has been the confusing evolution of the word). It is perhaps best not to use these words at all, but if one uses them, it is best not to use them in the loose and virtually meaningless way that is customary. For in such usage, they can have no more than emotive meaning. Such usage is name-calling, a "liberal" being somebody you dislike if you are a "conservative," and vice versa. It is better just to stipulate that the expression 'old-fashioned liberal' will be used to mean, say, anybody who puts liberty first.

Stipulation may also be used to reduce vagueness, to set limits on the use of a word. A law providing welfare relief to all "poor" people would be unenforceable. A poverty line must be drawn. Conversely, you couldn't tax just the "rich." Your tax laws need to specify income levels. Nor could you define your territory by saying, "My land goes as far as the eye can see." To prevent fights over land rights, it is necessary to draw precise boundaries.

Stipulations are also in order when established usage embodies some positive error. Once physicists defined 'matter' as 'impenetrable stuff'. Now they know that no stuff is impenetrable, but they still use the term 'matter' to denote the stuff they once mistakenly thought impenetrable; 'impenetrability' is just no longer part of its definition. Sometimes, too, scientists find that things once grouped under one heading are best considered under another. According to customary usage, whales are fish because they live in the sea and are shaped accordingly, but biologists have come to regard them as mammals because they have lungs and warm blood. Specialists also use an old word in a new way when the new usage is more fruitful. For example, economists do not use the word 'demand' in the customary way, to denote the quantity of goods wanted at some particular time, but to denote the quantity of goods wanted as that quantity is a function of such variables as price. Their reason is that the latter, more general, notion is more useful to economic theory than the former, more common, usage.

Finally, we may violate usage to correct objectionable evaluations. One argument for changing verbal usage respecting black people was to subvert the invidious discrimination that older usages symbolized and reinforced. Verbal habits are not separable from other institutions. We couldn't move toward justice while continuing to call blacks "niggers." Stipulating that the term 'black', on a par with 'white', be used instead facilitates desirable social change.

In general, there is no objection to stipulations that introduce a new word for a new idea, reduce ambiguity and increase precision, or correct other deficiencies in existing usage. In such cases, stipulations are not only appropriate; they are requisite. When, however, stipulations promise no definite gain, conservatism in word usage is the rule and adherence to customary practice the obligation.

Defects in Definitions

Stipulations, we have seen, are objectionable when lexical definitions would be more appropriate, but that is not the only way in which an attempt at "definition" can be defective. Here are some more failings to which putative definitions are subject.

Circularity, the attempt to define an expression by using the very expression you are defining, is a defect in any definition, lexical or stipulative. You ask what a liberal is and are told that it is someone who is liberal, someone characterized by liberality. You are no better off than you were. Instead of clarification, you got only repetition. To enlighten you, a definition must define words you don't understand using words you do. If you already understood the word 'liberal', you wouldn't need to ask what was meant by it. The circles in some definitions are larger than others, but that doesn't improve them. A dictionary of mine defines a cause as anything that has an effect and then defines an effect as anything that has a cause. This is no more informative than defining a cause as a cause, just wordier.

Just as bad as circular definitions are negative definitions, attempts to tell you what is meant by telling you what is not meant. "Spiritual entities are entities that are not tangible, not visible, and so on." No doubt, but what are they? Defining something in negative terms is like looking at a forest and saying, "See that tree. Well, it is not the one I mean." Then which one do you mean? Suppose I told you that a gibble is a being that is not a fish, not a tree, not an insect, and so on. I could go on in that way for quite a little while without your getting any idea at all of what I meant by the word 'gibble'.

Definitions phrased in metaphorical and emotive terms have the same defects as negative and circular definitions. "Love is a many-splendored thing, the light of my life and the inspiration of poets" is pretty, but the definition would be more enlightening if it were plainer. "Democracy is the greatest form of government" tells me that you like democracy, whatever it is, but it doesn't tell me what you think it is.

Also objectionable are definitions that make use of unintelligible jargon, gobbledygook. "By 'teaching' I mean the implementation of educational policy to effect the achievement of pedagogical ends in view on a long-term basis" is no more informative or intelligible than "By a 'frammalump' I mean a goozledook that is frizzlelump." Sometimes, of course, it is necessary to use technical terms in order to give clear definitions. There is no way to resolve the ambiguity of the word 'average' except by telling you that it is used to signify the mean, the median, or the mode, thereby using terms with which you may be less familiar. These latter words can, however, be defined using words you already understand: the mean score on a test is the score you get when you divide the total of all scores by the number who took the test; the modal score is the score that was scored most often; the median is the score that half the people surpassed and the other half did not reach. Technical language that can be thus clearly defined is intelligible and often helpful.

The rule is: don't define the obscure by means of the obscure; don't try to lighten somebody's darkness by providing a lamp without oil in it. Use words that your hearers understand or that can be made intelligible to them. Clarify the ambiguous by means of the unambiguous. Render the unspecific specific and the vague precise. In a word, let your hearers know what you are talking about. Make it impossible for them to misunderstand you. Circular definitions and definitions expressed in metaphorical, negative, or unintelligible words all break this rule, and should all be avoided.

A Test of Intelligibility

If definitions are not always as pellucid as they might be, perhaps part of the reason is that people often don't know when they aren't clear about something, such discrimination being much harder than you might think it. For many people, the test of intelligibility is just familiarity: they think they understand a word if they have heard it often enough. Familiarity, however, not only breeds contempt; it also fosters a complacent illusion of comprehension. Think of the word 'freedom'. It is a familiar word, but does that mean we know what it denotes ? If so, why are there so many verbal disputes over "freedom," and why can't any definition of the word get agreement ? Another example is the notion of "rights." We all demand our rights, but what sort of thing are we demanding ? Something that ought to be respected—no doubt, but what determines which "rights" ought to be respected and which ought to be denied ? That we know no clear answer to these questions indicates that the word 'right' is more familiar than clear.

Well, if familiarity is no guide to intelligibility, what is ? How do we tell whether what is being said, or what we ourselves are saying, makes sense ? Roughly speaking, it is a matter of knowing how (that is, when and where) the word is used and how (when and where) to use it ourselves. You know what the word 'red' means because you know that it means the color of fire trucks, rubies, cardinals, and so on, but not the color of grass, the sky, ebony, and so on. That is, you know what the word 'red' means because you know that it may be used to describe things in the first list but not things in the second. And what goes for 'red' goes for any other word. Understanding a word is knowing its applications, knowing when it would be right to use that word and when wrong. If you don't know how to use a word, or how others use it, you don't understand it. I tell you to pick out the frammalumps in the room. You can't do it. I call a typewriter and a cup "frammalumps." You don't know whether my remark is true or false, and you suspect it is neither. That uncertainty shows that the word 'frammalump' has no meaning for you.

Here are some more examples. You understand how to distinguish intelligent adults from unintelligent adults; so you understand talk of intelligence. You don't know how to tell intelligent babies from unintelligent babies; so you don't understand talk of inborn intelligence. You know how to distinguish a ripe apple from a green apple; so the terms 'ripe' and 'green' are intelligible when applied to apples. On the other hand, you don't know how to distinguish a "spiritual apple" from a "physical apple" so the distinction 'spiritual' and 'physical' means nothing to you when applied to apples. And so on. Do you know how to use the word ? Only then do you understand it.

We have learned two rules: (1) don't stipulate a use for a word that already has a use; and (2) when you do make a stipulation, make it in language that will be intelligible and informative, language that will leave no doubt how you intend the word to be used. The first of these rules follows from the fact that the legitimate business of a stipulation is to decrease ambiguity, not to increase it. The second follows from the fact that the business of any definition, whether stipulative or lexical, is to say what a word means in terms that can be understood. Keep these goals in mind, and it will be easy to remember the rules.

Exercises

A. Criticize the following attempts at definitions.

1. Extrasensory perception is perception by other means than the senses.

2. Freedom is having choices.

3. A free will is an unfettered will.

4. Love is something spiritual, something that transcends the physical.

5. Hunger is being hungry.

6. Intelligence is being smart.

7. The beautiful is what deserves to be admired.

8. Perceiving is apprehending entities or verities with the mind.

9. Being is the transcending of the transcendent.

10. A book is a thing like what I am reading now.

11. A thing is heavy if it feels heavy when you try to pick it up.

12. Mental illness is that condition of the mind that a person is in when he or she is emotionally sick.

13. The mentally ill are people whose behavior is abnormal or deviant.

14. The mentally ill are people who are ill but not physically so.

15. Insanity is ignorance of the moral quality of one's actions.

16. A person who is psychotic is out of touch with reality.

17. Gravity is a force that makes things fall to earth.

18. A cause is whatever causes something to happen.

19. A husband is any person with a wife, and a wife is any person with a husband.

20. Right is what God commands.

21. Your duty is your obligations, your responsibilities.

22. Hunger is wanting food.

23. A compulsion is an overpowering urge to do something.

24. The id is the basic psychic energy.

25. Psychic energy is the opposite to physical energy.

26. By 'God' is meant the supreme being.

27. By 'God' is meant the ultimate concern.

28. Theism is belief in God.

29. God is the incomprehensible.

30. By 'God' I mean the universe.

31. I define a square as a plane figure with three sides.

32. For me, God is whatever you want him to be.

33. True liberty is obeying the will of your husband.

34. The right thing to do is the natural thing to do; the wrong thing is unnatural.

35. Money is the God of the bankers.

B. Which of the items in (A) were intended as lexical definitions? Which as stipulations?

5 / *Definitions as Equations*

In the foregoing chapter I distinguished stipulations from lexical definitions. Then, for the most part, I discussed the legitimacy and uses of defining by stipulation. Here I want to make another point about definitions: that they are equations.

Ostensive "Definitions"

Now, when I say 'definitions' I mean statements of the meaning of an expression, not training in its use. Sometimes a distinction is made between "ostensive definitions" and "verbal definitions." Ostensive definitions define words by pointing to samples of the things the words denote. For example, one defines, or attempts to define, the word 'chair' ostensively by pointing to chairs while saying the word. This procedure differs considerably from that of telling someone what a word means by using other words, as you do when you say, "A chair is a piece of furniture used primarily for sitting." The latter is verbal definition.

As I shall here use the word, all definition is verbal. "Ostensive definition" is better thought of as training, and the training would have to be very thorough to count as definition. Merely pointing out a few examples defines nothing, for it sets no limits on one's use of a word. Suppose a child or a foreigner wants to know the meaning of the word 'red'. I point out a fire truck and a barn, intoning the word each time. Since both objects are large, my pupil just calls the next elephant he sees "red." Such are the hazards of defining by example. If one is to teach by ostension, one must point to a random selection of examples, and one must discourage incorrect uses as well as encourage correct ones. Only when one has done this so well that one's pupil has no doubt about when it is and when it is not appropriate to use the word in question may one claim to have defined it for him.

To be sure, we can't define words by using other words that are themselves defined in terms of still other words, ad infinitum. Definitions must come to an end somewhere, and they end with words we understand because we were trained to use them. Or, rather, that is where they begin. We learned to say "Mama" because it got the bottle filled again. Then we learned to say "milk" because Mama wouldn't fill the bottle if we didn't. In this way we eventually acquired a fund of words; we were introduced to definitions as devices for increasing our vocabularies in the absence of appropriate objects. Therefore, definitions presuppose knowledge of words that we learn without definitions, and these words can't be defined at all, only taught. No one can tell you what the word 'red' means, using other words. You must be shown. So "ostensive definition" is not only important; it is indispensable. It is just not definition in the strict sense of the word.

Definitional Equation

Strictly speaking, definitions are *equations*, statements to the effect that one expression means much the same as another. Let us call the expression being defined the *definiendum* and the expression being used to define it the *definiens*. The definition says that the definiendum is synonymous with the definiens.

Consider an example. Suppose we want a definition of the word 'bachelor'. Someone undertakes to satisfy our desire by declaring

(1)   A bachelor is a man who has not married.

This lexical definition amounts to the claim that, as words are normally used, the definiendum 'bachelor' means the same as the definiens 'a man who has not married'. So we may rewrite (1) as

(2)   a bachelor = a man who has not married,

replacing the word 'is' by the equal sign. In this respect (1) resembles

41

(3)   3 + 2 is 5

and differs from

(4)   A bachelor is a person.

We can rewrite (3) as

(5)   3 + 2 = 5,

replacing the word 'is' by the equal sign, but we could not rewrite (4) as

(6)   A bachelor = a person.

Conversion and Substitution

The measure and proof of this distinction is that equations are convertible *salva veritatae* (saving truth value): you can turn them around without changing their truth value. If you convert (1) into

A man who has not married is a bachelor,

it remains true, as does (3) when converted to

5 is 3 + 2.

On the other hand, if you convert (4) into

A person is a bachelor,

you change a truth into a falsehood. Therefore, (4) won't do as a definition, but (1) will.

The importance of noting that definitions are equations lies in another trait of equations: equals may be substituted for equals *salva veritatae*. Suppose we know

George has three plus two secretaries

to be true. Then, knowing equation (5), we know

George has five secretaries

to be true. Here the expression on the right-hand side acts as a proxy for the expression on the left-hand side. Similarly, knowing

(7)   George is a bachelor

42

and knowing definition (2), we may infer

(8)   George is a man who has not married,

replacing the definiendum 'bachelor' by the definiens 'man who has not married', there being no way that (2) and (7) could be true without (8) also being true.   If the definition is true, substituting the definiens for the definiendum, or vice versa, preserves truth value.

Should substitution change a truth into a falsehood, the definition is false.   Here is an illustration.   Someone proposes that a bachelor is just a stupid boor.   We write this definition as

(9)   Bachelor $\stackrel{df}{=}$ stupid boor,*

using the *sign of definitional equation* to distinguish definitions from arithmetical equations.   Substitution in (7) on the basis of (9) would yield

(10)   George is a stupid boor.

If, however, it happens that George is intelligent and refined, then (7) is true while (10) is false.   That shows that (9) is false, as false as

$$3 + 2 = 6.$$

Consider another example.   Someone offers the following definition of the word 'chair':

(11)   chair $\stackrel{df}{=}$ a thing you can sit on.

I find a rock and sit on it.   This rock is not a chair.   That is, the statement

(12)   This rock is not a chair

is true; employing the definition (11), we would rewrite true (12) as

(13)   This rock is not a thing you can sit on.

That (13) is false shows that (11) is false.   You cannot substitute the expression 'thing you can sit on' for the word 'chair' without turning some truths into falsehoods.   So you can't claim that 'chair' means the same as 'thing you can sit on'.

---

* If we were being strict, we would write this as

(9)   'Bachelor' $\stackrel{df}{=}$ 'stupid boor'.

But so much care would be pedantic for present purposes.

Counterexamples to Definitions

This same point can be put another way. Take the word 'bachelor'. It applies to a number of things, to all the things that can be called "bachelors." Now take the phrase 'stupid boor'. It applies to all the things that can be described as "stupid boors." If (9) were a true definition, the first group would be identical with the second. Everything that could be called a bachelor could also be called a stupid boor, and vice versa. As it turns out, however, George is a bachelor but not a stupid boor. He is a *counterexample* to the definition (9).

The rock is a counterexample to definition (11). Take the definiendum 'chair'. There is a group of objects it truly describes. Now take the definiens 'thing you can sit on'. There is a group of objects it truly describes. The rock belongs in the latter group but not in the former. It can be sat upon but is not a chair. Therefore, the group of things that can be truly described as chairs is not identical with the group of things that can be sat upon. The two groups have some things in common, but there are some things that belong to the one group and not to the other. So (11) is not a good definition.

In summary, recognizing that definitions are equations gives us a test, or, rather, two tests, for the truth of a lexical definition: conversion and substitution. If a definition is true, it will remain true when converted; and all true statements will remain true when the definiens has been substituted for the definiendum. Someone wants a definition of 'E'. The following equation is asserted:

$$E \overset{\text{df}}{=} D$$

If this is right, then $D \overset{\text{df}}{=} E$, and anything that can be truly called an "E" can be truly called a "D" and vice versa. The Es and the Ds comprise the very same group of things. If they don't, if there are things among the Es that are not among the Ds or vice versa, then the definitional equation is false. That is, should there be some object x such that x is an E but not a D, then the equation "$E \overset{\text{df}}{=} D$" is false.

Up to now, we have been discussing mostly lexical definitions, statements of what an expression means when it is used in the customary way. With slight modifications, the same remarks apply to stipulations. Suppose Sue offers you (9) as a stipulation. She does not claim that the word 'bachelor' is normally used to mean the same thing as the expression 'stupid boor'. She just proposes herself to use the two expressions interchangeably. Suppose, further, that George is a friend of hers and known to her to be a bachelor. We can point out that her stipulation commits her to regarding George as a stupid boor. If she does not wish to do that, she must give up (9) as inconsistent with her own usage. Hence, substitution is as good a test of stipulations as of lexical definitions. The only difference is that any stipulation that fails the test is thereby found to be inconsistent with the speaker's usage, whereas any lexical definition that fails is thereby found to be inconsistent with standard usage.

Extension and Intension

Nothing that fails the substitution test counts as a good definition, but some logicians believe that a definition could pass this test and still not be satisfactory. Let us illustrate their point and then try to explain it. Consider the following definition:

(14) x is an equilateral triangle $\stackrel{\text{df}}{=}$ x is a triangle with three equal angles.

By our test, this definition is true, all equilateral triangles being also equiangular triangles. Yet, one might reasonably object that the definiens is not synonymous with the definiendum. For when one is talking about an equilateral triangle, one has its sides, not its angles, in mind. So, even though the class of equilateral triangles is identical with the class of equiangular triangles, there being nothing in one that is not also in the other, we could not truly say that 'equilateral triangle' has the same meaning as 'equiangular triangle'.

What this objection shows is that the word 'meaning' is ambiguous. Up to now we have spoken as if the *meaning* of an expression were constituted by the things it meant, by its *denotation* or *extension*. According to this way of talking, the meaning of the word 'chair' is chairs, all the things that can truly be described as "chairs." According to this way of talking, the expressions 'equilateral triangle' and 'equiangular triangle' have the same meaning because they have the same extension. In short we have been talking about meaning as extension.

The point of our example is that the word 'meaning' also has another meaning. Different descriptions of the same objects call attention to different features of those objects. The word 'equilateral' calls attention to the sides, the word 'equiangular' to the angles. Sometimes, what is meant by "the meaning" of an expression is not the objects it denotes or describes but the features of those objects to which the description calls especial attention, the features that are thought most critical for the discussion in progress, the "essential" features. These features are said to constitute the *intension* of the expression. So the intension of the expression 'equilateral' is the equal sidedness of the triangles, equal sidedness being the feature we have uppermost in mind. Likewise, the intension of the expression 'equiangular' is the equal angularity, that being the feature most at issue when we use the word. Equilateralness and equiangularity being different features of the same things, the words 'equiangular' and 'equilateral' have different intensions.

Words that have no extension, words like 'unicorn' and 'satyr', also show why we must distinguish intension from extension. Since there are no unicorns or satyrs, the two words denote exactly the same things, namely, nothing. Being names of no objects, they are not true of different objects. So, by extensional criteria,

$$x \text{ is a unicorn} \overset{\text{df}}{=} x \text{ is a satyr}$$

is a good definition. Yet a unicorn is a one-horned horse, whereas a satyr is a creature with a horse's body and a man's head. So even though the two words mean (that is, refer to) the same things, they are not synonymous (that is, they have different intensions).

The test for identity of intension is also substitution, but with a difference. If two terms could be substituted for each other without changing truth value, we said they had the same extension. We may similarly say that two terms have the same intension if they may be substituted for each other for the purposes at hand. Now, 'equiangular' can be substituted for 'equilateral' without changing any truths into falsehoods, but it cannot be substituted for all purposes. As we have seen, the word 'equilateral' often has a function that would not be equally well served by the term 'equiangular'. Likewise, since nothing can be called either, anything that can be called "a unicorn" can also be called "a satyr" and vice versa, but a myth about unicorns would be quite a different story if we substituted the word 'satyr' for the word 'unicorn'. Since the myth wasn't true to start with, the substitution wouldn't turn a truth into a falsehood, but it would turn a coherent story into an incongruous one. Let us say, then, that the test of identity of extension is substitutability *salva veritatae*, but the test of identity of intension is substitutability *salva congruitatae* (saving congruity).

Whether two expressions serve one's purposes equally well depends on what one's purposes are. A mathematician thoroughly familiar with the fact that no triangles are equilateral unless also equiangular can let the one term act as a proxy for the other in anything he says. This is not the case for a person who has the idea that a triangle can be equilateral without being equiangular, or a person who wishes to talk about the sides without mentioning the angles. Someone with no interest in mythology will have little use for the distinction between 'unicorn' and 'satyr', but that distinction will mean a great deal to anyone studying Greek classics. It is clear, then, that intension is a somewhat more elusive and variable thing than extension.

Because of the elusiveness and subjectivity of intensions, it is the usual practice in logic, mathematics, and science to restrict one's talk to extensions. That will also be our policy here. Henceforth, the sign of definitional equation will mean, not that two expressions have the same intension, but only that they are substitutable *salva veritatae*. In short, having mentioned intensions, I propose to ignore them for the duration of the book.

Exercises

A. Produce counterexamples to the following putative definitions.

1. A book is anything you can read.

2. The word 'actor' means any person who regularly appears on TV.

3. A good teacher is an open and friendly person.

4. The truth is what the majority believe.

5. Democracies are countries with free enterprise, capitalist economies.

6. Christians are people who believe in God.

7. Religion is belief in God.

8. Man is a tool-using animal.

9. 'Fruit' means apples, pears, or oranges.

10. Happiness is having a new car.

11. 'Violence' means any sort of mistreatment of a person, including verbal abuse.

12. 'Violence' means any sort of aggressive behavior.

13. Rape occurs any time a man molests a woman in any way.

14. A criminal is any person who has ever broken the law.

15. Murder is taking another human life.

16. War is conflict between one nation and another.

17. Freedom is being able to do what you want.

18. To say that one is "free" means that one's thoughts are not in the power of others.

19. One is responsible for what one is conscious of doing.

20. A thought is something intangible.

B. Which of the following pairs of terms have the same extension; which the same intension?

1. (a) round square
   (b) married bachelor

2. (a) democracy
   (b) republic

3. (a) line whose points are equidistant from a common point
   (b) line enclosing the largest area of any line of the same length

4. (a) God
   (b) Creator of the Universe

5. (a) president with training in nuclear engineering
   (b) president who was a peanut farmer

UNIT II

Truth Functions

6 / Compounding and Analyzing Statements

Compounds and Components

Given the simple sentences

(1)   John is bald

and

(2)   John is fat,

you know how to combine them to get the *compound sentence*

(3)   John is bald and John is fat.

Then, having got (3), you know how to shorten it, by eliminating repetition of the subject and verb, to get a sentence with a *compound predicate*:

(4)   John is bald and fat.

Similarly, given

(5)   Mary is irascible

and

(6)   Susan is irascible,

you know how to combine them to get the compound sentence

(7)   Mary is irascible and Susan is irascible

and then how to shorten this sentence to

(8)   Mary and Susan are irascible,

which has a *compound subject.*

Not only may we combine sentences to get compounds, we may also reverse the process and analyze sentences into *components.* Thus, presented with a sentence like (8), we may think of it as a shortened version of (7), which is a compound of (5) and (6). Likewise, (4) is analyzable as a compound of (1) and (2).

Both (4) and (8) are obvious examples of compounding. Almost as obvious is

This is a red car,

which is the result of combining "This is red" with "This is a car." Not so obvious, however, is the apparently simple sentence

George is a bachelor.

But this may be regarded as equivalent by definition to

George is a man who has not married,

which results from the combination of

George has not yet married

with

George is a man.

Similarly, the apparently simple statement "Susan has the flu" can be thought of as abbreviating some such extended compound as "Susan has a cough and Susan has a fever and . . ." (the three dots mean, "Keep on going until you have listed all that goes into the definition of influenza"). Likewise, "Gary is intelligent" is perhaps an abbreviation of "Gary learns easily and Gary solves problems quickly and . . ." In general, any time a short predicate has a long definition, any apparently simple sentence containing that predicate can be regarded as a brief surrogate for a much longer and more complicated sentence.

Be careful, however. Analyzing predicates is not a mechanical business. You have to think about it. You can't treat every case like others that it superficially resembles.

This is a sea horse

is certainly not to be construed as compounding "This is a sea" and "This is a horse"; its component words are syncategorematic. Nor, probably, is

That is a hammer head

to be thought of as short for "That is the head of a hammer."

In the way that short and apparently simple predicates may be abbreviations for long and complex definitions, so short and apparently simple subjects may be surrogates for compound subjects. This is obviously true of sentences with plural subjects, which may be analyzed as compounds of sentences with singular subjects. For example

My family are nice

may be construed as compounding "My mother is nice" with "My father is nice," and so on through the list of members of my family. Similarly,

(9)   Humans are mortal

may be thought of as short for the indefinitely extended compound "Human$_1$ is mortal and human$_2$ is mortal and ...," through a list of humans, past, present, and future. And what applies to the plural 'humans' often applies as well to the abstract singular 'human'.

(10)   Man is mortal

may seem to be a simple statement about one entity, but it is best understood as a compound statement about indefinitely many, being equivalent to (9). Of course, there are times when 'man' is a genuinely singular subject. An example is:

Man has been on earth for fifty million years.

This cannot be analyzed as "Human$_1$ has been on earth for fifty million years and ..." The statement concerns the duration of the species, not of its members; it is about the collective, not about each member of that collective. Another illustration of the same sort is the term 'cotton'. "Cotton is white" may be equivalent to the compound "This cotton is white and that cotton is white and ...," but "Cotton is scarce" hardly means "This cotton is scarce and that cotton is scarce and ..."

Obviously, if statements can be compound in their subjects or compound in their predicates, they can be compound in both ways at once. The statement "All the people who were exposed caught the flu" is short for a compound of statements about each person who was exposed, and each of these statements is short for a compound of statements specifying the elements that go into the definition of influenza. So what seems on the surface to be a very simple statement turns out on examination to be multiply complex.

Let us say that we *analyze* a statement when we break it down into its components, revealing complexity where there may have seemed to be simplicity. Skill at analyzing statements is the basic logical skill and one of the most useful skills a person can have. In a sense, one thoroughly understands a statement only if one knows how to analyze it, as one understands the workings of a car only if one knows how it is constructed. That is why a mechanic has a better understanding of your car than you: she knows how to take it apart and put it back together. When you learn how to take statements down into their constituent parts and reassemble them you will understand them much better. People think they understand statements if they know how to use them, as people think they understand cars if they know how to drive them. And, in a sense, they do. But we find out how little we understand what we say when communication breaks down, as we find out how little we understand our cars when they break down. Learning how to analyze and reassemble statements is the best insurance against a breakdown.

The best way to learn to analyze statements, however, is not to start with very complicated statements of the kind you are likely to meet with and use in ordinary discourse. That would be like starting you off by asking you to disassemble an electronic fuel injection engine. A better procedure is to begin with artificially simple statements and learn how to break them down and put them together again. Once you see how they go together, you will be better able to see how to take on more complicated statements. Of course, simple and artificial examples aren't very interesting or very exciting. But if you don't learn to disassemble and reassemble simple toy motors, you will never learn to be a mechanic of electronic fuel injection engines.

Truth Functions

The main reason we want to learn to analyze compound statements is that they are often *truth functions* of their components. That is to say, the truth value of the compound is determined by the truth values of its components. Consider some examples. You know that

(11)   Istanbul is in Turkey

and

(12)   Bogotá is in Columbia

are both true statements. So you also know that

(13)   Istanbul is in Turkey and Bogotá is in Columbia

is true; but that

(14)   Istanbul is not in Turkey

and

(15)   Bogotá is not in Columbia

are false. Also false are

(16)   Istanbul is in Turkey but Bogotá is not in Columbia,

(17)   Istanbul is not in Turkey but Bogotá is in Columbia,

and

(18)   Istanbul is not in Turkey and Bogotá is not in Columbia.

Knowing the truth values of (11) and (12), you are able to determine the truth values of (13)–(18). The latter are truth functions of the former.

Notice that the converse relation does not hold. Components are not truth functions of compounds. You can sometimes but not always compute the truth values of the components by knowing the truth values of the compound. Suppose I inform you that the statement

(19)   Harold is handsome and Iona is intelligent

is false. Then you know that either

(20)   Harold is handsome

or

(21)   Iona is intelligent

is false, but you don't know which. Only if you know that (19) is true do you know the truth values of both (20) and (21). So the truth values of (20) and (21) are not determined by the truth value of (19).

We have stated that some compound sentences are truth functions of their component sentences. Now we should note that some are not. Consider

(22)   Susan believes that Harry is dishonest.

Suppose Harry is dishonest. That doesn't mean that Susan believes it. She might and she might not. The truth value of (22) is not determined by the truth value of

(23) Harry is dishonest.

In this respect, (22) differs considerably from

(24) It is false that Harry is dishonest,

which is false if (23) is true and true if (23) is false.

Notice that we said that (22) is not a truth function of its component (23). We did not say that (22) is not a truth function. Every statement is a truth function in a trivial sense, being a truth function of itself, and so is (22). Moreover, a statement whose truth value is not determined by its sentential components may have its truth value determined by the components of another statement that is equivalent to it by definition. Hence, as we saw earlier,

> John is a bachelor

is a truth function of the statements

> John has not married

and

> John is a man,

by virtue of the definition

> a bachelor $\stackrel{\text{df}}{=}$ a man who has not married.

If we had an adequate definition of belief, we might be able to discern statements of which (22) is similarly a truth function. Suppose, for example, that (22) were equivalent by definition to something like " Susan says that Harry is dishonest, and Susan distrusts Harry, and . . ." In that case (22) would be a truth function of the components of this definition, whose components are " Susan says that Harry is dishonest," and " Susan mistrusts Harry," and so on.

Another exception to the rule that compound sentences are truth functions of their components is

(25) Julia is quick because she is strong.

The truth values of "Julia is quick" and "Julia is strong" are not irrelevant to the truth value of (25), but they are also not sufficient to determine it. (25) is false if Julia is either not quick or not strong, but suppose she is both.

Consistently with that supposition, (25) can be either true or false. So knowing that

Julia is quick

and

Julia is strong

are both true would not enable you to declare that (25) is also true. It might be and it might not be.

To determine the truth value of (25), we need more information. In particular, we need to know whether all or most people who are quick are also strong. Saying that one thing A causes another thing B is saying that there is some general relationship between A and B such that, when A happens, so does B. So, to decide whether (25) is true, we need to know not only whether quick Julia is strong, but whether quick Sam, Sue, George, and Mary are also strong.

There are other things we need to know, too, but it is somewhat harder to say what they are. To spell them out would be to give a definition of 'because', to lay down its *truth conditions*, to say under what circumstances a statement in which it is used would be true and under what circumstances false. I shall not undertake that definition here: defining 'cause' is a task for a book, not a page, and a rather sophisticated book at that.*

Exercises

A. Which of the following are truth functions of "Mary was exposed to the flu" and "Mary is ill"?

1. Mary was exposed to the flu and is ill.

2. Mary was not exposed to the flu and is not ill.

3. Mary is ill as a result of having been exposed to the flu.

4. John saw that Mary is ill and saw her being exposed to the flu.

5. John said that Mary is ill and that she was exposed to the flu.

6. I wish that Mary had been exposed to the flu and gotten ill.

---

* For a good one, see Ernest Nagel, *The Structure of Science* (New York: Harcourt, Brace and World, 1961).

7. Mary's illness was not the result of having been exposed to the flu.

8. Either Mary is ill or Mary was not exposed to the flu.

9. Mary was exposed to the flu if and only if she is ill.

B. Suppose that Mary was exposed to the flu and is ill. Which of the items in (A) are true? Which false? Which are indeterminate on this information alone?

C. Suppose that Mary is ill but was not exposed to the flu. Which of the items in (A) are true? Which false?

D. Suppose that Mary is not ill but was exposed to the flu. Which of the items in (A) are true? Which false?

E. Suppose that Mary neither is ill nor was exposed to the flu. Which of the items in (A) are true? Which false?

F. Rewrite the following as compounds of simpler sentences.

   1. Dobbin, Corso, and Birdy are all horses.

   2. The horse is a mammal. (Hint: Assume a list of horses, $H_1, H_2, H_3, \ldots$)

   3. Mammals have lungs and a four-chambered heart.

   4. Mary is an intelligent woman.

   5. George threw two stones.

   6. Nothing is a unicorn. (Hint: Think of this as "Everything is a non-unicorn.")

   7. George is popular in our group (which includes Sue, Sam, and Flo).

   8. Meat is expensive.

G. Discuss whether "Dobbin is a beautiful horse" can be analyzed as "Dobbin is beautiful and Dobbin is a horse."

H. Which of the following sentences can be regarded as having compound subjects? Compound predicates?

   1. Diamonds are rare.

   2. Bartender, this is a pink lady.

   3. She is a nice person.

   4. He is a perfect crook.

58

5. They are foolish.

6. Fools are common.

7. The elephant weighs over a ton on the average.

8. Water is wet.

9. Martin and Rossi are funny and rich.

10. The team of Martin and Rossi is funny and rich.

7 / Conjunction and Denial

Two basic truth functions are *denial* and *conjunction*. All others are reducible to these.* So let's learn them.

Denial

Consider the sentence

(1)   God exists.

We can affirm this sentence or deny it, assert it or dispute it, say it or gainsay it. One way to assert it is to say simply, "God exists." Another way is to say, "I believe that God exists." Still another is to say, "It is evident that God exists." One can even assert it by asking rhetorically, "How can you doubt that God exists?" or declaring, "It is absurd to deny that God exists." There is a way of asserting to suit every fancy and every occasion.

There are also many ways to deny (1). One is to say, "I deny that God exists." Another is to say, "God does not exist" or "God lacks existence." Still another is to say, "The belief that God exists is false" or "It is false that God exists." And if theists may have recourse to rhetorical questions, so may atheists, who may ask, "How can you believe anything so absurd as that God exists?" One can also deny that God exists by saying, "I don't believe that God exists," but this is ambiguous and may mean "I

---

* Of course, these in their turn are also reducible to the others.

believe that God does not exist" (which expresses atheism—disbelief) or "I don't know whether to believe that God exists" (which may express mere agnosticism—lack of belief).

Obviously, there are innumerable ways to deny a statement; but, since they all come to the same thing, it will be convenient to have one standard way of indicating denial. We shall indicate it by putting a *tilde*, ~, before a statement being denied. Thus, we shall write denials of (1) as

(2)   ~ God exists,

which you are to read as "It is false that God exists" or "God does not exist" (or you may use any other idiom of denial that is to your taste).

Obviously, (2) is a truth function of (1); denial is a truth function of affirmation. For if (1) is true, then (2) is false; and if (1) is false, then (2) is true. Denials and affirmations have opposite truth values; they contradict each other. Hence, knowing the truth value of any statement will enable you to determine the truth value of its denial.

Obviously, too,

(3)   ~ ~ God exists,

which is the denial of (2), is also a truth function of (1), being true if (1) is true and false otherwise. Denials of denials are tantamount to affirmations.

Don't confuse denying a statement with asserting its opposite. Consider the following colloquy:

> *A:* George is short.
>
> *B:* No. George is tall.
>
> *C:* No. George is not tall.

Since *C* may believe that George is neither tall nor short, but of medium height, *C*'s denial of *B*'s statement is not tantamount to endorsement of *A*'s. But *B* did not confine himself to denying *A*'s statement. He also asserted the opposite, and it is that assertion of the opposite that *C* is denying. Had the conversation gone

> *A:* George is short.
>
> *B:* No. George is not short.
>
> *C:* No. It is false that George is not short,

then *C* would have been asserting essentially the same thing as *A*.

You should also not confuse denying a denial with doubling a denial. There is a considerable difference between

(4)   I ain't got no money

and

(5)   It is false that I don't have money.

(4) affirms poverty and (5), affluence. Only (5) can be written

~ ~ I have money.

The doubling of negatives in (4) must rather be construed as a form of repetitive emphasis:

~ I have money; ~ I have money.

Conjunction

Another basic truth function besides denial is *conjunction*. We conjoin two (or more) statements when we assert that both (or all) are true. Thus, we conjoin

Pococatapetl is a volcano

and

Vesuvius is a volcano

when we assert,

(6)   Pococatapetl is a volcano and Vesuvius is a volcano,

or any variant such as "Pococatapetl and Vesuvius are both volcanoes" or "Vesuvius is a volcano and so is Pococatapetl."

Likewise, we conjoin "Elephants are plentiful" with "Unicorns don't exist," when we say "Elephants are plentiful but unicorns don't exist," which has exactly the same truth value as "Elephants are plentiful and unicorns don't exist."   The only thing we lose when we replace 'but' by 'and' is emphasis on the contrast between the affirmative first conjunct and the negative second conjunct, but since this rhetorical difference makes no difference to truth value, it has no logical importance.   From the purely logical point of view, 'but' is merely another term for conjunction, as are 'although' and 'while', which also differ from 'and' in rhetorical force.

62

"Although elephants are plentiful, unicorns don't exist" and "While elephants are plentiful, unicorns don't exist" are true if elephants are plentiful and unicorns don't exist, and are false otherwise.

Since there are many different words for conjunction, as there were for denial, we shall need one standard symbol, as we did for denial. Our symbol for conjunction will be the ampersand, &. Don't confuse it with a plus sign, +, which means something else. The plus sign signifies that two numbers are being added, and we are not talking about adding numbers but about conjoining statements. Conflating the two symbols will cause you to confuse the two ideas later on when it will be important to keep them distinct.

Using the ampersand, we shall write (6) as

(7)   Vesuvius is a volcano & Pococatapetl is a volcano.

'And' usually means conjunction, but not always. So don't think you can always replace the English word 'and' by the ampersand. "You pay me well and I will work for you" does not assert either "You pay me well" or "I will work for you," much less both. It is not a conjunction but a conditional, meaning "If you pay me well, I will work for you." Another use of 'and' is to mean 'with'. Thus, "I like scotch and soda" cannot be regarded as short for the conjunction "I like scotch and I like soda." It means "I like scotch mixed with soda," and this may be true of a person who likes neither scotch nor soda separately. Similarly, 'while' often signifies conjunction, but "While she is painting I am doing the dishes" does not conjoin "She is painting" with "I am doing the dishes." Rather, it means "Whenever she paints, I do the dishes." Like many other words in English, words of conjunction do double duty. They are ambiguous. That is another reason, besides the diversity of English words for conjunction, for using one well-defined symbol to indicate conjunction.

Of course, (6) is true. On the other hand,

(8)   Everest is a volcano & Pococatapetl is a volcano,

(9)   Vesuvius is a volcano & the Matterhorn is a volcano,

and

(10)   Everest is a volcano & the Matterhorn is a volcano

are all false. A conjunction of statements is true if all the conjoined statements are true; otherwise, it is false. Both conjuncts of (6) are true, but (8) and (9) each have one false conjunct, and (10) has two. So (8), (9), and (10) are false, (8) and (9) no less so for having one true conjunct: half-truths are falsehoods.

So are two-thirds truths. The conjunction

(11)   Vesuvius is a volcano & Pococatapetl is a volcano & the Matterhorn is a volcano

is false, although it has two true conjuncts.

It doesn't matter in which order we write conjuncts. (7) remains true if written as

(12)   Pococatapetl is a volcano & Vesuvius is a volcano.

If false, it would remain false. In contrast, order is not always irrelevant in normal English. For example, "Sally got married and had a baby" says something different from "Sally had a baby and got married." The former means "Sally got married first and had a baby second," whereas the latter means "Sally had a baby first and got married second." Both are conjunctions, but they conjoin quite different statements, statements that indicate different orders of occurrence in time. Temporal order matters. Conjunctive order does not.

Denials and Conjunctions Together

Now that we have discussed conjunction and denial separately, let us discuss what happens when we conjoin denials and deny conjunctions. Take a statement like "Vesuvius is a volcano, but Pococatapetl is not." This statement is false. So are "Vesuvius is not, but Pococatapetl is, a volcano" and "Neither Vesuvius nor Pococatapetl are volcanoes." That is, all the following are false:

(13)   Vesuvius is a volcano & ~ Pococatapetl is a volcano,

(14)   ~ Vesuvius is a volcano & Pococatapetl is a volcano,

and

(15)   ~ Vesuvius is a volcano & ~ Pococatapetl is a volcano.

If it is not clear on inspection that each of these is false, it can be made graphically clear as follows. To save space, let us abbreviate "Vesuvius is a volcano" as "V" and "Pococatapetl is a volcano" as "P." Then we can write (7) as "$V \& P$," (13) as "$V \& \sim P$," (14) as "$\sim V \& P$," and (15) as

"$\sim V \& \sim P$." Then, knowing that "V" and "P" are both true, we can calculate the truth values of compounds of them as follows:

V P	$\sim V$ $\sim P$	$V \& P$	$V \& \sim P$	$\sim V \& P$	$\sim V \& \sim P$
T T	F F	T	F	F	F

On the extreme left are our two component statements, both true. Next are their denials, both false. After that come four conjunctions, all false but the first one.

When we want to deny a whole compound, say (7), we enclose it in parentheses and put a tilde before the parentheses, thus:

(16) $\sim (V \& P)$.

But don't confuse denying a conjunction with denying its components. That is, don't confuse (16) with (15). (15) says that neither Vesuvius nor Pococatapetl is a volcano. (16) says that at least one of the two isn't a volcano. In this case, both statements happen to be true; but compare

(17) $\sim$ (Wyoming is a state & Birmingham is a state)

with

(18) $\sim$ Wyoming is a state & $\sim$ Birmingham is a state.

In normal English, the distinction between these is the distinction between

(19)   It is false that both Wyoming and Birmingham are states,

which is true, and

(20)   It is both false that Wyoming is a state and false that Birmingham is a state,

which is false. (17) says that Wyoming and Birmingham aren't both states, which is true. (18) says that Wyoming isn't a state and also that Birmingham isn't a state, which is false. The distinction between these can easily be blurred in English. Suppose that someone says, "Wyoming and Birmingham aren't states." Does that mean (17) or (18)? The scope of the denial is not clear in the English statement.

By contrast, the scope of the tilde is unambiguous. The tilde functions much like the subtraction sign in arithmetic: $-(2 \times 9) = -(18)$; $-2 \times -9 = +(18)$. A tilde denies the statement immediately following, but in (17) the statement immediately following the tilde is the whole conjunction "Wyoming is a state & Birmingham is a state." The tilde therefore does not apply to the two conjuncts separately, as do those in (18). (17) truly denies the conjunction of a truth with a falsehood; (18) falsely conjoins a falsehood with a truth. Using obvious abbreviations for the component statements, we can see how the truth values work out:

W	B	~W	~B	~(W & B)	~W & ~B
T	F	F	T	T	F

On the left you see the truth values of the components. Next are given the truth values of their denials and then the truth values of (17) and (18).

The rule in computing truth values is to start with the values of the simple components; then compute the values of denials of those; then compute the values of conjunctions of the simple components with each other or with denials; then compute denials of those conjunctions; and so on. Consider, for example, the statement "It is not true that it is false that neither Eisenhower nor MacArthur were great generals," abbreviated as

(21) $\sim\sim(\sim E \,\&\, \sim M)$.

We compute the truth value of that statement as follows:

E	M	~E	~M	~E & ~M	~(~E & ~M)	~~(~E & ~M)
T	T	F	F	F	T	F

Working left to right, we see that (21) is false.

A somewhat more graphic method for computing the truth value of a conjunction, knowing the truth values of its components, is illustrated below. Consider (17) and (18) again. Their truth values are determined as follows:

Here you see that we start with the truth values of the abbreviated statements "W" and "B." We put the opposite values under denials of these statements. The lines then show how to proceed. The resulting truth values are here circled, but they would be plain without being circled, and we shall not continue to circle them.

In summary, to determine truth values, just reverse the procedure used to analyze a statement. To analyze, work inward, breaking the whole up into its constituents, then breaking those constituents up into their constituents. To determine truth value, go in the opposite direction, starting with the simple constituents and working up to the whole compound.

Exercises

A. Declare each of the following true or false.

1. Einstein was a physicist & Newton was a physicist.

2. Einstein was a physicist & ~Newton was a physicist.

3. ~Einstein was a physicist & Newton was a physicist.

4. ~Einstein was a physicist & ~Newton was a physicist.

5. ~(Einstein was a physicist & Newton was a physicist).

6. ~(Einstein was a physicist & ~Newton was a physicist).

7. ~(~Einstein was a physicist & Newton was a physicist).

8. ~(~Einstein was a physicist & ~Newton was a physicist).

B. Match each of the following with one of the items in (A).

1. Einstein and Newton were both physicists.

2. Neither Einstein nor Newton was a physicist.

3. Einstein was a physicist but Newton wasn't.

4. Although physics was Einstein's profession, it wasn't Newton's.

5. Either Einstein or Newton was a physicist.

6. It is false that neither Einstein nor Newton was a physicist.

7. At least one of the pair, Einstein and Newton, was a physicist.

8. I deny that Einstein wasn't a physicist but Newton was.

9. I deny that Einstein wasn't a physicist and I deny that Newton was.

10. "Einstein and Newton were both physicists" is false.

11. It is a myth that Einstein and Newton were both physicists.

12. The life of physics claimed Newton but passed Einstein by.

C. Redo (A), replacing 'Newton' by 'Columbus'.

D. Here is a list of abbreviated statements. "A" is true, "B" false. Say which are true and which false.

   1. $\sim(A \,\&\, B)$

   2. $\sim A \,\&\, B$

   3. $\sim A \,\&\, \sim B$

   4. $\sim(\sim A \,\&\, \sim B)$

   5. $\sim \sim(A \,\&\, B)$

E. If "A" abbreviates "Al loves Mary" and "B" abbreviates "Bill loves Mary," what, in idiomatic English, do the items in (D) say?

8 / Disjunction

We have learned two truth functions, conjunction and denial. Here we want to learn another, *disjunction* (also called *alternation*). Here is an example:

(1)   Either Babe Ruth or Wilt Chamberlain was a basketball player.

This disjunction is a truth function of two *disjuncts* (alternatives),

(2)   Babe Ruth was a basketball player

and

(3)   Wilt Chamberlain was a basketball player.

Since one of these disjuncts, namely, (3), is true, so is (1). Had they both been false, then (1) would have been false as well, as is

(4)   Either Babe Ruth or Joe Namath was a basketball player.

The Ambiguity of 'either/or'

All that is clear. A question arises, however, when both disjuncts are true, as in

(5)   Either Wilt Chamberlain or Bill Russell was a basketball player.

Given that both were basketball players, is (5) true, or is it false? Some people will insist that it is true, others that it is false; still others will be in doubt. This is because (5) is ambiguous, meaning either

69

(6)   Wilt Chamberlain or Bill Russell was a basketball player, but both weren't,

which is false, or

(7)   Either Wilt Chamberlain or Bill Russell was a basketball player, and perhaps both were,

which is true.

We shall call (6) an *exclusive* disjunction, because (6) says that its two disjuncts exclude each other, that they can't both be true. (7) is not an exclusive disjunction.* Its being true is compatible with both its disjuncts being true. If we are unable to decide whether (1) is true or false, it is because we don't know whether to take it as an exclusive disjunction or not.

Doubtful cases like (1) occur because there are times when we use the words 'either/or' to declare the alternatives mutually exclusive, and there are other times when we do not. Generally, if one says to one's child,

You may have either pie or cake,

one means

You may have either pie or cake, but you may not have both.

On the other hand, if one promises one's child either a bicycle or a sled for her birthday, one will not deserve reproach for reneging by deciding at the last minute to give both. Nor will the weatherman be found at fault for predicting either sleet or snow if we end up getting both. So the same words represent disjunctions that are meant to be exclusive and others that are not. Hence the ambiguity of (5).

Resolving the Ambiguity

In legal documents, this ambiguity is often resolved by using the monstrosity 'and/or' when the alternation is not meant to be exclusive. Thus the defendant has no cause for complaint if the judge gives him both a fine and a jail sentence on the basis of a clause in the law prescribing a penalty of 'five years and/or five thousand dollars." Unfortunately, this device is not systematically enough used to make it clear that the judge is

---

* Disjunctions that are not exclusive are sometimes said to be *inclusive*. That term is misleading in its suggestion that both alternatives are being asserted. *Nonexclusive* is better, but barbarous. So I avoid both.

wrong if she gives a fine and a penalty on the basis of a law that prescribes "five years or five thousand dollars" without indicating whether the two penalties are meant to be mutually exclusive.

Latin has a more satisfactory solution, two different words: *aut* for disjunctions that are exclusive and *vel* for disjunctions that are not. Hence

(8)   Wilt Chamberlain was a basketball player *aut* Bill Russell was

is equivalent to (6) and is therefore false, whereas

(9)   Wilt Chamberlain was a basketball player *vel* Bill Russell was

is equivalent to (7) and is therefore true.

We shall here follow Latin in employing two symbols. Unless we want to say that our alternatives exclude each other, we shall write a ' ∨ ' (wedge) between them. When we want to say that the alternatives exclude each other, we shall put a slash in the wedge: ' ⩝ '. Hence we shall write false (6) as

(10)   Wilt Chamberlain was a basketball player ⩝ Bill Russell was a basketball player,

but we shall write true (7) as

(11)   Wilt Chamberlain was a basketball player ∨ Bill Russell was a basketball player.

We shall also write false (6) as

(12) $(C \lor R) \& \sim(C \& R)$,

abbreviating "Wilt Chamberlain was a basketball player" as "C" and "Bill Russell was a basketball player" as "R". Like (10) and (6), (12) says that one or the other was a basketball player, but not both. All this is summarized in the following table:

C R	C ∨ R	C ⩝ R	$(C \lor R) \& \sim(C \& R)$
T T	T	F	F

As you see here, the exclusive disjunction is false when both disjuncts are true, but a disjunction that is not exclusive is true in that same case. In other cases, there is no difference.

We now know how to state our own disjunctions in unambiguous language, but what about the ambiguous disjunctions of others? How are we to interpret them? When we encounter a statement like (5), shall we read it after the fashion of (6) or after the fashion of (7)? Shall we read it as an exclusive disjunction, or not? If the author of (5) is close at hand, we can ask him. Let those who create ambiguity resolve it. If he is not available, we must look to context. But if that is insufficient, what shall we do then?

Without a clear context, a great many people would read (5) as an exclusive disjunction. To the question whether it is true or false they would reply, "Since both Chamberlain and Russell were basketball players, the statement that only one of them was is false." Such people would be taking (5) as meaning (6). That seems to be a mistake. The reverse policy seems to be better. That is, you shouldn't take a disjunction as exclusive unless there is clear reason to believe it is so intended.

There are several good reasons for adopting this policy. One is simple charity. If we can, we should take a person's ambiguous remark in the most plausible way, the way that will make it most likely to come out true. Now a disjunction that is not exclusive has a better chance of being true. Imagine (5) said by a man unfamiliar with professional basketball. He has just heard the two names 'Wilt Chamberlain' and 'Bill Russell', and knows in a vague way that at least one of the two is connected with basketball. He records this by declaring (5). Would you say that he is wrong? Surely not. You would interpret him as declaring that at least one of the two was a basketball player, which is exactly right. When you can, you should give someone the benefit of the doubt. It is true that people don't always deserve charity and also true that we mustn't expect any in return. Expect others to read your own disjunctions as exclusive unless you warn them against doing so.

Another reason for adopting a policy of not interpreting ambiguous disjunctions as exclusive is self-interest. Suppose a man offers to sell you, cheaply and sight unseen, two barrels of apples. He says that he is selling them cheaply because "One or the other contains a great many rotten apples." It is in your interest to read his statement as leaving open the possibility that both barrels may be rotten. Should you buy the barrels only to discover that both contained defective fruit, you would have only yourself to blame. The seller did not lie to you: he didn't say that one barrel was good, just that one or the other was bad. Admittedly, you could claim that he had misled you, especially if he knew all along that both barrels were bad. In that case he failed to tell you all that he knew. Yet being misled in such a case is your own fault. *Caveat emptor:* let the buyer beware. The seller was guilty of sharp practice but not of false representation. Failing to tell the whole truth is not the same thing as telling a lie.

A third, and even more compelling, reason to resist the tendency to read disjunctions as exclusive is that denial does not combine naturally with exclusive disjunction. True denials of false disjunctions wrongly turn out false when the disjunctions are thought of as exclusive. Consider an example. Suppose someone wants to deny (5). That is, she says, "It is not true that either Chamberlain or Russell was a basketball player." Now we would normally declare this false. But if we read (5) as (6) then it will be true. For (6) is false. So its denial is true. To see this, look at the following table:

C R	$C \vee R$	$\sim(C \vee R)$	$C \veebar R$	$\sim(C \veebar R)$
T T	T	F	F	T

You see here that the denial of the exclusive disjunction is true. Only the denial of the nonexclusive disjunction is false, as it should be.

For these reasons and others, it is usually best to read disjunctions as exclusive only when there is clear indication that they are so intended. This policy not only insures the most charitable interpretation of what is said but is also more coherent with the rest of our discourse. Anyone who wishes her remark to be taken as an exclusive disjunction can always indicate as much by adding a rider to that effect, as we did in (6). Of course, there are perils in this policy, but as long as people don't say exactly what they mean, we are at peril, and the policy will lead us right more often than wrong.

Restated, our policy will amount to reading 'either/or' as ' $\vee$ ' (rather than as ' $\veebar$ ') unless there is clear indication to the contrary. We shall treat an ambiguous disjunction as true when both disjuncts are true, as false only when neither disjunct is true. So, we shall render (5) as (11), which is true.

The Ambiguity of 'unless'

What applies to 'either/or' applies in equal measure to 'unless', another term of disjunction that shares exactly the same ambiguity. Consider

(13)   You will be fired unless you work hard.

This promise is clearly falsified if you do not work hard and are not fired, clearly verified if you do not work hard and are fired or do work hard and are not fired. But what if you work hard and are fired nevertheless? Has your employer lied to you? To ask such a question is to ask whether (13) should be understood as

(14)   You will be fired ∨ you will work hard,

or as

(15)   You will be fired ⩡ you will work hard.

Many people will read (13) as the exclusive disjunction (15). To do so is, however, as wrong as reading the corresponding statement

You will either work hard or you will be fired

as excluding the prospect that you will both work hard and be fired. Suppose you work hard but your employer finds that you are incompetent, or that he has no further need of your services. Then he may fire you in spite of your hard work. What he promised by uttering (13) was not to keep you on if you worked hard, no matter what else might happen. He merely promised not to keep you on if you did not work hard.

If this point is not clear, consider another example, one cited by the *Oxford English Dictionary* from Stuart Chase

(16)   Modern man is obsolete . . . unless he can stop world wars.

This rules out the possibility that modern man is not obsolete and does not stop world wars, but it is consistent with all other possible states of affairs. In particular, it leaves open the possibility that modern man stops world wars but becomes obsolete because of some other failure. So, (16) must be read as declaring

(17)   Modern man is obsolete ∨ he stops world wars.

Don't be discouraged if this point keeps slipping away from you just when you think you have it firmly in hand. Many people have the same problem. The tendency to read 'unless' as signifying exclusive disjunction is widespread. People often take 'p unless q' as short for 'if q, then not p' when it means rather 'if not q, then p'. Hence they misunderstand (16) as declaring that modern man is not obsolete if he does stop wars when it means rather that modern man is obsolete if he does not stop wars. As we shall see when we take up conditional statements, statements of the form 'if p then q', this misunderstanding is connected with an unfortunate tendency to confuse 'if not p then not q' with 'if p then q', and therefore with 'if not q then not p'. In the meanwhile, the moral of the story is this: translate 'unless' using the wedge except when there is clear reason to regard it as signifying an exclusive disjunction. That is, follow the same policy you learned regarding 'either/or', and for the same reasons.

As we have noted, not only may disjunctions be affirmed; they may also be denied. The standard idiom of denial is 'neither/nor'. Hence, the denial of (1) is

(**18**)   Neither Babe Ruth nor Wilt Chamberlain was a basketball player.

This must not be confused with

(**19**)   Either Babe Ruth or Wilt Chamberlain was not a basketball player,

because (18) is false and (19) true. Denial applies in (18) to the whole disjunction, in (19) to each of its disjuncts. This distinction becomes clearer in our notation. Using obvious abbreviations, and our special symbols, we rewrite (1) as

$$R \vee C,$$

(18) as

$$\sim(R \vee C),$$

and (19) as

$$\sim R \vee \sim C.$$

The truth values of these three statements are shown below:

R C	R ∨ C	~(R ∨ C)	~R ∨ ~C
F T	T	F	T

To compute the truth values of alternations or denials, just follow the procedure used in computing the truth values of conjunctions. First work out the truth values of the simple components and of their denials; then work out the truth values of alternations of these; and so on.

Exercises

A. Declare each of the following true or false.

    1. Einstein was a physicist $\vee$ Newton was a physicist.

2. Einstein was a physicist $\vee$ Newton was a physicist.

3. ~Einstein was a physicist $\vee$ Newton was a physicist.

4. ~Einstein was a physicist $\vee$ Newton was a physicist.

5. Einstein was a physicist $\vee$ ~Newton was a physicist.

6. Einstein was a physicist $\vee$ ~Newton was a physicist.

7. ~Einstein was a physicist $\vee$ ~Newton was a physicist.

8. ~Einstein was a physicist $\vee$ ~Newton was a physicist.

9. ~(Einstein was a physicist $\vee$ Newton was a physicist.)

10. ~(Einstein was a physicist $\vee$ Newton was a physicist.)

11. ~(~Einstein was a physicist $\vee$ Newton was a physicist.)

12. ~(~Einstein was a physicist $\vee$ Newton was a physicist.)

13. ~(Einstein was a physicist $\vee$ ~Newton was a physicist.)

14. ~(Einstein was a physicist $\vee$ ~Newton was a physicist.)

15. ~(~Einstein was a physicist $\vee$ ~Newton was a physicist.)

16. ~(~Einstein was a physicist $\vee$ ~Newton was a physicist.)

B. Abbreviating "Einstein was a physicist" as "E" and "Newton was a physicist" as "N," and using our special symbols, paraphrase each of the following. Then compute their truth values.

1. Either Einstein was a physicist or Newton was.

2. Neither Einstein nor Newton was a physicist.

3. Either Einstein or Newton was a physicist, but both weren't.

4. It is false that either Einstein or Newton was a physicist.

5. It is false that neither Einstein nor Newton was a physicist.

6. It is false that Einstein was a physicist or that Newton was.

7. It is either false that Einstein was a physicist or false that Newton was.

8. It is not either false that Einstein was a physicist or false that Newton was.

9. It is not false either that Einstein was a physicist or that Newton was.

10. It is not false either that Einstein was not a physicist or that Newton was not.

11. Einstein was a physicist unless Newton was.

12. Einstein was not a physicist unless Newton was not.

13. Einstein was a physicist unless Newton was not.

14. It is false that Einstein was not a physicist unless Newton was.

15. It is not false that Einstein was a physicist unless Newton was.

C. Redo (A) after replacing 'Newton' by 'Houdini'. Abbreviations will help.

D. If "A" abbreviates "Al loves Mary" and "B" abbreviates "Bill loves Mary," what, in idiomatic English, do the following say?

1. $A \lor B$

2. $\sim(A \lor B)$

3. $\sim A \lor B$

4. $\sim A \lor \sim B$

5. $\sim(\sim A \lor \sim B)$

9 / *Grouping*

We have seen how denial combines with conjunction and with alternation. We now want to investigate the combination of conjunction and alternation with each other. The result is a level of complexity that poses problems with which all of us need to learn to deal. Consider the true statement

(1) Either Maine and Vermont both voted for Roosevelt or neither did.

That statement, simple as it may first appear, has a fairly complicated logic. How is it to be analyzed?

Well, we begin by noticing that it is an alternation and can be written:

(2) Maine and Vermont both voted for Roosevelt ∨ neither Maine nor Vermont voted for Roosevelt.

The *grouping words* 'either/or' help us to see this. They divide the sentence up into two parts; the word 'either' marks the first part and the word 'or' the second. Now our problem reduces to analyzing the two alternatives.

Clearly, the first is a conjunction and can be written

(3) Maine voted for Roosevelt & Vermont voted for Roosevelt.

The second can also be regarded as a conjunction:*

(4) ~ Maine voted for Roosevelt & ~ Vermont voted for Roosevelt.

So the whole can be written

---

* We could also regard it as a denial of an alternation, as "~ (Maine voted for Roosevelt ∨ Vermont voted for Roosevelt)." As we will see later, it comes to the same thing.

(5)   (Maine voted for Roosevelt & Vermont voted for Roosevelt) ∨
        (∼ Maine voted for Roosevelt & ∼ Vermont voted for Roosevelt).

Parentheses

Notice the parentheses. Without them, (5) would be hopelessly ambiguous. How would you interpret

(6)   Maine voted for Roosevelt & Vermont voted for Roosevelt ∨
        ∼ Maine voted for Roosevelt & ∼ Vermont voted for Roosevelt?

So written, the statement is neither clearly an alternation nor clearly a conjunction. We need the parentheses to resolve the ambiguity by marking the limits of the components. In (1) that is done for us by the device of speaking of Maine and Vermont in the same breath as subjects of one predicate. That is, it is done by *subject compression*.

Just as it contains many ways of indicating denial, conjunction, and alternation, English contains many devices for indicating how a sentence is to be divided up and how its various parts are to be grouped together. As before, however, logical analysis will be facilitated if we make use of one standard device. Hence, we shall use parentheses whenever we want to group compounds that are themselves components of larger compounds. These parentheses will make it plain to the eye how the parts of the sentence are to be grouped, and they will thus make computation of the truth values of very complex sentences quick and easy. To see how quick and easy, consider (5), knowing that Maine did not vote for Roosevelt and neither did Vermont. The second component, (4), is clearly true and so, therefore, is (5).

The need for unambiguous indicators of grouping can be illustrated by considering another example:

(7)   Either Georgia voted for Roosevelt or Maine voted for Roosevelt
        and Vermont voted for Roosevelt.

Are we to take this as the alternation

(8)   Georgia voted for Roosevelt ∨ (Maine voted for Roosevelt &
        Vermont voted for Roosevelt),

or should we read it as the conjunction

79

(9)   (Georgia voted for Roosevelt ∨ Maine voted for Roosevelt) &
        Vermont voted for Roosevelt ?

Since Georgia voted for Roosevelt, (8) is true; but since Vermont did not,
(9) is false. So whether (7) is true or false depends on which grouping is
intended.

The grouping achieved by parentheses in (8) and (9) is managed in
English by other devices. One way to amend (7) so that it says (8) is to
insert the word 'both' after 'or' and compress the last two statements into
a single statement about two subjects, thus:

(10)   Either Georgia voted for Roosevelt or both Maine and Vermont
        voted for Roosevelt.

Perhaps the simplest way to make (7) clearly mean (9) is to put a comma
before the word 'and', thus:

(11)   Either Georgia voted for Roosevelt or Maine voted for Roosevelt,
        and Vermont voted for Roosevelt.

Another way is by compression of subjects:

(12)   Either Georgia or Maine voted for Roosevelt, and Vermont voted
        for Roosevelt.

We have so far seen how parentheses can do the work of (a) grouping
words, like 'either/or' and 'both/and'; (b) punctuation, like commas; and
(c) compression.* We also saw in earlier chapters how parentheses help
to make clear the scopes of denials, by distinguishing, for example, between

(13)   ∼ (John is stupid & Mary is stupid)

and

(14)   ∼ John is stupid & Mary is stupid,

which read respectively in standard English as

(15)   John and Mary are not both stupid

and

(16)   John is not stupid but Mary is.

---

* We have here illustrated only compression of subjects, but there can be similar
compression of predicates; for example, "Mary is either sick or malingering but
Sam is well and at work."

This is a lot of work to do, but parentheses do it well and provide a clear model for the job being done by a multitude of devices in natural languages. So it is worth learning to use them, and we can learn to use them best if we first learn to read them.

Reading Parentheses

The idea behind parentheses is very simple. As in arithmetic, they are used to enclose any complex expression that we wish to treat as a component unit of a larger expression. We just put a left-hand parenthesis, (, in front of such an expression and a right-hand parenthesis,), at the end. What occurs in between two facing parentheses is to be regarded as one indissoluble unit. Units thus enclosed in parentheses can be denied by putting tildes in front of them. Thus

$$\sim (M \,\&\, V)$$

is a denial of the unit "$M \,\&\, V$" but not of any of the components of that unit. Units enclosed in parentheses can also be compounded with other units. Hence,

$$\sim M \,\vee\, (M \,\&\, V)$$

disjoins the units "M" and "$M \,\&\, V$", forming a very different expression from

$$(\sim M \,\vee\, M) \,\&\, V,$$

which conjoins the units "$\sim M \,\vee\, M$" and "V".

We shall frequently write statements that are compounds of components that are themselves compounds. An example is (6), abbreviated as

(17) $(M \,\&\, V) \,\vee\, (\sim M \,\&\, \sim V).$

Here the mating lines show how to match parentheses. The lines are drawn according to the rule: mate each left hand parenthesis to the nearest succeeding unmated right hand parenthesis. The same result is achieved by following the rule: don't let mating lines crisscross.

We shall also have occasion to write statements so complex that we shall need a hierarchy of grouping signs. In these cases we shall follow the common mathematical practice of using square brackets to group units enclosed in parentheses, and braces to group units thus enclosed in brackets. The following two examples will illustrate this practice.

(18) $M \mathbin{\&} [V \lor (\sim M \mathbin{\&} \sim V)]$

(19) $\sim M \lor \{M \mathbin{\&} [V \lor (\sim M \mathbin{\&} \sim V)]\}$

Once again, our mating lines guide your eye, but you will need to learn to do the guiding yourself, for the lines will appear no more in this book.

The most common fallacy in reading parentheses is to suppose that, because a statement is within the scope of an ampersand, wedge, or tilde, so are its components. The assumption is incorrect.

$M \mathbin{\&} (V \lor G)$

says that Maine voted for Roosevelt and either Vermont or Georgia did, too. Don't confuse it with

$(M \mathbin{\&} V) \lor G,$

which says that either Maine and Vermont voted for Roosevelt or else Georgia did. To repeat, parentheses enclose compounds that are to be thought of as units in a larger compound. Those units are, as whole units, within the scopes of adjacent ampersands, wedges, or tildes, but no part of either unit is.

If this explanation is confusing to you, don't despair. You will soon understand it without even trying. Looking at what (18) says when it is spelled out in standard English will help: (18) says

(20)   Maine voted for Roosevelt, and either Vermont did, too, or both Maine and Vermont did not.

Paraphrasing

It is instructive to see how to get from (20) to (18) and back again. That there is a complete sentence before 'and' helps us to see that (20) is a conjunction. Then the pair of grouping words 'either/or' helps us to see that what comes after the 'and' is an alternation. The word 'or' divides that alternation into two alternatives, "Vermont did, too," and "Both

Maine and Vermont did not." Using obvious abbreviations, that much analysis yields

M and either V or both $\sim M$ and $\sim V$,

which we render as (18).

Since (20) is already a rather clear English sentence, you may wonder why we bother to turn it in this laborious way into (18). We do so to help us appraise its truth value. Just by looking, it is a little hard to decide whether (20) is true or false, and one can easily get confused trying to decide. Rendered as (18), however, the truth value of (20) is easy to appraise. We simply use methods now familiar to you:

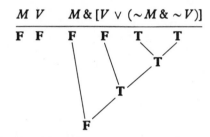

In this way you discover that (18) and therefore (20) are false. There can no longer be any doubt or any dispute. By making it perfectly clear which compounds are themselves components of which compounds, the parentheses guide computation of truth value. Therefore, you have a perfectly mechanical and nearly foolproof method for deciding the truth value, no matter how complicated, of any compound, provided only that you know the truth values of its components.

With practice, you should be able to analyze fairly complicated compounds and, knowing the truth values of their components, to compute their truth values. For practice, let us look at another case, the statement

(21)   Either Alabama voted for Roosevelt or Georgia did, but either Maine or Vermont did not.

In this case the first step should probably be to replace all statements by obvious abbreviations. That will make the logical structure more perspicuous. The result is:

(22)   Either A or G, but either not M or not V.

Now we must decide whether (22) is an alternation or a conjunction. Although it starts with 'either', the sentence is clearly a conjunction. We see this from the comma, which indicates that the scope of the 'either/or' ends at the word 'but'. That comma tells us to read (21) as the conjunction

(23)   (Either *A* or *G*) & (either not *M* or not *V*).

(Without the comma it might be possible to read (21) as the alternation "*A* ∨ (*G* and either ∼*M* or ∼*V*)." You see how much difference even so small a thing as a comma can make.)

Now that we have reduced (21) to (23), we can analyze its components, getting

(24)   (*A* ∨ *G*) & (∼*M* ∨ ∼*V*),

which is true, as the following computation indicates:

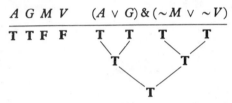

Remember the rule: work inward to analyze; work outward to compute truth value. If you do it by stages it will be easier. First try to decide whether the whole statement is a conjunction, a disjunction, or what—as we did when we transformed (1) into (2). If the components of this statement are themselves complex, enclose them in parentheses. Then break up the components into their components—as we did when we transformed (2) into (5). Finally, when you have got down to components that are not themselves compounds, abbreviate them. The result will be a nice picture of the grammatical and logical structure of the whole.

Why bother? Because doing so is one way to be quite sure you understand a statement well enough to decide its truth value with confidence. Remember, you understand what you can analyze into its truth conditions.

Exercises

A. Letting *A* = Art is prospering, *B* = Business is prospering, *S* = Science is declining, and *R* = Religion is declining, abbreviate and paraphrase the following into our special notation. Be sure to use enough punctuation to make the results unambiguous.

   1. Business and art are prospering but either science or religion is declining.

2. Business is not prospering but either art is or else science and religion are not declining.

3. Either business and art are prospering or neither science nor religion is declining.

4. Science is not declining and religion is not declining but either business or art is not prospering.

5. Business is prospering but either art is not prospering or else religion and science are both declining.

6. It is false either that business is not prospering or that art is not prospering, and false either that science is not declining or that religion is not declining.

7. It is either false that both religion and science are declining or false that business and art are prospering.

8. Either business is prospering or else art is prospering and religion and science are both declining.

9. It is false that business and art are prospering but not false that religion and science are declining.

10. Business, but not art, is prospering and religion, but not science, is declining.

B. Suppose that "*B*" and "*A*" are true but that "*S*" and "*R*" are false. Which of the preceding ten statements are true? Which false?

C. If "*A*," "*B*," "*R*," and "*S*" abbreviate the same statements as in (A), what, in idiomatic English, do the following say?

1. $A \lor [B \& (S \lor R)]$. (Hint: 'It is true that', like 'it is false that', helps with grouping.)

2. $(A \lor B) \lor (S \lor R)$

3. $\sim(A \lor B) \& \sim(S \lor R)$

4. $(\sim A \lor \sim B) \lor (S \& R)$

5. $\sim[(A \lor B) \& (S \lor R)]$

10 / Equivalence

Usually, there are several ways of saying much the same thing. Knowing these ways enables you to add variety to your speech and writing. It also helps resolve verbal disputes, and, as every shoe salesman will testify, saying the same thing in different ways can determine how people react to it: it is better to tell someone sensitive about the size of his feet that the left foot is smaller than to tell him that the right foot is larger. Another advantage of knowing different ways of saying the same thing is that some ways of saying a thing are clearer than others. For example,

Love is a many-splendored thing

says the same thing as

It is false that love is not a many-splendored thing;

but more people will find the first, direct way of stating it easier to understand. So it is helpful to be able to recognize that the second could be eliminated in favor of the first.

Up to now, we have depended on your being able to recognize different ways of saying the same thing. As the examples get more complicated, however, recognition gets more difficult. So it will be worthwhile to learn a method to help with hard cases. Learning this method will also sharpen your understanding of what it means to say, as we shall often have occasion to say, that two statements are *equivalent*.

The first point to be noticed is that equivalence is not just sameness of truth value. Statements that have unlike truth values aren't equivalent, but consider two statements that have like truth value:

      Prisms refract light

and

      Mirrors reflect light.

Though both are true, they are not equivalent. But if equivalence is not just identical truth value, what is it?

    A rough but accurate answer is that equivalent statements not only have the same truth value but couldn't conceivably have different truth values.* Let us explain what that means by looking at the dummy statement†

(1)   Ned is nearsighted

and its equivalent

(2) $\sim \sim$ Ned is nearsighted.

You don't know whether (1) is true or false. But whichever it is, (2) must have the same truth value, as the following *truth table* shows:

N	$\sim N$	$\sim \sim N$
T	F	T
F	T	F

Here (1) and (2) are abbreviated in an obvious way, and two possibilities are considered. The first line considers the possibility that (1) is true, and points out that, in that case its denial is false and the denial of that denial, namely, (2), is true. The second line considers the possibility that (1) is false and points out that, in that case, (2) is also false. Since two lines exhaust the possibilities, (1) and (2) have the same truth value, whatever it is. There is no way they could have different truth values.

    Consider another example, the conjunction

(3)   Ned is nearsighted and so is Shirley.

This example is equivalent to its *converse,*

---

   * We shall give a more exact definition later.

   † A dummy statement is just a sentence that no one has asserted. So it has no definite truth value. But as we can learn artificial respiration by practicing on dummies, which we can pretend are human, so we can learn logic by practicing on artificially fabricated sentences, which we are pretending to be statements. Hence, where truth tables for statements had only one line, truth tables for dummy statements have several. We pretend that the dummy is true on some of these lines and on others false. A real statement, being either true or false and not both, cannot be so treated.

(4)   Shirley is nearsighted and so is Ned,

as this truth table shows:

N S	N & S	S & N
T T	T	T
T F	F	F
F T	F	F
F F	F	F

Once again you are ignorant of the truth values of the components. But if they have truth values, both are true, or both are false, or one is true and the other false. Thus, there are four possibilities. The truth table considers all four and points out that (3) and (4) have the same truth value no matter what the truth values of "N" and "S," their abbreviated components.

So we may provisionally define equivalence of statements as sameness not merely of truth value but of *truth table*.★ Two compound statements are equivalent if and only if they would be true under the same conditions, false under the same conditions, whatever the conditions. You can better appreciate what this means if you compare (3) to a statement that is not equivalent to it, namely,

(5)   Ned is nearsighted ∨ Shirley is nearsighted.

N S	N & S	N ∨ S
T T	T	T
T F	F	T
F T	F	T
F F	F	F

As this table points out, the conjunction is true only when both conjuncts are true; the alternation is false only when both alternates are false. Thus, there are two cases—one where "N" is true but "S" false and one where "S" is true but "N" false—in which the conjunction and the alternation will have different truth values.

Now that you have a clearer understanding of what equivalence is, let us review some of the equivalences noted in earlier chapters. We have already noted the equivalence between the conjunction (3) and its converse conjunction, (4). There is a similar equivalence between the alternation (5)

★ This definition will have to be qualified later.

and its converse,

> Shirley is nearsighted ∨ Ned is nearsighted.

The order of conjuncts or of alternatives makes no difference to truth value.

None of the equivalences so far noted needed truth tables to make them obvious, but here is one that might. Compare

(6)   Ned isn't nearsighted and Shirley isn't nearsighted

to

(7)   Neither Ned nor Shirley is nearsighted.

That these are equivalent is not clear at first but it becomes clear once we rewrite (6) as

(8) $\sim N \,\&\, \sim S$

and (7) as

(9) $\sim(N \vee S)$

and then compare them using a truth table, thus:*

N S	$\sim(N \vee S)$	$\sim N \,\&\, \sim S$
T T	F	F
T F	F	F
F T	F	F
F F	T	T

Here we see that (8) and (9), our symbolic paraphrases of (6) and (7), come out having the same truth value on every line of the truth table. No matter whether their common components are taken as true or as false, these compounds have the same truth value.

The equivalence of (8) to (9) is a special case of what is known as *De Morgan equivalence,* after the logician Augustus De Morgan (who deserved the honor of having the equivalence named after him even if he wasn't its discoverer). Another form of De Morgan equivalence is that of

(10)   Either Ned is nearsighted or Shirley is

with

---

* As before, notice that we start on the left with the base components, then move right to denials of those, then to conjunctions or alternations of the base components or their denials, then to denials of those compounds, and so on. Later we will skip some of these steps.

(11)   That Ned is not nearsighted and that Shirley, too, is not near-sighted is false.

(10) and (11) are paraphrased and abbreviated as, respectively,

(12) $N \lor S$

and

(13) $\sim(\sim N \,\&\, \sim S)$,

which are shown by the following truth table to be equivalent.

N S	$\sim(\sim N \,\&\, \sim S)$	$N \lor S$
T T	T	T
T F	T	T
F T	T	T
F F	F	F

In what follows, we shall declare two statements to be equivalent by writing our sign of definitional equation between them. Thus, we shall write the two forms of De Morgan equivalence already noted, and several more, as:*

$$N \,\&\, S \overset{\mathrm{df}}{=} \sim(\sim N \lor \sim S)$$
$$N \,\&\, \sim S \overset{\mathrm{df}}{=} \sim(\sim N \lor S)$$
$$\sim N \,\&\, S \overset{\mathrm{df}}{=} \sim(N \lor \sim S)$$
$$\sim N \,\&\, \sim S \overset{\mathrm{df}}{=} \sim(N \lor S)$$
$$\sim(\sim N \,\&\, \sim S) \overset{\mathrm{df}}{=} N \lor S$$
$$\sim(\sim N \,\&\, S) \overset{\mathrm{df}}{=} N \lor \sim S$$
$$\sim(N \,\&\, \sim S) \overset{\mathrm{df}}{=} \sim N \lor S$$
$$\sim(N \,\&\, S) \overset{\mathrm{df}}{=} \sim N \lor \sim S$$

You should study these equivalences closely, using truth tables, to assure yourself that they all hold. Don't believe it just because I say it is so.

---

* Notice that the symbol '$\overset{\mathrm{df}}{=}$' occurs only between two whole statements. Accordingly, the first equivalence is to be read as declaring the whole statement "$N \,\&\, S$" equivalent to "$\sim(\sim N \lor \sim S)$". The sign of definitional equivalence, like the equal sign, has the greatest possible scope. Hence '$p \overset{\mathrm{df}}{=} q \lor q$' is to be read as an assertion of equivalence, not as a disjunction—as '$4 = 2 + 2$' is an equation, not a summation. That is, the equivalence is to be read as if it were punctuated '$p \overset{\mathrm{df}}{=} (q \lor q)$', not as if it were punctuated '$(p \overset{\mathrm{df}}{=} q) \lor q$'.

As we have noted, sameness of truth tables indicates equivalence; difference indicates nonequivalence. So we can also use truth tables to reinforce some of our earlier lessons about the scope of denial. Notice, again, that

(14) $\sim N \vee S$

is equivalent neither to

(15) $\sim(N \vee S)$

nor to

(16) $\sim N \vee \sim S$:

N S	$\sim N \vee \sim S$	$\sim N \vee S$	$\sim(N \vee S)$
T T	F	T	F
T F	T	F	F
F T	T	T	F
F F	T	T	T

You see the nonequivalence of (14) with (15) in the first and third lines, the nonequivalence of (15) with (16) in the second and third lines, and the nonequivalence of (14) with (16) in the first and second lines.

You will get comparable results if you compare the following three nonequivalent statements:

$\sim N \& S$ $\sim(N \& S)$ $\sim N \& \sim S$

So far we have looked at statements whose truth values were unknown to us—or, rather, at dummy statements having no definite truth value. What we have learned applies as well, however, to statements whose truth values we know. Compare

Mirrors reflect light and prisms refract it

to

Prisms refract light and mirrors reflect it.

Even if we did not know that both these statements are true, we could ascertain that they are equivalent by constructing a truth table like the ones we have been using. And, from a similar table, we could see that neither is equivalent to

Mirrors reflect light or prisms refract it.

Briefly stated, the importance of equivalence is that a statement and its equivalent do the same logical work. Since they differ in form, but not in truth value, one may be substituted for the other in full assurance that no change in truth value will result. That, as it turns out, makes recognition of equivalences extremely useful. You will have some idea just how useful when you reflect on the uses of the same principle in arithmetic.

Obviously, two statements that are each equivalent to a third are equivalent to each other.

Exercises

A. Which of the following have the same truth value? Which are equivalent to "Elephants have trunks but oxen don't"?

1. It is false that elephants and oxen both have trunks.

2. It is false either that elephants lack trunks or that oxen have them.

3. It is either false that elephants lack trunks or false that oxen have them.

4. It is false that elephants don't have trunks, but oxen do.

5. It is false that elephants don't have trunks and false that oxen do.

B. Which of the following have the same truth value? Which are equivalent to "Neither elephants nor oxen have trunks"?

1. Either elephants or oxen do not have trunks.

2. It is false that either elephants or oxen have trunks.

3. It isn't true that either elephants or oxen have trunks.

4. It is false that elephants don't have trunks but oxen do.

5. It is false that oxen don't have trunks but elephants do.

6. It isn't false that neither elephants nor oxen have trunks.

7. Elephants don't have trunks and oxen don't have trunks.

8. It is false that elephants and oxen both have trunks.

9. It is false that elephants and oxen don't both have trunks.

10. It is false that elephants and oxen don't both lack trunks.

C. By means of truth tables, show the equivalence of "$\sim(O \vee \sim E)$" to "$\sim O \,\&\, E$" and its nonequivalence to "$O \,\&\, \sim E$."

II / *Consistency and Implication*

In the preceding exercise we learned what it is for two statements to be equivalent to each other. Here we want to learn what it is for two statements to be consistent with each other or for one statement to imply another.

Consistency

Roughly speaking, to say that two (or more) statements are *consistent*★ means that they could both (or all) be true. Consider the dummy statements

(1)   Harold is handsome

and

(2)   Iona is intelligent.

Not knowing who Harold and Iona are, you don't know whether either of these statements is true; but for all you know, they could both be true. (1)'s being true does not rule out (2)'s being true. By contrast, (1) does exclude the truth of

(3)   Harold is not handsome.

(1) and (2) are consistent; (1) and (3) are not.

★ When we are talking about several statements, "consistent" is short for "consistent with each other." Later, when we discuss single statements, "consistent" will mean "consistent with itself."

As there was a truth table test for equivalence, so there is one for consistency. The following truth table shows that (1), abbreviated "*H*," is not consistent with (3), abbreviated "~*H*":

H	~H
T	F
F	T

Here we consider all possible truth values for "*H*" and see that there is no way in which "*H*" can be true while "~*H*" is true.

Another statement inconsistent with (1), as you see below, is

(4) ~Harold is handsome & Iona is intelligent:

H I	~H	~H & I
T T	F	F
T F	F	F
F T	T	T
F F	T	F

This table considers all possible combinations of truth values for the two component statements "*H*" and "*I*." You see that there is no combination that will make "*H*" come out true while also making "~*H* & *I*" come out true.

There is one limitation on the truth table test of consistency: it assumes components that are *independent* of each other, components consistent both with the other components and with denials of the other components. Let us illustrate. Try to compare (1) with

(5) Harold is ugly

by means of the following truth table:

	H U
Impossible	T T
	T F
	F T
	F F

The first line represents an impossibility, there being no way Harold can be at once handsome and ugly. So it should be ruled out.

Also not independent of (1) is

(6)   Harold is physically attractive.

Because (6) is inconsistent with the denial of (1), and (1) with the denial of (6), the second and third lines of the truth table would be ruled out:

	H	A	~H
	T	T	F
Impossible	T	F	F
Impossible	F	T	T
	F	F	T

Before we can use the truth table as a test of consistency, then, we need to make sure that the statements being compared have components that are independent of each other. That is sometimes harder done than said. Consider the following two statements:

(7)   God is omnipotent

and

(8)   God is perfect.

Most people would say that both are true. But there is a real question whether they are consistent. Does (7) mean that God could tell lies if he wanted to? Does (8) mean that he couldn't? Then (7) and (8) are inconsistent with each other. If, as most theologians think, perfection excludes moral fault while omnipotence includes the power to do what any morally deficient human being could do, then perfection and omnipotence exclude each other. The question is a difficult one and indicates that more detailed analyses of (7) and (8) are in order before truth tables will be appropriate.

In the case of Harold and Iona, however, there seems to be no problem. We know no reason why (1) and (2) couldn't both be true or both be false. So we may assume until further notice that they are independent of each other, provided we keep in mind that our assumption may need revising in the light of new information.

Remember that a truth table assesses the consistency of two statements by seeing whether there is any line of the truth table in which both are true. If there is, they count as consistent.

We have used truth tables to ascertain whether two statements are inconsistent with each other, but there are different sorts of inconsistency, and we may also use truth tables to distinguish them. Consider (3) and (4) again. Although they are equally inconsistent with (1), there is a difference

10. If 'p' is inconsistent with 'q', then 'q' is inconsistent with 'p'.

11. 'p', 'q', and 'r' are consistent with each other if there is no way in which they could all be false.

C. Using truth tables, decide which of the following (a) are consistent with, (b) imply, (c) are implied by, (d) are equivalent with, or (e) contradict "$\sim H \vee \sim I$."

    1. $H \vee I$

    2. H

    3. $\sim H \& \sim I$

    4. $\sim(H \vee \sim I)$

    5. $\sim(H \& I)$

D. Which of the following pairs are logically independent of each other?

    1. (a) John is tall.
       (b) John is short.

    2. (a) John is tall and fat.
       (b) John is short and skinny.

    3. (a) $A \& B$
       (b) $A \vee B$

    4. (a) A
       (b) $A \vee B$

    5. (a) $A \& B$
       (b) $\sim A \& \sim B$

12 / Statement Forms

In the last chapter we used truth tables as tests of consistency, implication and equivalence, but we noted that the test has limits. These limits exist because truth tables apply primarily to *statement forms* and only secondarily to statements. Let me explain what this means.

To begin with, statements have forms. For example, the statements

(1)   Rabbits are cute & rabbits are fearsome

and

(2)   Friends are rare & friends are valuable

both have the form

(3) $p \& q$,

the form of all conjunctions. Similarly, all disjunctions have the form

(4) $p \lor q$,

and all denials have the form

(5) $\sim p$.

The form of a statement is a mere diagram, a schema, a skeleton of a statement, not a statement. The 'p' and 'q' in (3), (4), and (5) do not stand for particular statements. They are merely place markers for any statements you please. Unlike (1) and (2), therefore, (3), (4), and (5) have no truth values. They are mere formulas, like the algebraic formula

$$x + y = z,$$

101

which is neither true nor false, but is the formula for countless arithmetical equations that are true or false, equations like

$$2 + 3 = 6$$

and

$$3 + 5 = 8.$$

Statement forms like (3) containing lower case letters from the end of the alphabet are therefore not to be confused with *abbreviated statements* like

(6) $C \& F,$

which contain upper case letters that are abbreviations for statements. Being an abbreviation of the statement (1), (6) is itself a statement with a truth value, the very same truth value as (1).

Substitution Instances

Now every statement may be thought of as a *substitution instance* of some statement form, as the result of replacing the statement letters by statements. For example, (1) and (2) are substitution instances of (3), (1) being the result of replacing 'p' by "Rabbits are cute" and 'q' by "Rabbits are fearsome," (2) being the result of replacing 'p' by "Friends are rare" and 'q' by "Friends are valuable." Similarly, disjunctions may be regarded as substitution instances of (4), and denials may be counted as substitution instances of (5).

Statements are said to *have* the forms of which they are substitution instances. Hence (1) and (2) have the form (3). Indeed, having a form and being a substitution instance of a form come to the same thing.

In short, statement forms may be pictured as the logical skeletons that remain when you have stripped off the statemental flesh, and statements may be thought of in their turn as the results of reversing the process and putting flesh back on the bones. Alternatively, statement forms may be regarded as maps, statements as mapped territories.

Don't let the fact that one statement form can have many different substitution instances confuse you. In any given statement form, substitution must be *uniform*: you must always put the same statements for different occurrences of the same letter. For example, consider

(7) $p \& (p \lor q).$

102

You must not substitute one statement for the first occurrence of 'p' and a different statement for the second occurrence.

(8)   John is ill & (John is ill ∨ Sue is mad)

is, but

(9)   John is ill & (Mary is impertinent ∨ Sue is mad)

is not a substitution instance of (7). (9) is, rather, a substitution instance of

(10) p & (r ∨ q)

When we go further and extend uniform substitution to two different statement forms, putting the same statements for the same letters in both forms, we get *simultaneous* substitution instances of those two forms. For example, suppose we start with (3) and (4), putting "Love is a many-splendored thing" for 'p' and "Hate is a many-sided evil" for 'q'. Then we will get the following pair of simultaneous substitution instances.

(11)   Love is a many-splendored thing & hate is a many-sided evil

and

(12)   Love is a many-splendored thing ∨ hate is a many-sided evil.

Our substitutions were simultaneous in that we did them at the same time.

The New Definitions

We are now in a position to define equivalence, implication, and consistency somewhat more strictly than before. I begin with equivalence: two statement forms are equivalent with each other if their simultaneous substitution instances have the same truth values; otherwise not. To see what this means, compare 'p ∨ q' to its equivalent 'q ∨ p'. You will see that there is nothing you can substitute for 'p' and 'q' in both that will make one come out true while the other comes out false. That is what the following truth table assures us.

p q	p ∨ q	q ∨ p
T T	T	T
T F	T	T
F T	T	T
F F	F	F

You see here that any substitutions for 'p' and 'q', whether true or false, that will make '$p \vee q$' come out true will also make '$q \vee p$' come out true. Similarly, any substitutions for 'p' and 'q' that will make '$p \vee q$' come out false also make '$q \vee p$' come out false.

By contrast, the forms '$p \vee q$' and '$p \& q$' are not equivalent, there being substitution instances of each that are true while simultaneous substitution instances of the other are false, as the following truth table reveals.

p q	$p \vee q$	$p \& q$
T T	T	T
T F	T	F
F T	T	F
F F	F	F

We see from the second line of this table that we could replace 'p' by a true statement and 'q' by a false one and get a true substitution instance for '$p \vee q$' and a false one for '$p \& q$'. It wouldn't matter which statements we used, just so we put a true statement for 'p' and a false one for 'q'. For example, putting "Elephants have tusks" for 'p' and "Oxen have tusks" for 'q' would do it. So would putting "Donkeys bray" for 'p' and "Horses sing" for 'q'. A similar point is made in the third line, which shows that replacing 'p' by a false statement, while replacing 'q' by a true one, would make '$p \vee q$' true, while making '$p \& q$' false.

So much for equivalence. Now for consistency. Two statement forms are consistent if and only if they have simultaneous substitution instances that are both true. Hence, '$p \vee q$' and '$p \& q$' are consistent with each other, as the first line of the preceding table shows. Just replace both 'p' and 'q' by true statements and the results will be true statements. For example, replace 'p' by "Oxen have horns" and 'q' by "Elephants do not have horns." The result will be a true disjunction and a true conjunction.

By contrast, the forms '$p \& q$' and '$\sim(p \& q)$' are not consistent with each other, there being no substitutions for 'p' and 'q' that will make both come out true. Indeed, they contradict each other, for there are also no substitutions that have the same truth value.

Implication is, of course, just the obverse of consistency. One statement form implies another if and only if the first is inconsistent with the denial of the second. Put another way, the first implies the second if and only if no substitution instance of the first is true while the simultaneous substitution instance of the second is false. Hence, '$p \& q$' implies '$p \vee q$', but not the other way round, as a truth table will show. Construct one and see.

Now that we understand consistency, implication, and equivalence of statement forms, what about statements ? It would be nice if I could tell the same story regarding statements, nice if I could say that statements are consistent (or whatever) if and only if they are simultaneous instances of forms that are consistent (or whatever), but neither life nor logic is so simple. Truth tables provide reliable tests of the consistency (or whatever) of statement forms, but not of statements. I regret this, but there is nothing I can do about it besides explain it.

Causes of the Unreliability of Truth Tables

This situation has two causes, one of which we noted in the last chapter: substitution instances of different forms are not always logically independent of each other. Recall the statements "John is ugly" and "John is handsome." There is no way they could both be true. Yet the first is a substitution instance of 'p' while the second is a substitution instance of 'q', and these two statement forms are consistent with each other. So we have inconsistent statements that are simultaneous substitution instances of consistent statement forms. Hence, consistency of truth tables is no proof of consistency of statements. As we noted before, truth tables are in order only after full analysis of logically related statements into logically independent statements. Only when we have analyzed "John is ugly" as, say, "John is not handsome but is physically repulsive" can we use truth tables to see the inconsistency that was not obvious before.

The other cause of the unreliability of truth tables as tests of consistency (and so on) of statements is that every compound statement is a substitution instance of at least two statement forms, one of which reveals more of its logical structure than the other. For example, (11) is not only a substitution instance of '$p \& q$', but also of 's'. Similarly, (12) is not only a substitution instance of '$p \lor q$' but of 'r'.* In consequence, whether you will see that (11) implies (12), or vice versa, will depend on which forms you think of them as instantiating. If you think of (11) as a substitution instance of '$p \& q$', you will conclude that (11) implies (12) but (12) does not imply (11). On the other hand, if you think of (11) as a substitution instance of

---

* The principle here is the same as in Algebra. "$x + y = z$" is not only the formula for "$2 + 5 = 7$" but also for "$2 + (4 + 1) = 7$", which also has the formula "$x + (t + w) = z$."

'r' while thinking of (12) as a substitution instance of 's', you will conclude that neither implies the other.

This means, once again, that truth tables are reliable only when the statements in question have been analyzed fully so as to reveal all of their logical structure. Logical forms are like maps, and some maps reveal more detail than others. A very detailed map of the same territory will show things that are not evident on a somewhat less detailed map. Every conjunction is a substitution instance of both '$p \& q$' and 'p', but '$p \& q$' shows more of its logical form, and a truth table is reliable only when all the logical form has been exposed.

The moral of the story is that truth tables provide reliable tests of the consistency, implications, and equivalence of statement forms, but not of statements. What we were really doing when we used truth tables to test the consistency (or whatever) of statements was to abstract their forms and then test the consistency (or whatever) of those forms. (That this is so will be obvious to you if you will reflect that truth table tests of consistency (or whatever) have more than one line, and that truth values vary from line to line, whereas a statement has only a one-line truth table because it has only one fixed truth value). In this way we can discover whether the statements in question have consistent (or whatever) forms, but not always whether they are consistent (or whatever). We can count on doing the latter only when we are sure that we have, by full analysis, exposed all of the logical form. When we cannot be sure that further analysis would not reveal more logical structure, we must limit ourselves to conclusions justified by the following generalizations:

First, if two statements are simultaneous substitution instances of inconsistent forms, they are inconsistent. Statements may, however, be simultaneous substitution instances of consistent forms without being consistent. So don't conclude from a failure to discover inconsistency that it doesn't exist.

Second, if a statement S_1 has a statement form SF_1 that implies another form SF_2, then S_1 implies simultaneous substitution instance S_2. S_1 may, however, imply S_2 even though SF_1 does not imply SF_2. So don't conclude from the failure to discover implication that it doesn't exist.

Third, if two statements are simultaneous substitution instances of forms that imply each other, they are equivalent. Statements may also be equivalent, however, even when their forms are not. So don't conclude from a failure to discover equivalence that it doesn't exist.

In short, truth table tests of statements will prove inconsistency, implication, or equivalence, but they will not prove consistency (absence of inconsistency), absence of implication, or absence of equivalence.

Exercises

A. (a) Which of the following are inconsistent with '*p*'? (b) Which are equivalent with '*p*'? (c) Which are implied by '*p*'? (d) Which contradict '*p*'? and (e) which are logically independent of '*p*'?

1. $p \lor q$

2. $\sim p \lor q$

3. $p \,\&\, q$

4. $p \,\&\, \sim q$

5. $\sim(p \lor q)$

B. The statement "Marigolds are offensive & (petunias are nice ∨ I am a monkey's uncle)" is a substitution instance of which of the following?

1. p

2. q

3. $p \,\&\, q$

4. $p \,\&\, (q \lor r)$

5. $r \,\&\, (p \lor q)$

C. Which of the following are not substitution instances of "$\sim p \lor q$"?

1. Marigolds are not offensive ∨ petunias are nice.

2. ∼ Marigolds are offensive ∨ (petunias are nice and I am a monkey's uncle).

3. ∼ (Marigolds are offensive ∨ I am a monkey's uncle).

4. Marigolds are not offensive ∨ ∼ I am a monkey's uncle.

5. ∼ Marigolds are offensive & I am a monkey's uncle.

D. Find pairs of simultaneous substitution instances of '$\sim p \lor q$' and '$\sim q \lor p$' that show them to be consistent with, but not to imply, each other.

E. True or False?

1. If two statements are simultaneous substitution instances of equivalent statement forms, they are equivalent.

2. If two statements are equivalent, they are simultaneous substitution instances of equivalent statement forms.

107

3. If two statements are simultaneous substitution instances of consistent statement forms, they are consistent.

4. If two statements are consistent, they are simultaneous substitution instances of consistent statement forms.

5. If two statements are simultaneous substitution instances of inconsistent statement forms, they are inconsistent.

6. If two statements are inconsistent, they are simultaneous substitution instances of inconsistent statement forms.

7. If statement form$_1$ implies statement form$_2$, then statement$_1$ implies simultaneous substitution instance statement$_2$.

8. If statement$_1$ implies simultaneous substitution instance statement$_2$, then statement form$_1$ implies statement form$_2$.

13 / Tautology and Self-Contradiction

Truth Table Definitions

The simple statement "Harold is handsome" is true if Harold is handsome; and false otherwise. By contrast, the compound statement "Harold is handsome and not handsome" is false whether Harold is handsome or not, false under all conceivable conditions, false no matter what. If you made up a truth table for such a statement, you would see that it is false in every line. Abbreviate "Harold is handsome" as "H," and then examine the truth table:

H	$\sim H$	$H \& \sim H$
T	F	F
F	T	F

We shall say that such statements are *self-contradictory*. Statements that are not self-contradictory will be said to be *self-consistent*. "Harold is handsome" is self-consistent; "Harold is handsome and not handsome" is self-contradictory.

Just as there are statements that are false no matter what, so there are statements that are true no matter what. An example is "Harold is either handsome or not," which is true whether Harold is handsome, ugly, or just average looking. Statements such as these are *tautologies*.★ Tautologies are true in every line of their truth tables:

H	$\sim H$	$H \vee \sim H$
T	F	T
F	T	T

★ Tautologies are also called *laws of logic*.

109

You may be tempted to suppose that the denial of a consistent statement must be inconsistent, as the denial of a true statement must be false. Resist temptation! "Harold is not handsome" is as self-consistent as "Harold is handsome." They contradict each other, but they don't contradict themselves. Furthermore, don't confuse a statement's not being a tautology with its being a self-contradiction: "Harold is handsome" is not a tautology, but neither is it a self-contradiction.

It is denials of tautologies that are self-contradictory, false no matter what. Thus, the denial of "$H \lor \sim H$" is inconsistent, as the following table shows:

H	$\sim H$	$H \lor \sim H$	$\sim (H \lor \sim H)$
T	F	T	F
F	T	T	F

As all denials of tautologies are self-contradictions, so all denials of self-contradictions are tautologies. Thus, "$\sim (H \& \sim H)$" is a tautology, true no matter whether Harold looks like Valentino or like a toad.

Unlike simple truth and falsity, tautology and self-contradiction can be determined by inspection of the statement itself, or rather, by inspection of its truth table. Suppose you want to know whether Harold is handsome. The only way is to examine Harold, take a look at him. You can't determine the truth of the sentence "Harold is handsome" merely by understanding the sentence. You could understand that sentence perfectly without knowing whether it is true or false. By contrast, that "Harold is handsome $\lor$ $\sim$ Harold is handsome" is tautologous and that "Harold is handsome $\&$ $\sim$ Harold is handsome" is self-contradictory can be seen by inspecting the sentences themselves, without ever taking a look at Harold. We don't need to know a thing about Harold to know that he is either handsome or not, or to know that he isn't both handsome and not handsome. We just need a truth table.

Qualification of Truth Table Definitions

There is, however, a limitation on the truth table test of tautology and self-contradiction: its use presupposes a fully exposed statement form, which presupposes adequate analysis. Consider

Harold is handsome and ugly.

There is no way that this statement could be true, but suppose we abbreviate it as

$$H \& U$$

and run a truth table test. We shall find lines showing it true. What has gone wrong?

The answer is that we didn't analyze the statement sufficiently. A more nearly correct analysis would recognize that 'ugly' means something like 'not handsome and repelling'. With the benefit of this more detailed analysis, our statement comes out as "Harold is handsome and Harold is not handsome but is repelling," which abbreviates to

$$H \& (\sim H \& R)$$

and is self-contradictory, as a truth table would show.

Using a similar analysis of 'ugly', we see that

Harold is handsome or ugly

is not a tautology. Its full analysis abbreviates as

$$H \lor (\sim H \& R),$$

which is false if Harold is neither repulsive nor handsome.

Using similar reasoning, we might decide that

Harold is either handsome or not attractive

is a tautology, even though a truth table test of its abbreviation,

$$H \lor \sim A,$$

would show it false in some lines. Just substitute 'handsome' for its approximate synonymn 'attractive' and you get

$$H \lor \sim H,$$

which is clearly a tautology. Of course, if 'handsome' isn't a synonymn of 'attractive', then the substitution will be unjustified and the verdict of tautology will be a mistake.

In strictness, then, we should not claim that truth tables provide decisive tests of tautology or self-consistency in statements. They do so only under conditions of full analysis and of elimination of all synonymns. This complication is reminiscent of the similar complications we encountered when using truth tables as tests of the mutual consistency of pairs of statements, and it has the same explanation: truth tables are tests of consistency or tautology primarily of statement forms and only derivatively of their substitution instances. Strictly speaking, we should not say that statements with all 'T's in their truth tables are tautologies. Strictly speaking, statements don't have truth tables in which their truth value varies from line to line. A statement has one fixed truth value. Truth tables are therefore appropriate only to statement forms, whose substitution instances can vary in truth value. So, strictly speaking, we should define tautology and self-contradiction for statement forms. Let us now do so.

A statement form is *tautologous* if and only if every substitution instance is true; a statement form is *self-contradictory* if and only if every substitution instance is false. By these definitions, the statement form

$$p \lor \sim p$$

is tautologous, the statement form

$$p \mathbin{\&} \sim p$$

is self-contradictory, and the statement form

$$p$$

is neither, as this truth table shows:

p	$p \lor \sim p$	$p \mathbin{\&} \sim p$
T	T	F
F	T	F

You see that 'p' has both true and false substitution instances, but that '$p \mathbin{\&} \sim p$' has only false substitution instances and '$p \lor \sim p$' only true ones.

We may say that any substitution instance of a tautologous statement form is tautologous, but we may not say that no substitution instance of a nontautologous statement form is tautologous. The reason is that one and the same statement can be a substitution instance of two forms, one that is tautologous, one that is not. Consider

Harold is handsome $\lor$ $\sim$ Harold is handsome

This can, of course, be construed as a substitution instance of '$p \lor \sim p$', which is tautologous, but it can also be thought of as a substitution instance of 'q,' which is not.

A statement can also be a substitution instance of a form that is self-contradictory and of one that is not. An example is

Harold is handsome & ~ Harold is handsome,

which is a substitution instance of both 'p & $\sim p$' and of 'q'. The importance of this observation is that you might, when analyzing a statement, overlook the analysis that reveals it to be a tautology or self-contradiction, which wouldn't prove a thing: overlooking gold is not proving there is none in the stream.

As we have already noted, statement forms are diagrams and are therefore like maps. Now, there can be two maps of the same territory, one showing much more detail than the other because drawn to a much finer scale. If both maps are accurate, and the gross map shows topographical structure, the structure is there; but if the gross map fails to show topographical structure, you can't conclude that it isn't there. To justify that sort of negative conclusion, you need a map showing all the structure there is. The same goes for statement forms, which are maps of the logical structure of statements. Possessing a tautologous (or contradictory) statement form makes a statement tautologous (or contradictory), but a statement form revealing less of the logical structure of its substitution instance might not show the statement's tautologous (or contradictory) nature. To justify the conclusion that a statement isn't tautologous (or contradictory), you need the most detailed analysis possible.

So, as soon as your analysis of a statement reveals that it has tautologous or self-contradictory form, you need go no further. That discovery settles the question. What does not do so is the failure of your analysis to prove that the statement in question has either tautologous or self-contradictory form.

Further Matters

That point having now been sufficiently labored, let us go on to other matters. To begin with, it is interesting to note that a statement form not consistent with itself is also not consistent with any other, as the following table shows:

p q	p & $\sim p$
T T	F
T F	F
F T	F
F F	F

Notice that the form '$p \& \sim p$' is false on every line. So there is no line on which both it and 'q' are true. Two statement forms are mutually consistent, however, if and only if they have true simultaneous substitution instances.

This same table also shows that a self-contradictory statement form implies every statement form. For notice that there is no line on which '$p \& \sim p$' is true while 'q' is false, there being no line on which '$p \& \sim p$' is true. So '$p \& \sim p$' implies 'q', and all substitution instances of the former imply all simultaneous substitution instances of the latter. Hence, "God can make squares that are not square" implies both "God does not exist" and "God does exist."

A similar table and similar reflections show that tautologous statement forms are consistent with all statement forms except self-contradictory ones, and that tautologous statement forms are implied by all statement forms whatsoever:

p	q	$p \vee \sim p$
T	T	T
T	F	T
F	T	T
F	F	T

You will notice that there are no lines on which '$p \vee \sim p$' and 'q' are both false, there being no lines on which '$p \vee \sim p$' is false. So '$p \vee \sim p$' is consistent with 'q'. Similarly, there are no lines on which '$p \vee \sim p$' is false while 'q' is true, there being no lines on which '$p \vee \sim p$' is false. Therefore, 'q' implies '$p \vee \sim p$'.

So far, we have illustrated the concepts of tautology and self-contradiction by using extremely simple examples. There are, of course, more complex examples. An example of a slightly more complex tautology is:

$$\sim p \vee (\sim q \vee p).$$

Its truth table is

p	q	$\sim p$	$\sim q$	$\sim q \vee p$	$\sim p \vee (\sim q \vee p)$
T	T	F	F	T	T
T	F	F	T	T	T
F	T	T	F	F	T
F	F	T	T	T	T

A slightly more complex self-contradiction would be the denial of this same tautology, namely,

$$\sim[\sim p \vee (\sim q \vee p)].$$

Exercises

A. Which of the following statement forms are tautologous, which are self-contradictory, and which are neither?

   1. $\sim p \vee \sim (q \,\&\, \sim p)$

   2. $\sim p \,\&\, (\sim q \vee p)$

   3. $\sim p \,\&\, (\sim q \,\&\, p)$

   4. $(p \,\&\, q) \vee (\sim p \,\&\, \sim q)$

   5. $(p \vee q) \,\&\, (\sim p \vee \sim q)$

B. Which of the following statements have contradictory statement forms? Which have tautologous statement forms?

   1. Either rabbits are not fearsome or rabbits are neither cute nor fearsome.

   2. Either rabbits are both not cute and not fearsome or rabbits are both cute and fearsome.

   3. Either rabbits are not cute or else it is false that rabbits are both fearsome and not cute.

   4. Rabbits are not fearsome and either rabbits are not cute or they are fearsome.

   5. Rabbits are either cute or fearsome and they are either not cute or not fearsome.

C. True or false?

   1. A statement with a tautologous form is a tautology.

   2. A substitution instance of a nontautologous form is not tautologous.

   3. A statement of self-contradictory form is self-contradictory.

   4. All substitution instances of self-contradictory forms are false.

   5. A statement may be tautologous even though it is the substitution instance of a statement form that is not.

6. Any self-contradiction implies any tautology.

7. Any self-contradiction is inconsistent with every tautology.

8. All tautologies are equivalent.

9. All self-contradictions are equivalent.

10. No tautologies imply anything but other tautologies.

11. No self-contradictions imply anything but other self-contradictions.

12. No self-contradictions are implied by anything but other self-contradictions.

13. Every self-contradiction contradicts every other statement.

14. Every tautology is consistent with every other statement.

15. Every tautology contradicts every self-contradiction.

14 / Conditional Statements

We have lavished considerable attention on the little words 'not', 'or', and 'and'. They deserve it. You use these words no matter what you may be talking about, whether it be rocks or rockets, moons or moonies, stirring or streaking. They remain constant with every change of subject. They constitute the logical structure of whatever you say upon any subject. They make up the logical form of any sentence. For this reason, they are often called *logical constants*. Logic may be defined as the study of such logical constants.

Truth Values of Conditionals

Here we want to begin to study another familiar logical locution, 'if-then'. We use this expression to make *conditional statements* like

(1)   If Mary is at the dance, then so is Sam.

Spelled out, this statement has two components:

(2)   Mary is at the dance

and

(3)   Sam is at the dance.

(2) is called the *antecedent* of (1) and (3) its *consequent*.
    Don't confuse the conditional statement (1) with the *inference*

117

(4)   Since Mary is at the dance, so is Sam.

(4) affirms both that Mary is at the dance and that Sam is; (1) affirms neither. What (1) does is, rather, to deny the combination of Mary's presence at the dance with Sam's absence. That is, it asserts

(5)   ~ (Mary is at the dance & ~ Sam is at the dance).

This being so, we could, if we wished, just rewrite (1) as (5). In general, we could rewrite every conditional of the form

(6)   if p then q

as

(7)   ~ $(p \mathbin{\&} \sim q)$.

We shall not, however, generally do so. Conditionals occur often enough to deserve their own special symbol, and one has accordingly been invented for the purpose. Using a horseshoe shaped symbol, we shall paraphrase (1) as

(8)   Mary is at the dance ⊃ Sam is at the dance.

Or, in general, we shall rewrite conditionals of the form (6) in the form

(9) $p \supset q$,

which, as the following truth table shows, says the very same thing as its obverse, (7):

p	q	$\sim q$	$p \supset q$	$\sim(p \mathbin{\&} \sim q)$
T	T	F	T	T
T	F	T	F	F
F	T	F	T	T
F	F	T	T	T

Notice that a conditional statement counts as true except when its antecedent is true and its consequent is false. Put another way, it counts as true provided either that the consequent is true or that the antecedent is false. This may strike you as odd. Consider (1) again. Knowing that Mary is at the dance but Sam is not, you will have no hesitation pronouncing (1) false. Suppose, however, that neither Mary nor Sam is at the dance. In that case, you might balk at declaring (1) either true or false. You might reply that, since Mary isn't at the dance, there is no question of (1)'s being either true or false. We don't normally assert a conditional except by way of granting a license to infer the truth of the consequent given the truth of the antecedent. Granting such a license has no point if we already know the antecedent and consequent to be both false. Indeed, it has no point if either the antecedent is known to be false or the consequent is known to be true.

Given these reflections, you might prefer that a truth table for conditionals show question marks where we put 'T's. Let us abbreviate (1) as

(10)   If M then S;

you might then think its truth table ought to be

M S	If M then S
T T	?
T F	F
F T	?
F F	?

rather than

M S	M ⊃ S
T T	T
T F	F
F T	T
F F	T

These intuitions will be further reinforced if you look at a conditional like

(11)   If the moon is green cheese, I am a monkey's uncle.

Is this true or false? You are likely to protest that it doesn't follow, that the constitution of the moon has nothing to do with my kinfolk. Since (11) seems to suggest otherwise, you will be reluctant to pronounce it true simply on the grounds that the antecedent is false, just as you would be reluctant to pronounce

(12)   If the moon is rock, I am a human being

true simply on the grounds that the consequent is true.

If these are your intuitions, they are shared by a great many people. Nevertheless, they seem to be wrong. Such misgivings may be the result of confusing conditional statements with statements of implication. Look at (11) again. You protested that the conclusion doesn't follow, that the antecedent has nothing to do with the consequent. Your observation is accurate, but it is irrelevant unless (11) is read as an assertion that the moon's being green cheese implies that I am a monkey's uncle. If (11) were so read, then, of course, (11) would be false; for even if the moon were green cheese, it wouldn't follow that I am a monkey's uncle. Still, this fact doesn't show that (11) is false. It merely shows that

(13)   "The moon is green cheese" implies "I am a monkey's uncle"

is false, and we shouldn't confuse (11) with (13) or (1) with the assertion that Mary's being at the dance implies that Sam is there, too. That assertion is false, but (1) may be true. Indeed, it is true unless Mary is there but Sam isn't.

Granted, we don't normally assert a conditional except by way of issuing a license to infer the consequent, given the antecedent, and this is as much as to say that the antecedent plus the conditional imply the consequent. Hence, if I assert (1), you may infer (3) if you know that (2) is true. The conjunction of (1) and (2) imply (3). To admit this implication, however, is not to admit that the conditional all by itself implies its consequent or asserts that its antecedent does. The conditional is not by itself an inference ticket leading from antecedent to consequent.

Besides, our question is not whether (3) is true given that (2) is; our question is whether (1) is true given that (2) is not. At the moment, we are interested in the truth value of the conditional given the truth value of its components, not vice versa.

In what follows, then, we shall regard conditional statements as being true except when they are false, which is only when their antecedents are true and their consequents false. Hence, statements like (11) will count as true. This doesn't say that I am a monkey's uncle, although I have been called worse. Since I am not a monkey's uncle, it just says that the moon isn't green cheese.

Being perceptive, you will notice that this policy has the paradoxical result of making true both

(14)   The moon is green cheese ⊃ I am a monkey's uncle

and

(15)   The moon is green cheese ⊃ I am not a monkey's uncle.

This paradox bothers some people. Since (14) and (15) seem to be contradictories, how can they both be true? The explanation is that (14) and (15) are not contradictories; only their consequents are contradictories.

CHAP. 14 / Conditional Statements

Once again: don't confuse a conditional statement with a statement about either or both of its components. That is the mistake we made when we misread (14) as (13).

If we want the contradictory of (14), it is

(16)   ~(The moon is green cheese ⊃ I am a monkey's uncle),

which is equivalent to

(17)   The moon is green cheese & ~ I am a monkey's uncle.

Before we go on, let me summarize: read statements of the form

(6)   If p then q

as

(9) $p \supset q$

and as true except when 'p' is true and 'q' is false; do not confuse such conditional statements with categorical statements of implication or with inferences. That understood, let us proceed.*

Converses and Contrapositives of Conditionals

We have noted that we may paraphrase statements of the form (6) by writing (9); (9) is also an acceptable paraphrase of the following:

If p, q;
q, if p;
Given p, q;

and

p only if q.

All these are just so many different ways of saying the same thing. They are all true except when 'p' is true and 'q' is false.

None of these statements is to be confused with converses like the following:

$q \supset p$;
If q then p;
If q, p;
Given q, p;

and

q only if p.

---

* For a more thorough discussion of conditionals, see W. V. Quine, *Methods of Logic*, 3rd edition, Holt, Rhinehart and Winston, Inc., pp. 19–23, 42–44.

All these phrasings say that 'q' is false unless 'p' is true, which is very different from saying that 'p' is false unless 'q' is true. To see this difference, compare (1) with its *converse*:

(18)   If Sam is at the dance, then so is Mary.

(1) denies the combination of Mary's presence with Sam's absence; (18) denies the very different combination of Sam's presence with Mary's absence. Whereas (1) makes Sam's presence a *necessary condition* of Mary's presence, (18) makes it a *sufficient condition*.

For some unfathomable reason, people find this distinction hard to keep straight. They confuse conditionals with their converses, indentifying "If Fred is handsome, he is popular" with "If Fred is popular, he is handsome," forgetting that there are ways to be popular besides being handsome. That this is a mistake can be demonstrated by an example: "If Hank is a horse, he is a mammal" is true, but its converse, "If Hank is a mammal, he is a horse," is false. Order makes no logical difference to conjunctions or to alternations, but you have a different statement if you reverse the order of the components of a conditional, as a truth table will show:

p q	$p \supset q$	$q \supset p$
T T	T	T
T F	F	T
F T	T	F
F F	T	T

You see here that the conditional and its converse have different truth values in the middle two lines.

If we want a statement that says the same thing as a conditional of the form '$p \supset q$', we should look, not to its converse, but to its *contrapositive*— a corresponding statement of the form

$$\sim q \supset \ \sim p.$$

Hence, the equivalent of (1) is

(19)   If Sam is not at the dance, then Mary is not.

Once again, (19) is not to be confused with its converse,

(20)   If Mary is not at the dance, then Sam is not,

which is the contrapositive, not of (1), but of its converse.

122

Perhaps these points will be clearer to you after you have compared the following columns:

Conditionals	*Their converses*	*Their contrapositives*
$p \supset q$	$q \supset p$	$\sim q \supset \sim p$
if p then q	if q then p	if not q then not p
if p, q	if q, p	if not q, not p
q, if p	p, if q	not p, if not q
p only if q	q only if p	not q only if not p

All formulas within one column are equivalent to others in that same column. No formulas in the middle column are equivalent to any formulas in the other two. All formulas in the extreme two columns are equivalent to one another. All those in the extreme two columns declare that the truth of 'q' is a necessary condition of the truth of 'p' and that the truth of 'p' is a sufficient condition of the truth of 'q'. That is, they all assert '$\sim(p \,\&\, \sim q)$'. By contrast, the formulas in the middle column assert '$\sim(q \,\&\, \sim p)$'.

Biconditionals

The only conditionals that can be converted without running the risk of changing truth value are *biconditionals*, conditionals that we express in English by saying

(21) p if and only if q

and that we shall paraphrase here by writing

(22) $p \equiv q$.

Biconditionals are symmetrical; they say exactly the same thing as their converses,

   q if and only if p

and

   $q \equiv p$.

The explanation of this symmetry is that biconditionals are really conjunctions of conditionals with their converses. Accordingly, (21) amounts to the conjunction

123

(23) $(p$ only if $q) \& (p$ if $q)$,

as (22) amounts to the conjunction

(24) $(p \supset q) \& (q \supset p)$.

Because they are conjunctions, (23) and (24) are convertible *salva veritatae*.

Biconditionals like (21) and (22) also amount to the declaration that 'p' and 'q' are either both true or both false, as this truth table shows:

$p \ q$	$p \equiv q$
T T	**T**
T F	**F**
F T	**F**
F F	**T**

You see here that the biconditional is true only when 'p' and 'q' have the same truth value.

Don't confuse biconditionals with statements of equivalence. That is, don't confuse (22) with

(25) $p \overset{\mathrm{df}}{\equiv} q$.

To do so would be as bad a mistake as confusing the conditional with a statement of implication; in fact, it would be the same mistake made twice over. So resist any tendency to read (22) as declaring that 'p' is equivalent to 'q', just as you should resist any tendency to read '$p \supset q$' as declaring that 'p' implies 'q'. Such misreadings can cause serious confusion.

One final point: we have learned that '$p \supset q$' is equivalent to '$\sim(p \& \sim q)$', which is equivalent to '$\sim p \lor q$'. If you doubt me, check me with a truth table. While you are at it, you might also verify the following equivalences:

$$p \equiv q \overset{\mathrm{df}}{\equiv} (p \& q) \lor (\sim p \& \sim q)$$
$$p \equiv q \overset{\mathrm{df}}{\equiv} (\sim p \lor q) \& (\sim q \lor p)$$
$$p \equiv q \overset{\mathrm{df}}{\equiv} \sim(p \& \sim q) \& \sim(q \& \sim p).$$

Exercises

A. Paraphrase each of the following, using the tilde ($\sim$), the horseshoe ($\supset$), or the triple bar ($\equiv$) and the abbreviations 'H' and 'M'. Then declare the results true or false.

124

1. If honey is sweet, then the moon is made of green cheese.

2. The moon is green cheese only if honey is sweet.

3. Honey is sweet if the moon is green cheese.

4. If the moon is green cheese, then honey is sweet.

5. Honey is not sweet if and only if the moon is green cheese.

6. That the moon is not green cheese if honey is sweet is false.

7. If honey is sweet, then the moon is not green cheese.

8. It is false that if the moon is not green cheese, then honey is not sweet.

9. It isn't true that the moon is green cheese and that honey is not sweet.

10. The moon is green cheese if and only if honey is sweet.

B. Check all the following that say the same thing as "$H \supset G$."

   1. $\sim G \supset \sim H$

   2. $\sim(H \,\&\, \sim G)$

   3. $G \supset H$

   4. $\sim G \supset H$

   5. $\sim(G \supset H)$

   6. $\sim(G \,\&\, \sim H)$

   7. $\sim H \,\&\, \sim G$

   8. $\sim\sim(H \supset G)$

   9. $H \supset \sim\sim G$

  10. $\sim H \supset \sim G$

C. Consider: "If honey is sweet, the moon is green cheese." Which of the following say the same thing in a different way? Which contradict the statement?

   1. It is not true that honey is sweet and that the moon is not green cheese.

   2. If the moon is not green cheese then honey is sweet.

   3. If the moon is green cheese, then honey is sweet.

   4. Honey is not sweet unless the moon is green cheese.

   5. Honey is sweet and the moon is not green cheese.

6. Honey is sweet only if the moon is green cheese.

7. If it is false that the moon is green cheese then honey is sweet.

8. If the moon is not green cheese, then honey is not sweet.

9. If honey is sweet, the moon is not green cheese.

10. Honey is sweet if and only if the moon is not green cheese.

D. Write the contrapositive and the converse of "If honey is sweet, the moon is green cheese."

E. Does "The moon is green cheese" imply "Honey is not sweet"?

F. Identify (a) the tautologies and (b) the self-contradictions.

1. $p \supset (q \supset p)$

2. $p \supset (q \vee \sim q)$

3. $(p \,\&\, \sim p) \supset q$

4. $(p \vee \sim p) \supset (q \,\&\, \sim q)$

5. $\sim[(p \supset p) \supset \sim(p \supset p)]$

15 / Complex Cases

Up to now we have confined ourselves deliberately to considering statements that were the result of compounding no more than two components. Sometimes we have treated compounds of compounds of two components, but we have gone no further in complexity. We have had a good reason for this limitation; in fact, we have had two reasons. The first is that it is best to learn simple cases before going on to complex cases. The second is that, since the simple cases are the ones that occur most often, they are the ones it is most urgent to understand, the ones that will prove most useful. It is time, however, to lift our limitation and notice that the methods of analysis and evaluation we have been learning apply as well to highly complex statements. We want, then, to look at compounds of three components, 'p', 'q', and 'r', or even of four or more. That is, we want to look at statements having forms like

$$p \,\&\, (q \vee r)$$

and

$$(p \vee q) \supset [q \,\&\, (r \vee s)].$$

Don't let the complexity of these forms frighten you. Their study requires no new principles, just repeated applications of the same old principles. It is like addition and multiplication. Once you know how to add or multiply two numbers, you know how to multiply three numbers or four or more: just multiply two of them, then multiply the result by the third, and so on. Similarly, to add several numbers you just add two, then add the third to the sum, and so on. You can also multiply one number by

127

a second, then add the result to a third, and so on. In the same way, to find out the truth value of statements of the form

(1) $(p \lor q) \& r$,

you first find out the truth value of '$p \lor q$' and then investigate the result of conjoining its truth value with that of 'r'. Hence, if 'p' and 'q' are both true but 'r' is false, (1) will be false, being the conjunction of a falsehood with a truth. Under the same assumptions, statements of the following forms will all be true:

$p \& (q \lor r)$;
$r \supset \sim(p \lor q)$;
$\sim r \& (p \& q)$;

and

$p \lor (q \lor r)$.

Complexity does, however, have one important result: it increases the lengths of truth tables. As the following truth table illustrates, each new component doubles the combinations of truth values to be considered:

p q r	$\sim p$	$q \& r$	$\sim p \lor (q \& r)$
T T T	F	T	T
T T F	F	F	F
T F T	F	F	F
T F F	F	F	F
F T T	T	T	T
F T F	T	F	T
F F T	T	F	T
F F F	T	F	T

Where we had four-line truth tables, now we have an eight-line truth table. These eight lines represent all the possible combinations of truth and falsity for three different components, 'p', 'q', and 'r'. The first line considers the possiblity that all three are true; the next three lines consider the ways that two of them can be true while a third is false; and so on. Starting with these eight combinations of truth values on the left, we work in the usual way to compounds of 'p', 'q', and 'r' on the right, and then to compounds of the compounds. As before, each line of the table shows what truth value the compound on the right has, given the truth values of its components on the left.

To deal with statement forms with four compounds, we require a truth table of sixteen lines, twice as many again. A statement form with five components would require thirty-two. The formula is 2^n, where 'n' represents the number of components and 2 is the number of truth values. You can see this doubling effect in the following branching tree:

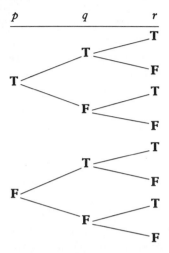

The simplest way to tabulate all the necessary combinations is to list all components from left to right. Then start on the left and go down, writing 'T' in one-half the lines, 'F' in the remaining one-half lines. Then go right and write 'T' in the first and third one fourths of the lines, 'F' in the second and fourth one fourths of the lines. If you will look at the longish truth table used above, you will see that this is the method used there.

If, of course, we never in real life encountered any statements with three components or more, we wouldn't need here to worry about such complexity; but we do. Even very ordinary English sentences can contain enormous complexity. If you don't believe it, undertake the analysis of the following simple warranty:

> In case the product proves defective in either parts or workmanship, the company agrees at its option either to refund the price of purchase or to repair the product. The provisions of this warranty are, however, valid only under the conditions specified, and only if the product has not been tampered with. Should there be evidence that the product was tampered with, the warranty is null and void.

This warranty contains three complicated statements. How shall we analyze them? Give it a try, and then read the procedure outlined here to see whether you went about it in the right way and got the right result.

Begin with the first statement. You should notice first that it is a conditional statement. "In case..." is just another way of saying "If...". Having noticed the conditional, you should also notice that the comma divides the antecedent condition from the consequent condition. Therefore, we can write the sentence as "The product proves defective in either parts or workmanship ⊃ the company will either refund purchase price or repair the product." Now the problem is reduced to analyzing the compounds that occur before and after the horseshoe.

Begin with the antecedent. It is obviously an alternation and should read, "The product is defective in parts ∨ the product is defective in workmanship." If we abbreviate the first alternate "P" and the second "W," we can abbreviate the alternation "$P \vee W$."

Now for the consequent. Obviously, it, too, is an alternation and should read, "The company will refund purchase price ∨ the company will repair the product." If we abbreviate the first alternate "R" and the second "F" (for 'fix'), the whole abbreviates to "$R \vee F$."

So we have "$P \vee W$" as antecedent and "$R \vee F$" as consequent. We may therefore abbreviate the entire sentence "$(P \vee W) \supset (R \vee F)$." In this abbreviated and schematic form, its logical structure is obvious at a glance. Making it thus obvious was the point of the exercise.

If you also got "$(P \vee W) \supset (R \vee F)$," congratulate yourself. Don't be so self-congratulatory, however, if you got "$P \vee W \supset R \vee F$." The parentheses are essential. Without them, the statement is hopelessly ambiguous. Whoever reads "$P \vee W \supset R \vee F$" will be at a loss whether to take the horseshoe or one of the two wedges as having the greater scope. In the absence of punctuation no one can tell whether the statement is a conditional or one of two alternations, "$P \vee (W \supset R \vee F)$" or "$(P \vee W \supset R) \vee F$." Even these contain ambiguous compounds; for "$P \vee (W \supset R \vee F)$" might mean "$P \vee (W \supset R) \vee F$," which reads in English "Either P, or if W then R, or F"; or it might mean "$P \vee [(W \supset (R \vee F)]$," which is in English "Either P or if W then either R or F." Similarly, "$(P \vee W \supset R) \vee F$" is ambiguous between "$P \vee (W \supset R) \vee F$" and "$[(P \vee W) \supset R] \vee F$," the first of which reads "Either P, or if W then R, or F" and the second, "Either if either P or W then R or F." So make sure you enclose both the antecedent compound and the consequent compound in parentheses to get "$(P \vee W) \supset (R \vee F)$," which reads "If either P or W, then either R or F."

That completes our discussion of the first statement. Now for the second: "The provisions of this warranty are, however, valid only under the conditions specified, and only if the product has not been tampered with." How shall we deal with this sentence?

Well, we must notice first that it, too, is a conditional statement, not an 'if' statement, but an 'only if' statement, the converse of an 'if' statement. Then, remembering that a conditional is indicated by a horseshoe, we can begin our analysis by rewriting the statement as "The provisions of this warranty are valid $\supset$ (the conditions specified were met & the product has not been tampered with)." You will notice that the parentheses are essential. Without them we would have "The provisions of this warranty are valid $\supset$ the conditions specified were met & the product was not tampered with," which is ambiguous between a conditional and a conjunction. We need parentheses to show that the statement is a conditional and only its consequent is a conjunction.

Having got this far, we need to analyze the antecedent and consequent conditions. What are the "provisions of this warranty"? And what are the "conditions specified"? Well, the provisions of the warranty are to refund or fix, that is, "$R \lor F$." The conditions specified are that the product have defective parts or show poor workmanship, that is, "$P \lor W$." So we may write the second sentence as "$(R \lor F) \supset [(P \lor W)$ & the product was not tampered with]." If we abbreviate "The product was tampered with" as "T," this sentence becomes "$(R \lor F) \supset [(P \lor W)$ & $\sim T$]," which makes its logical structure obvious. For we now see that, where the first sentence promised to refund or fix if there were bad parts or workmanship, the second sentence promises to refund or fix only if there are bad parts or bad workmanship and, furthermore, only if the product has not been tampered with.

Notice, once again, that the parentheses are all essential. To see the difference they make, compare "$[(R \lor F) \supset (P \lor W)]$ & $\sim T$" with "$(R \lor F) \supset [(P \lor W)$ & $\sim T]$." The first says, "The company will either refund or fix the product only if either the parts or workmanship are bad. Furthermore, the product has not been tampered with." So it states, categorically, that the product has not been tampered with. By contrast, the second does not deny that the product has been tampered with. It just says that the company will honor the warranty only if the product has not been tampered with.

Compare, too, "$(R \lor F) \supset [(D \lor W)$ & $\sim T]$" with "$(R \lor F) \supset [D \lor (W$ & $\sim T)]$." The first says, "The company will either refund or fix the product only if it is defective in either parts or workmanship and only if it has not been tampered with." The second reads, "The company will either refund or fix the product only if either it is defective in parts or it both is defective in workmanship and has not been tampered with." These are quite different statements, having quite different truth conditions.

Speaking of truth conditions, let us compare the truth conditions of the first statement of our warranty with those of the second. Only in this way can we be sure we understand the difference between them. We shall write them in order:

(2) $(P \vee W) \supset (R \vee F)$;

(3) $(R \vee F) \supset [(P \vee W) \& \sim T]$.

Notice that (2) is true in every case except when "R" and "F" are both false and either "P" or "W" is true. That is to say, the company is telling the truth unless it won't refund and won't fix a product that is defective in either parts or workmanship. Now notice that (3) is true except in the case where either both "P" and "W" are false or "$\sim T$" is false and either "R" or "F" is true. That is, the company is prevaricating if it will refund your money for or fix a good and well-made product that has been tampered with.

Now for the third and final statement of the warranty: "Should there be evidence that the product has been tampered with, the warranty is null and void." Given the second statement, this statement is really redundant, for it says "$T \supset \sim (R \vee F)$." That is, it says that the company won't refund your money or fix the product if you have tampered with it, which is equivalent to saying that it will refund your money or fix the product only if you haven't tampered with it. So it adds nothing to the second statement.

You may think that the second statement also added nothing to the first, but that would be a mistake. Promising to do something under certain conditions (which the first statement does) is not the same as promising to do it only under those conditions. That is, it is not the same as saying that the promise won't hold under other conditions as well. As a truth table comparison will show, "$(P \vee W) \supset (R \vee F)$" is not the same as, nor does it imply, "$(R \vee F) \supset (P \vee W)$."

Exercises

A. Using the same abbreviations as were used in the text, paraphrase the following in our notation. Be careful to use enough punctuation to remove all ambiguity.

   1. Unless the product has been tampered with, the company agrees at its option either to refund the purchase price or to repair any product that either is defective in parts or shows signs of poor workmanship.

132

2. The company will neither repair nor refund the purchase price on any product that has been tampered with or on any product that is free from defects both in workmanship and in parts, but it will repair or refund the purchase price on a product that has not been tampered with and is defective either in parts or in workmanship.

3. The company will refund the purchase price or repair any product if and only if it has not been tampered with and either is defective in parts or shows poor workmanship.

B. Construct full truth tables to show under what conditions each of the following statement forms would be true and under what conditions each would be false.

1. $p \supset (q \,\&\, r)$

2. $[p \vee (q \supset r)] \,\&\, s$

3. $\sim [p \,\&\, (q \supset r)] \vee \sim s$

4. $(p \vee q) \,\&\, (\sim p \vee r)$

5. $\sim p \supset [q \supset (r \supset s)]$

6. $\sim \{p \,\&\, [q \,\&\, (r \,\&\, s)]\}$

C. Construct full truth tables to reveal the truth conditions of the statements you analyzed in (A).

UNIT III

Arguments

16 / Arguments: Valid, Sound, and Good

You have learned how to analyze and appraise statements. Now you shall learn how to analyze and appraise arguments. We shall reverse the order, however, learning first how to evaluate previously analyzed arguments and then how to analyze them.

The Purpose of an Argument

By an _argument_ I don't mean a dispute. I mean an attempt to show somebody that a statement is true. The attempt starts with premises already known or believed to be true and declares that these could not be true unless the conclusion, whose truth was in doubt, is true as well. Suppose a woman doesn't believe she will die. You try to convince her of her mortality by arguing, "All people die sooner or later. So you will, too." That is an argument. The first sentence states a reason for believing the second to be true.

Do not confuse an argument with a conditional statement. "If all people die, you will, too," is a conditional statement. "Since all people die, you will, too," is an argument. The argument asserts both that all people die and that you will, too; the conditional statement asserts neither.* Failure

---

* Except, of course, when the conditional statement is an enthymeme and elliptical for an argument. The existence of this exception is one of the things that causes confusion of conditional statements with inferences and statements of implication.

to observe this distinction can have unhappy results. The preacher says, "If fornication is right, sin is right." A shocked member of the congregation reports him as having said, "Fornication is right. So sin is right." Of course, the preacher said no such thing. On the contrary, he made his conditional statement in the course of arguing that fornication is wrong because sin is. The shocked parishioner was dozing.

Most people use the wrong standard to evaluate arguments. If the conclusion agrees with their preconceptions, or otherwise pleases them, they declare the argument good. If the conclusion challenges their prejudices, they condemn the argument. Hence, people who don't want to believe they are going to die pass "proofs" of immortality, however bad, without a second glance, but scan closely all criticisms of the doctrine. To such people, "The moon is green cheese; so you will live forever" seems a good argument; whereas "All people die; so you will, too," seems bad.

Clearly, most people put the cart before the horse. We should judge the conclusion by the argument, not the other way around. If the argument proves us wrong, we ought to change our minds, not close them. We ought to be grateful for having an error corrected, not resentful because a cherished delusion was destroyed. Furthermore, so as to correct the opposite tendency, we ought to be especially critical of arguments that seem to bolster conventional wisdom and personal bliss.

The Virtues of Arguments

If most people use the wrong test, what is the right one? How can we tell good arguments from bad? What are the distinguishing marks of good arguments? The answer, briefly stated, is that good arguments have three virtues: (1) their premises imply their conclusions, (2) their premises are true, and (3) they carry conviction. Arguments that have the first virtue are *valid*; those that have the first two virtues are *sound*, and those that have all three are *good*.

The first requirement of sound argumentation is validity: the conclusion must follow from the premises; the premises must imply the conclusion. This, as you already know, means that there must be no way that the conclusion could be false consistently with the premises' being true. It does not mean that the premises must be true, or that the conclusion can't be false. Arguments with false premises or false conclusions can nevertheless be valid. Here is an example with both:

(1)   The moon is green cheese. So the moon is cheese.

The false conclusion is a defect, but it doesn't make the argument invalid. Nor does a true conclusion make an argument valid.

(2)   The moon is a satellite of the earth. So it reflects light.

has a true premise and a true conclusion, but it is not valid. The conclusion could be false consistently with the premise being true. So, don't judge the validity of an argument by the truth of the premise or conclusion. A valid argument can have true premises or false ones, and true conclusions or false ones, and it can have them in any combination except one: the premises can't be true while the conclusions are false.

Given that the conclusion follows from the premises, the next requirement of good argument is that the premises be true. When the premises not only imply the conclusion but are also true, the argument is not just valid; it is sound. Being sound is better than being valid. A sound argument is valid and has true premises whereas a valid argument might not have true premises. An argument can fail to be valid only by having a conclusion, whether true or false, that does not follow from its premises, whether true or false, but an argument can fail to be sound either by having false premises or by having conclusions that don't follow from the premises. (2) is unsound in the second way, (1) is unsound in the first, and (3) is unsound in both ways.

(3)   The moon is green cheese. So it does not reflect light.

Not only are the premises of (3) false, but the conclusion does not follow.

Sound arguments, then, are valid arguments with true premises. This means that their conclusions are also true, and no argument is good that does not have a true conclusion. So no argument is good that is not sound, but an argument that is sound must satisfy one further condition in order to be good: it must carry conviction. This follows from the purpose of an argument, which, you will remember, is to advance knowledge, to show to be true something that was not already known to be true. An argument, however sound otherwise, that leaves its hearer unpersuaded of the truth of its conclusion has failed to carry conviction, and is insofar, not a good argument.

Consider, for example,

(4)   God exists. Therefore God exists.

Even if the premise is true and implies the conclusion, (4) is a bad argument—sound, but not good. It is bad because it wouldn't convince anyone who wasn't already convinced. In particular, it wouldn't convince an atheist or an agnostic, the only sort of person who needs convincing. Like all *circular arguments*, all arguments that *beg the question*, (4) assumes what was to be proved; it takes for granted what was in doubt. (4) is good argument only if repetition constitutes good argument, and it doesn't. Good arguments start with premises any reasonable person will have to admit. Then they go on to point out how admitting the premises is inconsistent with denying the conclusion. So persuasion is part of good argumentation.

Don't, however, identify good argument with persuasion. Good argument involves persuasion, but there is more to it. People can be persuaded of what is false, but a good argument always concludes with the truth. Arguments which are merely persuasive without tending towards truth are good from a purely rhetorical point of view, but from the point of view of logic, they are very bad. From the point of view of logic, a good argument does not merely persuade you that its, perhaps false, conclusion is true; a good argument shows you that its conclusion is true. Getting you to believe that the conclusion is true is not enough. What is required is that the argument make you to know that the conclusion is true. It must advance knowledge, and an argument can advance knowledge only if (1) it starts with premises that are known to be true and (2) it goes on to show that there is no way those premises could be true if the conclusion were false.

How can we know whether the premises are, as we believe, true? How can we tell whether our belief is a mere opinion or genuine knowledge? Sometimes the answer is that we know that the premises are true because we can prove them. That is, we can start with premises we already know to be true and construct another argument that shows to be true the premises of the argument in question. Sometimes, that is to say, we can see that the premises are true because they follow from things that we already know to be true.

At other times, the truth of the premises is evident without proof. I know that the earth is round because of proofs, but I do not need a proof to know that I have a headache. That is all too obvious without proof. You know that the earth goes around the sun because of proofs, but your knowledge that this is a book you are reading is not a product of proof. You don't need a proof that this is a book, and anyone who does need a proof wouldn't be helped by one.

Appeals to what is evident without proof have a great advantage over other arguments: no one can reasonably question your premises. Hence the very best arguments have premises which everyone already knows to be true, without the need for further argument. Such arguments short circuit the demand for proofs of your proofs to infinity. That is why producing such proofs is often described as producing *evidence* for your conclusions.

Isn't evidence relative to persons? Yes and no. It is relative in the sense that what is evident to some people may not be so to others. What is evident to those with eyes or to those who are in a position to see may not be evident to the blind or to those who are too far away. What is evident to the chemist is not evident to her pupil, who lacks the knowledge necessary to detect what is obvious to his professor. Evidence is not, however, relative in the sense that thinking something to be evident makes it so. It was "evident" to people in the Middle Ages that the earth is flat and that the sun rises. Now we regard it as established by argument that the earth is round and that the horizon falls. This example shows that we can make a mistake in thinking something evident: it never was really evident that the earth is flat or that the sun rises; people just mistakenly thought so. We have to be careful about what we count as evident, especially when it is inconsistent with the rest of what we know, or has been challenged by others. The "evident" is not evident, but doubtful, when it conflicts with the rest of our knowledge or with what other reasonable people believe. That the earth is flat did not conflict with anything most people in the Middle Ages knew; so they mistakenly thought it evident.*
It conflicts with what we know; so we rightly count it false.

Once the truth of the premises has been made evident, one should go on and make the conclusion evident too. How can one do that? We shall see in some detail later on, but the answer, in brief, is: step by painful step. A good argument is a demonstration, a showing. It makes perfectly clear that there is no way for its premises to be true while its conclusion is false. It makes you see that. It makes clear to you that the conclusion follows from the premises, and therefore must be as true as they are.

In summary, a good argument is one whose premises are known to be true and whose conclusion clearly follows from its premises. Such an argument is good because it does its job, which is to show that its conclusion is true. Being good, such an argument is sound, and being sound it is valid, but an argument can be valid without being sound, and it can be sound without being good. That is, an argument can be valid without

---

* Actually, there was evidence sufficient to prove the earth round even before the Middle Ages. Aristotle believed on good evidence that the earth was round.

having true premises, or have true premises without being valid, and it can be both valid and have true premises without doing its job, which is to show you that its premise is true.

Some Warnings

Let me conclude by issuing a few warnings.

The first is: don't confuse saying that an argument is invalid, unsound, or otherwise poor with saying that its conclusion is false. Very bad arguments often have true conclusions; for example:

The moon is a piece of green cheese. So it is a satellite of the earth.

The argument is defective in every conceivable way, but nonetheless, the conclusion is perfectly true. To declare an argument deficient in some way is not to declare the conclusion false, but just to say that the argument has failed to prove the conclusion true. Failing to prove something true is not, however, the same as proving it false. Indeed, the contrary supposition is the fallacy known as *arguing from ignorance.*

You haven't proved that God exists; so God does not exist

is an invalid argument. The premise may be true. The conclusion doesn't follow and might, consistently with the premises, be false.

If this is a point people often miss, perhaps it is because they confuse saying that a good argument has a true conclusion (which is true) with saying that a bad argument has a false conclusion (which is false).

Our next warning is: don't call arguments "true" or statements "valid." Arguments are composed of statements that are true; and the arguments may properly be described as "valid," but the statements that compose them may not. The conclusion is validly or invalidly inferred from the premises, but the conclusion is not itself valid or invalid. It is either true or false. Using the words in any other way causes confusion.

Finally, don't say that the premises "infer" the conclusion or that the speaker "infers" so and so by what he says. To do so is bad grammar. Premises imply conclusions, and so do speakers who assert the premises. Their assertions may result in hearers inferring conclusions from what the speakers say. But the speakers no more infer conclusions by what they say than the listeners imply conclusions from what the speakers say.

142

Exercises

A. Mark every statement true of a valid argument with a *V*, every statement true of a sound argument with an *S*, and every statement true of a good argument with a *G*.

1. It has true premises.

2. It has a true conclusion.

3. Its conclusion follows from its premises.

4. It has a form that has no substitution instances having true premises and false conclusions.

5. Its premises are known to be true.

6. Its conclusion is clearly implied by the premises.

7. It advances our knowledge by showing us to be true something we did not already know.

B. True or false?

1. If it has a true conclusion, it is valid.

2. If it has a true conclusion, it is sound.

3. If it has a true conclusion, it is good.

4. If it is valid, it is good.

5. If it is valid, it is sound.

6. If it is sound, it is good.

7. If it is valid, it has a true conclusion.

8. If it is sound, it has a true conclusion.

9. If it is good, it has a true conclusion.

10. If it is good, it is valid.

11. If it is sound, it is valid.

12. If it is good, it is sound.

13. If an argument convinces us of its conclusion, it is good.

C. I once said to a class,

> There is no proof that electro-shock therapy does anybody any good.

A student took me as saying,

> Electro-shock therapy does people harm.

Explain the error.

D. What is wrong with begging the question, reasoning in a circle?

17 / Validity: Long and Short Tests

The Long Test

In the preceding chapter, I said that an argument is good if its premises are known to be true and the conclusion clearly follows. We discussed, albeit briefly, how one knows whether the premises are true. Here we want to get clear how to tell whether the conclusion follows.

Briefly and roughly speaking, the conclusion of an argument follows if and only if it is implied by the premises, if and only if there is no way the premises could be true consistently with the conclusion's being false. Now, you already know what it means for one statement to imply another. So you have some knowledge of how to tell whether an argument with one premise is valid. Sometimes, however, arguments have several premises, no one of which implies the conclusion. Such arguments may nevertheless be valid: they are valid if there is no way for all the premises to be true while the conclusion is false. Let us illustrate this situation and then define it somewhat more rigorously.

Consider the dummy argument "Carol is either ill or at work. She is not at work. So she is ill." The conclusion that Carol is ill follows from neither of the two premises alone. It is, however, implied by the two of them together. For there is no way both premises could be true while the conclusion is false: its being false is inconsistent with both premises being true. Hence, the argument is valid.

By contrast, the argument "If Carol is not ill, then she is at work; she is at work; so she is not ill" is an invalid argument whose premises imply the conclusion neither jointly nor separately, there being no inconsistency in affirming both of them and denying the conclusion.

144

We have illustrated one way to define a valid argument. A better way is to define it in terms of the notion of argument form. You remember that a statement form is like a statement except that it contains lowercase letters instead of statements, the same letter standing for the same statement at each occurrence. Well, an *argument form* is like an argument except that it contains lowercase letters instead of statements, the same letter each time standing for the same statement. Consider an example: "If I am a monkey's uncle, you are, too; but you aren't; so I am not." This has the form

$$p \supset q, \quad \sim q, \quad \therefore \sim p$$

(the symbol, $\therefore$, means 'therefore'). Another argument having that same form is "If the moon is green cheese, then there is a man in the moon; but there is no man in the moon; so the moon isn't green cheese." Arguments having the same form will be said to be *substitution instances* of that form, as statements having the same form were said to be substitution instances of that form. Now, an argument is valid if it is a substitution instance of a form that is valid—valid, that is, if it has a valid form: validity is a matter of form.

What does it mean for an argument form to be valid? Just this: that there is no substitution instance of that form which has true premises and a false conclusion. The preceding argument form is called *modus tollens*. *Modus tollens* is valid, as the following truth table shows:

p q	$p \supset q,$	$\sim q,$	$\therefore \sim p$
T T	T	F	F
T F	F	T	F
F T	T	F	T
F F	T	T	T

You see that the conclusion is true in every line in which both premises are true and false only in those lines in which at least one premise is false. Therefore, no matter how you interpret the letters 'p' and 'q' (provided only that you substitute the same statements for the same letters throughout), you will not get an argument having true premises and a false conclusion.

By contrast, the argument form '$p, \therefore p \,\&\, q$'* is invalid, as the truth table for the form shows:

---

* To avoid excessive punctuation, we adopt the convention that the scope of the symbol for 'therefore', $\therefore$, will extend past that of the symbols used for compounding statements—the ampersand, wedge, horseshoe, and tilde. Hence '$p, \therefore p \,\&\, q$'

p q	$p,$	$\therefore p \,\&\, q$
T T	T	T
T F	T	F
F T	F	F
F F	F	F

That the premise is true and the conclusion false in the second line shows that there are substitution instances of this argument form having true premises and a false conclusion. One is "Whales are mammals; so whales and trout are both mammals." The existence of one substitution instance having true premises and a false conclusion shows that an argument form is invalid.

A slightly more complicated example of an invalid argument is tested on the table below:

p q r	$p \supset q,$	$r \supset q,$	$\therefore p \supset r$
T T T	T	T	T
T T F	T	T	F
T F T	F	F	T
T F F	F	T	F
F T T	T	T	T
F T F	T	T	T
F F T	T	F	T
F F F	T	T	T

That the premises don't imply the conclusion is clear from the second line, in which the conclusion is false and both premises are true. Hence, the argument form

$$p \supset q, \quad r \supset q, \quad \therefore p \supset r$$

is invalid.

If no combination of truth values yields premises that are all true while simultaneously yielding a conclusion that is false, the argument form is valid. Take, for example,

$$p \supset q, \quad q \supset r, \quad \therefore p \supset r;$$

its truth table proves it valid:

---

will be read as an argument having the conjunction '$p \,\&\, q$' as conclusion; it will not be read as a conjunction of the argument '$p, \therefore p$' with the statement 'q'. That is, it will be read as if it were punctuated '$p, \therefore (p \,\&\, q)$', not as if it were punctuated '$(p, \therefore p) \,\&\, q$'.

p q r	$p \supset q$,	$q \supset r$,	$\therefore$ $p \supset r$
T T T	T	T	T
T T F	T	F	F
T F T	F	T	T
T F F	F	T	F
F T T	T	T	T
F T F	T	F	T
F F T	T	T	T
F F F	T	T	T

You see that there are only two lines in which the conclusion is false, but there is at least one false premise in each of those lines. So there are no lines in which the premises are all true while the conclusion is false. This arrangement proves that the argument form is valid, that there can be no substitution instances of this form having true premises and a false conclusion.

As you will see, when you undertake the exercises at the end of this section of the chapter, truth table tests of validity can become very long and tedious. Fortunately, there is a way to shorten the work, and we shall learn it in the next section. Meanwhile, it is necessary to learn the long method so that you will be able to understand the short one.

Exercises: The Long Test

A. Indicate which of the following arguments have the form '$p \supset q$, p, $\therefore$ q'.

1. If Carol is ill, then she is in bed. She is ill. Therefore she is in bed.

2. If Carol is in bed and has a fever, then she is ill. Carol is ill and in bed. So she has a fever.

3. If Carol is feverish or in bed, then she is either ill or sleepy. She is feverish or in bed. So she is ill or sleepy.

4. Carol is feverish only if she is in bed. She is feverish. So she is in bed.

5. Carol is in bed only if she is feverish or sleepy. She is feverish or sleepy. So she is in bed.

6. Unless she is ill, Carol is in bed. She is in bed. So she is ill.

7. If Carol is in bed, she is ill. She is in bed. So she is ill.

8. Carol is in bed only if she is ill. She is ill. So she is in bed.

147

9. If Carol is in bed, then she is both ill and in bed. She is both ill and in bed. So she is in bed.

10. Carol is not in bed unless she is ill. She is ill. So she is in bed.

B. Below is a list of argument forms. Using truth tables, decide which are valid.

1. $p \supset q$, p, $\therefore q$

2. $p \supset q$, $\sim q$, $\therefore \sim p$

3. $p \supset q$, q, $\therefore p$

4. $p \supset q$, $\sim p$, $\therefore \sim q$

5. $p \lor q$, $\sim p$, $\therefore q$

6. $p \lor q$, p, $\therefore \sim q$

7. p, $\therefore p \& q$

8. $p \& q$, $\therefore p$

9. p, $\therefore p \lor q$

10. $p \lor q$, $\therefore p$

11. $p \supset q$, $q \supset r$, p, $\therefore \sim r$

12. $p \supset q$, $q \supset r$, $r \supset s$, $\sim s$, $\therefore \sim p$

13. $p \supset q$, $q \lor r$, $\sim(r \& \sim s)$, $\therefore \sim s \supset \sim p$

14. $p \lor q \lor r \lor s \lor t$, $\therefore p \& q \& r \& s \& t$

15. $p \supset \{q \supset [r \supset (s \supset t)]\}$, $\therefore t \supset \{s \supset [r \supset (q \supset p)]\}$

The Short Test: Assigning Truth Values

You have just learned that an argument form is invalid if there is a line of the truth table in which the premises are all true while the conclusion is false. Constructing full truth tables is a tedious task when an argument form contains many letters. A full truth table for the invalid argument form '$p \supset q, q \supset r, r \supset s, s \supset t, \therefore p \supset t$' would require 32 lines, and the number of lines needed will double with each variable added. An argument with ten variables would contain 1024 lines! Fortunately, there is a way to shorten the truth functional evaluation of complex argument forms.

We need only remember that we are interested in discovering whether there are any lines in which the premises are true while the conclusion is false. Remembering that will help us to simplify our task, because it means that we need consider only those substitution instances that make the conclusion come out false. We can safely ignore the rest. (For, obviously, the lines in which the conclusion is true won't be lines in which it is false while the premises are true.) Then, we only need to see whether the premises come out true in any of those lines. If so, the argument form is invalid; if not, it is valid.

Consider the fallacy of *affirming the consequent*:

p q	$p \supset q,$	$q,$	$\therefore$ p
T T			
T F			

We begin by noting only those lines in which the conclusion is false, lines 3 and 4. Next, we ascertain that the first of these two lines has true premises.

p q	$p \supset q,$	$q,$	$\therefore$ p
F T	T	T	F
F F			F

The existence of this one line means that the argument form is invalid.

Let us now use this method to assure ourselves that an argument form is valid. Consider the form of argument known as *modus ponens*. Start by filling in only those two lines in which the conclusion is false:

p q	$p \supset q,$	$p,$	$\therefore$ q
T T			
T F			F
F T			
F F			F

Now observe that at least one of the premises is false in each of these two lines. *Modus ponens* is therefore a valid form of argument.

149

We can shorten the procedure even more if we don't bother to write out the entire list of values for our variables. Look again at the fallacy of affirming the consequent:

p	q	$p \supset q,$	$q, \therefore p$
F	**T**	**T**	**T** **F**

Notice, first, that the only way the conclusion can be false is for 'p' to be false. Then notice that if 'p' is false, the premise '$p \supset q$' will be true. There remains only the premise 'q' to consider, and nothing says it can't be true. So we see that the argument form has true premises and a false conclusion when we interpret 'p' as false and 'q' as true.

Put another way, what we are trying to do is see if we can *assign* truth values to the statement letters in a way that will make the conclusion come out false while making the premises all come out true. Consider another example, the fallacy of *denying the antecedent*:

p	q	$p \supset q,$	$\sim p, \therefore \sim q$
F	**T**	**T**	**T** **F**

Just make 'p' false and 'q' true. The premises will both come out true, while the conclusion comes out false. That arrangement shows that the argument form is invalid.

If it were valid, no such interpretation would be possible. Try to find an interpretation of 'p' and 'q' that will make the premises of *modus tollens*, '$p \supset q$, $\sim q$, $\therefore \sim p$', come out true while the conclusion comes out false. You can't do it. If you make the conclusion '$\sim p$' false (by making 'p' true) and the premise '$\sim q$' true (by making 'q' false), you simultaneously make the other premise, '$p \supset q$', false. So the only way you can get a false conclusion is to get at least one false premise. Of course, you could do it if you made 'p' or 'q' true in one place, false in another, but that wouldn't count: the same letters must be assigned the same truth values throughout.

A word of caution: you may conclude that an argument form is invalid when you find one line in which the premises are true while the conclusion is false; but you may not conclude that the argument form is valid until you make sure that there are no such lines, and to do so, you must go about eliminating possibly invalidating lines in a systematic way. If you do it haphazardly, you might overlook a line that would show the argument invalid. Let me illustrate. Consider the argument form '$p \lor q, \therefore p \,\&\, q$'.

Suppose you noted that the conclusion is false if both 'p' and 'q' are false and then noted that the premise is also false in that case. You shouldn't conclude that the argument is valid. There are two other ways the conclusion could be false, the premise true. Make either 'p' or 'q' false and the other true; that arrangement will yield a true premise and a false conclusion.

To be sure you have covered all possibilities in such cases, you should start your shortened truth table by listing all cases in which the conclusion is false, thus:

p q	$p \vee q$,	$\therefore p \& q$
T F	T	F
F T	T	F
F F		F

Then you will notice that the premise is true in the first two lines, if not in the third.

In summary, the method of assigning truth values is to begin with the conclusion, assigning values in such a way as to make it false; then to see whether, consistently with that assignment, you can make all the premises true. This method didn't save us much time in the simple examples we have so far used to illustrate it, but it will pay off in complicated cases. Consider once again the argument form we mentioned in the beginning:

p q r s t	$p \supset q$,	$q \supset r$,	$r \supset s$,	$s \supset t$,	$\therefore t$
F F F F F	T	T	T	T	F

A full truth table would occupy thirty-two lines. By assigning 't' a truth value of F and then noticing that the premise '$s \supset t$' will be true if we make 's' false and so on, however, we can isolate the one line that shows this argument invalid.

By using a similar procedure we show that the long *hypothetical syllogism*

$$p \supset q, \quad q \supset r, \quad r \supset s, \quad s \supset t, \quad \therefore p \supset t$$

is valid. For to make the conclusion '$p \supset t$' false, we must make 'p' true while making 't' false. If we make 't' false, we must also make 's' false in order to make the premise '$s \supset t$' true. Similarly, we must make 'r', 'q', and 'p' false. But we have already made 'p' true. So we can't find a consistent interpretation of the letters that will make the premises all true while making the conclusion false. Hypothetical syllogism is a valid form of argument.

Exercises: The Short Test

A. Specify assignments of truth values that show to be invalid all those that are invalid.

Example: p, $\therefore q$

$$\frac{p \quad q}{\text{T F}}$$

1. $p \vee q$, $r \vee s$, $\sim p \vee \sim r$, $\therefore q \vee s$ $p\ q\ r\ s$

2. $p \supset q$, $q \supset r$, $r \supset s$, $\therefore s \supset p$ $p\ q\ r\ s$

3. $p \supset q$, $r \supset s$, $p \vee r$, $\therefore q \vee s$ $p\ q\ r\ s$

4. $p \supset q$, $r \supset s$, $\sim p \vee \sim r$, $\therefore \sim q \vee \sim s$ $p\ q\ r\ s$

5. $p \,\&\, q$, $p \supset s$, $q \supset r$, $\therefore s \,\&\, r$ $p\ q\ r\ s$

6. $p \,\&\, q$, $s \supset p$, $r \supset q$, $\therefore s \,\&\, r$ $p\ q\ r\ s$

7. $p \supset q$, $p \vee r$, $\therefore q \vee s$ $p\ q\ r\ s$

8. p, q, $\therefore (p \vee r) \,\&\, (q \vee s)$ $p\ q\ r\ s$

9. $(p \,\&\, q)$, $\therefore (p \,\&\, q) \vee r$ $p\ q\ r$

10. p, $\therefore (p \,\&\, q) \vee r$ $p\ q\ r$

B. Explain what would be wrong with saying "An argument form could be valid in some cases, invalid in others."

18 / Refutation by Counterexample

Counterexamples to Argument Forms

We have learned that a form of argument is invalid if there is a substitution instance having true premises and a false conclusion. You can discover whether such an instance exists by constructing a full truth table or by assigning truth values; but if you are debating with someone, a more effective stratagem is to produce a counterexample. Suppose George argues: "If Sara is a communist, she is an atheist. Well, I happen to know that she is an atheist. So she must be a communist, too." You could reply that one might as well argue: "If Tabby (a cat) is a cow, then she is a mammal. She is a mammal. So she is a cow." Notice that this argument has the same form, true premises, and a false conclusion. It is a *counterexample*. It proves that the form of argument '$p \supset q, q, \therefore p$' is invalid.

Logically, refutation by counterexample is as good as refutation by truth table, and rhetorically, it is better. A counterexample will make an impression on people who wouldn't know a truth table from a Canadian goose. The only trouble with counterexamples is that it is sometimes difficult to think of one. In that respect, truth tables have a great advantage. Thinking of counterexamples takes imagination and ingenuity, but almost anybody can learn to work a truth table. Furthermore, the truth table, when worked rightly, settles the question: if there is no line with true premises and a false conclusion, the argument form is valid, but failure to think of a counterexample does not prove that none exist, and an invalidating line will demonstrate the possibility of a counterexample, even when you can't think of one.

153

For a counterexample to be effective, it should satisfy two conditions: first, it should definitely have the form to which it is offered as a counterexample; second, it should have premises that are indisputably true and conclusions that are indisputably false. Consider the fallacious argument

> If Smith is not a fool, he did not do it. He did not do it. So he is not a fool.

That has the form

$$\sim p \supset \sim q, \quad \sim q, \quad \therefore \sim p.$$

Somebody offers this "counterexample":

> If Kissinger was not president, Ford was not president. Kissinger was not president. So Ford was not president.

The only trouble is that the "counterexample" is no counterexample. It does not have the required form, and it has a false premise.

The following argument has the right form but the conclusion is true:

> If Kissinger was not president, Brzezinski was not president. Brzezinski was not president. So Kissinger was not president.

By contrast, the following has true premises and a false conclusion, but the wrong form:

> If Kissinger was not secretary of state and Ford was not president, Kissinger was not president. So Ford was not president.

Here, however, is a genuine counterexample:

> If Ford was not president, Kissinger was not president. Kissinger was not president. So Ford was not president.

This argument has the same form, true premises and a false conclusion.

Counterexamples to Arguments

As we have already noted, a counterexample to an argument form is just as good a proof of its invalidity as is a truth table, and in some ways it is better; but let us be clear what we do prove and what we do not prove by a counterexample or a truth table. All we prove is that a certain form of argument is invalid. We do not prove thereby that every argument having that form is invalid. Proving that an argument form is valid is sufficient to prove that any given substitution instance of that form is valid, but don't conclude that proving an argument form invalid is proving any given substitution instance invalid. To do that, you must not merely prove that the substitution instance has an invalid form; you must prove that it has no valid form. Let me explain why.

As you remember, a statement may be a substitution instance of more than one statement form, one tautologous, one not. Well, an argument may also be a substitution instance of more than one argument form, one valid and one invalid. Consider the argument

(1)   Varna was once named 'Odessa' and is on the Black Sea. So Varna was once named 'Odessa' or is on the Black Sea.

This argument is valid because it has the valid form

(2) $p \& q, \quad \therefore p \vee q.$

Paradoxically, however, it also has the invalid form

(3) $p, \quad \therefore q$

The latter form has substitution instances that will make the premise true while making the conclusion false. Here is one:

(4)   Washington was our first president. So he was our last.

Now, suppose you had set out to evaluate the validity of (1) by abstracting its form and constructing a truth table to test that form. Suppose further that you did not notice that the premise is a conjunction and the conclusion an alternation. You just took them as simple statements. That is, you interpreted (1) as a substitution instance of (3). Then, noticing that (3) is invalid, suppose you declared (1) invalid. Well, you would have made a mistake. (1) is indeed a substitution instance of (3), which is invalid; but you have overlooked the fact that (1) is also a substitution instance of (2), which is valid. Your analysis revealed that (1) has an invalid form, but it was too superficial to reveal that (1) also has a valid form. Having that valid form makes (1) valid.

Full Analysis Needed

The difference between the two argument forms (2) and (3) is like the difference between a more detailed and a less detailed map. That you cannot see a path from your origin to your destination on the less detailed map doesn't prove that there is no path. A more detailed map might show one. To justify a conclusion that there is no path, your map must show every detail.

The ease of overlooking an analysis that would yield a valid form is illustrated by the following case:

Felix is a mammal. So Felix has a four-chambered heart.

That argument has the form 'p, $\therefore q$', which is invalid. But the conclusion follows. If we know the definition of 'mammal', we know that "Felix is a mammal" means "Felix has a four-chambered heart and . . .," which implies that Felix has a four-chambered heart.

This example illustrates that there is a limitation on the truth table as a test of validity. Unless you make a mistake, an argument valid by the truth table test is valid. You shouldn't conclude, however, that an argument invalid by the truth table test is invalid. Such a conclusion presupposes a fully analyzed argument. It assumes that no more detailed and profound analysis would reveal a valid form. Of course, in many cases you can be quite confident that this assumption is correct, but not always; and it is something that you should never be absolutely certain about. If you keep this limitation in mind, it is all right to use truth tables as tests of validity and to draw tentative conclusions therefrom. I regret that things are so complicated, but logic can only make life less hazardous, not make it perfectly safe.

Anyhow, there is this much consolation: if a negative result of a truth table test won't prove an argument invalid, it will at least indicate that the argument is not clearly valid and thereby put the *burden of proof* back on the shoulders of whoever advanced it. Somebody argues: "Felix is a mammal. So Felix has a four-chambered heart." The conclusion follows, but, as you remember, if one can't clearly see that the conclusion follows, the argument is not a good one. The argument is valid. It is even sound. But if it doesn't do its job, which is to show us that the conclusion is true, then it is defective—not fallacious, but deficient. A negative truth table test will at least point out that deficiency and indicate the need for a demonstration that the argument has a form which is valid.

The same limitations and consolations exist when you are refuting arguments by constructing counterexamples. Strictly speaking, all you are doing is proving that the argument in question has an invalid form, and doing so is proof not that the argument is itself invalid, just that one of its forms is. To show that the argument itself is invalid, you would have to show that it is the substitution instance of no valid form, and that can't be done. Nevertheless, refutation by counterexample has considerable utility. Suppose the other party to the dispute, George, thinks that the argument "If Sara is a communist, she is an atheist" is good, because he thinks valid the fallacious form of argument '$p \supset q$, q, $\therefore p$'. In that case, your counterexample will demonstrate his mistake. On the other hand, if George is not guilty of the fallacy of affirming the consequent, if he thinks that there is an analysis of the argument by which it has a valid form, then your counterexample obligates him to produce the analysis. You have pointed out that the argument seems invalid on the most obvious analysis. If George claims that it is nevertheless valid, he ought to spell out the analysis that will show it valid. A counterexample, like a truth table, shifts the burden of proof back to the other side.

Exercises

A. True or False?

1. If you can construct a counterexample to an argument, it is invalid.

2. An argument with an invalid form is invalid.

3. If the premises of an argument are not known to be true, it is unsound.

4. You can refute an argument by pointing out that the premises are not evident, even when the premises happen to be true.

5. You can refute an argument by constructing a counterexample to it.

B. Construct counterexamples to the following.

1. $p \supset q$, $\sim p$, $\therefore \sim q$.

2. $p \vee q$, p, $\therefore \sim q$.

3. $p \supset q$, q, $\therefore p$.

4. $p \vee q$, $\therefore p \,\&\, q$.

5. $p \supset q$, $\therefore q \supset p$.

C. True or False?

1. An argument is invalid if it has an invalid form.

2. An argument is valid if it has a valid form.

3. An argument with no valid form may nevertheless be valid.

4. An argument with a false conclusion is invalid.

5. An argument with false premises is valid, for its premises can't be true while its conclusion is false.

6. Arguments can be shown invalid by constructing counterexamples to them—that is, arguments of the same form having true premises and false conclusions.

7. An argument with a valid form might nevertheless be invalid.

8. The premises of an argument imply the conclusion only if the argument is a substitution instance of a valid argument form.

9. If an argument form is invalid, every substitution instance of that form is invalid.

10. If an argument form is valid, every substitution instance is valid.

D. Decide which of the following arguments are valid. Can you declare the others invalid? Why not?

1. Men are irrational and if irrational, then perverse. So men are perverse.

2. If men are irrational, they are perverse. They are perverse. So they are irrational.

3. Men are either perverse or irrational, but they are not perverse. So they must be irrational.

4. Men are either perverse or irrational, and it is well known that they are irrational. So they must not be perverse.

5. If men are perverse, they are irrational. So, if they are not irrational, they must not be perverse.

6. If men are perverse, they are irrational. So if they are irrational, they are perverse.

7. If men do that, they are either perverse or irrational. They do not do that. So they are not either perverse or irrational.

8. Men are perverse or irrational. If perverse, they do bad things. If irrational, they do strange things. So they do either bad things or strange things.

9. Men do either bad things or strange things. If irrational, they do strange things. If perverse, they do bad things. So they are either perverse or irrational.

19 / Some Basic Forms of Argument

Conjunction and Alternation in Arguments

Some forms of argument are so elementary or so commonly used that it is worthwhile singling them out for special mention. Let us begin with the most obviously valid, *conjunction*:

$$p, \quad q, \quad \therefore p \,\&\, q.$$

Suppose you are told that men are present and also told that women are present. Then you may infer that men and women are present or, if you prefer, that women and men are present, sexual preference being indifferent to logic.

If conjoining statements is a valid mode of inference, so is *separating* them. That is, all arguments of the form

$$p \,\&\, q, \quad \therefore p$$

are valid. Suppose we know that women and men are present. We may conclude that women are present; and, since '$p \,\&\, q$' comes to the same thing as '$q \,\&\, p$', we may, if we wish, also infer that men are present.

As valid as conjoining true statements is *alternating* or disjoining them:

$$p, \quad q, \quad \therefore p \lor q.$$

Suppose women are present. Suppose men are present. Then either men or women are present. If this conclusion seems wrong, perhaps it is because you have misinterpreted the disjunction as being exclusive. Remember, saying "Either men or women are present" does not exclude both being present. It may also seem odd that anybody would conclude

To be sure, there are *pseudo dilemmas* that might look valid but aren't, for example,

$$p \supset r, \quad q \supset s, \quad \sim p \vee \sim q, \quad \therefore \sim q \vee \sim s$$

and

$$r \vee s, \quad p \supset r, \quad q \supset s, \quad \therefore p \vee q.$$

You will see immediately that the first of these commits the fallacy of denying the antecedent, and the second involves the fallacy of affirming the consequent. The argument is "Men are present only if there is drinking. Women are present only if there is dancing. Neither men nor women are present. So there is neither dancing nor drinking." Suppose that children are present and that they dance or drink. Then we have a counterexample. The same circumstances refute the argument "Men are present only if there is drinking. Women are present only if there is dancing. There is dancing or drinking. So there are men or women present."

Summary of Argument Forms

Here is a summary list of some forms of argument considered in this chapter, with shortened names. On the left are valid forms of argument. On the right are fallacious forms of argument that are often confused with the valid forms.

Valid	*Fallacious*
Conjoining	
$p, \; q, \; \therefore p \& q$	
$p, \; q, \; \therefore q \& p$	
Separating conjuncts	Separating disjuncts
$p \& q, \; \therefore p$	$p \vee q, \; \therefore p$
$p \& q, \; \therefore q$	$p \vee q, \; \therefore q$
Adding an alternative	Adding a conjunct
$p, \; \therefore p \vee q$	$p, \; \therefore p \& q$
$p, \; \therefore q \vee p$	$q, \; \therefore p \& q$
Disjunctive syllogism	Affirming an alternative
$p \vee q, \; \sim p, \; \therefore q$	$p \vee q, \; p, \; \therefore \sim q$
$p \vee q, \; \sim q, \; \therefore p$	$p \vee q, \; q, \; \therefore \sim p$

Valid	*Fallacious*

Modus ponens

$$p \supset q, \; p, \;\; \therefore q$$

Affirming the consequent

$$q \supset p, \; p, \;\; \therefore q$$

Modus tollens

$$p \supset q, \; \sim q, \;\; \therefore \sim p$$

Denying the antecedent

$$p \supset q, \; \sim p, \;\; \therefore \sim q$$

Hypothetical syllogism

$$p \supset q, \; q \supset r, \;\; \therefore p \supset r$$

Misplaced middle

$$p \supset r, \; q \supset r, \;\; \therefore p \supset q$$

Constructive dilemma

$$p \vee q, \; p \supset r, \; q \supset s$$
$$\therefore r \vee s$$

Pseudo dilemma

$$r \vee s, \; p \supset r, \; q \supset s,$$
$$\therefore p \vee q$$

Destructive dilemma

$$p \supset r, \; q \supset s, \; \sim r \vee \sim s$$
$$\therefore \sim p \vee \sim q$$

Pseudo dilemma

$$p \supset r, \; q \supset s, \; \sim p \vee \sim q,$$
$$\therefore \sim r \vee \sim s$$

Exercises

A. Name the form of argument used and declare it valid or invalid. Remember, soundness is not in question, just validity.

1. God is both wise and just. So he is wise.

2. God is wise. So he is wise and just.

3. God is wise. So he is wise or unwise.

4. If God created the earth, it exists. It exists. So he created it.

5. If God had not created the earth, it would not exist. He created it. So it exists.

6. Either God is wise or he is just. As he is wise, he is not just.

7. Either God is wise or compassionate. If wise, he would not create sinners. If compassionate, he would not punish them. So either God would not create sinners or he would not punish them.

8. If wise, God would not create sinners. He created them. So he is unwise.

9. If God created sinners, he created sin. If he created sin, he is evil. So, if God created sinners, he is evil.

10. If God is omnipotent he can eradicate evil. If he is good, he wants to. Either he doesn't want to or he can't eradicate evil. So he is either not good or not omnipotent.

11. $(F \lor G) \supset H$, $(F \lor G)$, $\therefore H$

12. $(F \lor G) \supset (H \& I)$, $(H \& I) \supset (J \& K)$, $\therefore (F \lor G) \supset (J \& K)$

13. $[F \lor (G \& H)]$, $\sim F$, $\therefore G \& H$

14. $(F \& H)$, $\therefore (F \& H) \lor (G \supset I)$

15. $(F \& H) \supset I$, $\sim(F \& H)$, $\therefore \sim I$

16. $(F \lor H) \& (J \supset I)$, $\therefore F \lor H$

17. $(F \& H) \lor (G \& I)$, $F \& H$, $\therefore \sim(G \& I)$

18. $F \supset (G \& H)$, $J \supset (G \& H)$, $\therefore F \supset J$

19. $F \supset (G \& H)$, $K \supset (L \lor J)$, $\sim F \lor \sim K$, $\therefore \sim(G \& H) \lor \sim(L \lor J)$

20. $(F \& G) \lor H$, $\sim(F \& G)$, $\therefore H$

20 / *Chain Arguments: Proofs*

Extended Proofs

Sometimes the conclusion you want to prove is not deducible from your premises by any single use of an elementary form of inference but is implied by the totality of your premises and can be inferred from them by a series of elementary inferences. In such cases your argument forms a chain. You start with what you know and deduce conclusions from that. Then you deduce conclusions from your conclusions and so on until you arrive at the conclusion whose truth you wish to demonstrate. The result is a chain of many arguments linked together by the fact that the conclusions of one are premises of the next. Such chains will support the weight attached to them if every link is good and if the other end is firmly anchored. However, if any link is broken, the whole chain is broken; and if it is not firmly anchored, it will support nothing. To speak more literally, your extended argument is valid if every component argument is valid and sound if your original premises are true; but if any component argument is invalid, the whole argument is invalid; and a false premise vitiates the proof of any conclusion, no matter how far removed.

You will understand better what this explanation means, and extend your powers of argument enormously, if you will learn to make up a valid chain argument from a series of small but valid steps. Let us look at an example. We begin with all that we know to be true and relevant to the conclusion we wish to prove:

Premises
1. The butler was not in the house.
2. If the butler did it, the butler was in the house.

167

3. If the butler did not do it, the maid or the chauffeur did it.
4. The maid couldn't have done it.

Now we believe, but our discussant does not, that the chauffeur did it. How shall we prove our belief true? Well, if our discussant will accept the four statements stipulated above, we can make our case as follows:

Deductions

5. The butler did not do it. How do we know that? From premises 1 and 2, which imply 5 by modus tollens.
6. The maid or the chauffeur did it. We know that because it follows from conclusion 5 and premise 3 by modus ponens.
7. The chauffeur did it. This follows from the preceding conclusion and premise 4 by disjunctive syllogism.

In this way we prove on the basis of the available evidence that the chauffeur did it. Of course, this proof is satisfactory only if the premises we started with are known to be true, and we do not here prove that they are. What we do here prove is that, granting these premises to be true, the conclusion is true as well. That is, we prove that the conclusion follows from the premises. We do this by *deducing* the conclusion from the premises.

Schematizing Proofs

Exactly what we have done is easier to see when we abbreviate and schematize the argument, thus:

1. $\sim H$	premise
2. $B \supset H$	premise
3. $\sim B \supset (M \lor C)$	premise
4. $\sim M$	premise
$\therefore 5.\ \sim B$	from 1 and 2 by modus tollens
$\therefore 6.\ M \lor C$	from 5 and 3 by modus ponens
$\therefore 7.\ C$	from 6 and 4 by disjunctive syllogism

On the left you see, abbreviated, the premises and conclusions. The first four are premises, and they are labelled as such on the right. The next three steps are deductions from those premises or from preceding deductions. On their right are indicated the premises or previous conclusions from which they are deduced and the valid forms of inference that are involved in these deductions.

When the prosecuting attorney can construct a chain of argument like this one, based on premises accepted by the defense, the chauffeur's only recourse is to plead innocent by reason of insanity or to throw himself on the mercy of the court. If, of course, the defense challenges any of the premises, then it will be necessary to extend the chain in the other direction. The premises themselves will become conclusions from other premises whose truth is not disputed similarly.

Such is the nature of a proof. It starts with premises accepted by all discussants and then proceeds by showing how the conclusion can be reached by a series of small and obviously valid steps. The result is to make obvious what might not have been obvious before.

Constructing such a proof is difficult, much harder than running a truth table test of validity. But skill in constructing proofs is very valuable. So let us look at some more examples and then get some practice.

Again, we start with what we know that may prove relevant. We know (1) that State U and State College will both win; (2) that State Tech and State Baptist will both lose; and (3) that if State Baptist loses and State U wins, Mom will be very disappointed. We want to show that Mom will be very disappointed. Let us begin by abbreviating everything. Then we can write our proof as follows:

1.	$U \& C$	premise
2.	$T \& B$	premise
3.	$(B \& U) \supset M$	premise
$\therefore$4.	B	from 2 by separating conjuncts
$\therefore$5.	U	from 1 by separating conjuncts
$\therefore$6.	$B \& U$	from 4 and 5 by conjoining
$\therefore$7.	M	from 3 and 6 by modus ponens

Notice that the important part of this proof is on the right, where there is a justification for every item on the left. You are told on the right that the first three items on the left are the premises from which all succeeding inferences proceed. Then you are told how each item is deduced from those premises or from some conclusion previously deduced from them, and you are told what form of inference is used in that deduction.

Proof Strategy

No one can give you a foolproof way to construct such a proof. It takes intelligence and imagination. But there is one strategy that might help:

start with the conclusion and look back at the premises while referring to the table of valid rules of inference given in the preceding chapter. If you spot your conclusion somewhere in the premises, then try to find a rule that will permit you to extract it from them. That was the strategy I followed in constructing the proof given above. My conclusion was "*M*," which occurs only in premise 3. But how was I to get "*M*" out of 3? I couldn't just detach the consequent of a conditional. I knew, however, that I could detach the consequent if I knew the antecedent to be true. Now my problem reduced to finding "*B & U*." "*B & U*" occurred in neither of the other two premises, but I noticed that its components occurred in them. Then I saw how to extract "*B*" from the first premise and "*U*" from the second and how to put them together to get "*B & U*." Now all I had to do was to turn that series of steps around to get my proof. The proof is so obvious that anybody who accepts the premises but denies the conclusion will have to be disregarded as an absolute idiot. People of minimal intelligence can follow such proofs, if not construct them.

The strategy just recommended will usually increase your chances of finding a proof, but not always. Consider the following case: we know that State U will win and that State Baptist will lose. We know that if State U wins, Mom will be disappointed and will bake no chocolate cake for supper. We want to prove that there will be either no chocolate cake or no roast beef for supper. Our problem here is going to be getting 'roast beef' into the conclusion. Now, the only way to get a statement that does not occur in the premises into a conclusion is by adding an alternative. So our problem reduces to figuring out where the other alternative comes from. We find it in the second premise, but not all by itself. So we have to extract it. The following proof shows how to proceed:

1. $U \& B$ premise
2. $U \supset (M \& \sim C)$ premise
∴3. U from 1 by separating conjuncts
∴4. $M \& \sim C$ from 3 and 2 by modus ponens
∴5. $\sim C$ from 4 by separating conjuncts
∴6. $\sim C \vee \sim R$ from 5 by adding an alternative

When constructing arguments, short or long, the most important thing to keep in mind is what you are trying to achieve. You want to end up showing that a certain statement is true. You want to show its truth to somebody who may doubt it, and you want to make it so clear that it can no longer be doubted. Now, to do that you must start with premises known to both you and the other person. Then you must proceed by a series of elementary and obvious steps to reach your conclusion. So you must restrict yourself to forms of inference that almost any person can see to be valid. Here we shall restrict ourselves to the forms listed at the end of the preceding chapter.

Exercises

A. Consulting the list of rules given in the preceding chapter, write out the justification for each line that is not a premise. (Hint: It will help to abbreviate statements to single letters.)

a. 1. If a war starts, it will be long.

   2. If it is long, many lives will be lost.

   3. If many lives are lost, there will be suffering at home.

   4. War is certain.

  ∴**5.** If war starts, many lives will be lost.

  ∴**6.** If war starts, there will be suffering at home.

  ∴**7.** There will be suffering at home.

b. 1. If there is disagreement or a misunderstanding, they will fight or they will negotiate.

   2. There will be a misunderstanding, but no negotiations.

  ∴**3.** There will be a misunderstanding.

  ∴**4.** There will be a disagreement or a misunderstanding.

  ∴**5.** They will fight or negotiate.

  ∴**6.** They will not negotiate.

  ∴**7.** They will fight.

c. 1. If we are to have pleasant lives, we must clean up the environment.

   2. If we clean up the environment, we will destroy jobs.

   3. We won't destroy jobs.

  ∴ **4.** We won't clean up the environment.

  ∴**5.** We won't have pleasant lives.

d. 1. If unemployment is reduced, inflation will increase.

171

   2. If inflation is increased, retired people will suffer.

∴**3.** If unemployment is reduced, retired people will suffer.

e. 1. They will marry or not.

   2. If love prevails, they will marry; and if good sense prevails, they will not marry.

∴**3.** If love prevails, they will marry.

∴**4.** If good sense prevails, they will not marry.

∴**5.** Either love will not prevail or good sense will not prevail.

B. The following "proofs" contain fallacies. Check each line that contains an error.

a. 1. If Smith is smart, she will take her losses and quit.

   2. Smith will take her losses and quit.

∴**3.** Smith is smart.   from 1 and 2 by '$p \supset q$, q, ∴p'

∴**4.** Smith is smart or rich.   from 3 by 'p, ∴$p \lor q$'

b. 1. Jones is either a teacher or a plumber.

   2. If Jones is not a plumber, he is a fireman.

   3. Jones is not a teacher.

∴**4.** Jones is a teacher.   from 1 by '$p \lor q$, ∴p'

∴**5.** Jones is not a plumber.   from 1 and 4 by '$p \lor q$, p, ∴$\sim q$'

∴**6.** Jones is a fireman.   from 2 and 5 by '$p \supset q$, p, ∴q'

c. 1. I ate it and got ill.

   2. If I got ill, it must have been spoiled.

   3. If it was poisoned, it was spoiled.

∴**4.** I got ill.   from 2 by '$p \supset q$, ∴p'

∴**5.** It was spoiled.   from 2 by '$p \supset q$, ∴q'

∴**6.** It was poisoned.   from 3 and 5 by '$p \supset q$, q, ∴p'

d. 1. Jones went but she didn't enjoy it.

   2. If Jones enjoyed it, it was pretty awful.

∴**3.** Jones did not enjoy it.   from 1 by '$p \& q$, ∴q'

∴**4.** It was not pretty awful.   from 3 and 2 by '$p \supset q$, $\sim p$, ∴$\sim q$'

e. 1. If it was good, she liked it.

  2. If she liked it, he liked it.

  3. He liked it.

∴**4.** If it was good, he liked it.   from 1 and 2 by '$p \supset q$, $q \supset r$, ∴ $p \supset r$'

∴**5.** It was good.   from 4 and 3 by '$p \supset q$, q, ∴ p'

C. In the following, use just the rules listed in the preceding chapter.

  1. You know that Fred is failing but Susan is passing. If Fred is failing, the course is hard. If Susan is passing, it is interesting. Show that the course is hard but interesting.

  2. You know that if they get married, they will fight but have children; and that if they don't get married, they will fight but have children. Given that they will get married or not, prove that they will have children or pets.

  3. You know that Smith is a good man but not too bright. You know that it takes a bright man to do the job. You know that there will be pay only if the job is done. Prove that there will be no pay.

  4. You know that if Carol is your friend, she will be your friend for life; but if she is your enemy, she will not be your enemy long. You also know that if you have been acquainted with Carol a long time, she is either your friend or your enemy. Finally, you know that she is not your enemy and that you have been acquainted with her a long time. Prove that she is your friend.

  5. You know that there is blood on the carpet and that there is blood only if somebody was hurt and the rug was not cleaned. Prove that either the rug was not cleaned or you are a monkey's uncle.

D. Show by a series of valid deductions that the conclusion follows from the premises.

  1. $(F \& H) \supset I$, $I \supset (G \& \mathcal{J})$, $F \& H$, ∴ G

  2. F, G, H, ∴ $[(F \vee \mathcal{J}) \& (H \vee I)] \& (G \vee L)$

  3. $F \& G$, ∴ $[(F \vee \mathcal{J}) \& (G \vee L)] \vee H$

  4. $F \vee G$, $H \& K$, ∴ $(F \vee G) \& K$

  5. $F \supset (G \& H)$, $(G \& H) \supset L$, $\sim L$, ∴ $\sim F$

21 / Transformation

Substituting Equals

Some ways of saying a thing are more perspicuous than others. Thus,

Debby and Patty both passed

is a clearer way of saying

It is false that either Debby or Patty failed.

Consequently, people sometimes doubt your claims, not because they doubt what you say, but because you say it in a way that is not clear to them. In such cases you need a clearer way of stating the same thing. Pointing out a clearer way is one use of the method of argument we are going to present here. We call it "transformation." *Transformation* is based on the principle that equals may be substituted for equals. This principle is as good in logic as it is in algebra.* Suppose

$$a^2 = b + c.$$

Then,

$$a \times a = b + c.$$

For

$$a^2 = a \times a.$$

---

* In fact, it is good algebra only because it is good logic.

Similarly, suppose

(1)   If Fred passed, then Patty and Debby both passed.

Then,

(2)   If Fred passed, it is false that either Patty or Debby failed.

For

(3)   Patty and Debby both passed $\overset{\text{df}}{=}$ It is false that either Patty or Debby failed.

So, if you knew someone who was sure that (1) is true but unsure whether (2) is true, you could point out that (2) is just a different way of saying (1) and therefore must be true if (1) is. Likewise, if (1) is false, so is (2). Substitution of equals for equals preserves truth value, whatever it is. That is what the equivalence stated in (3) assures us: we can replace the statement on the left by the one on the right, or vice versa, without making any change in the truth value of the sentence in which the replacement occurs.*

Truth value is preserved whether the substitution is for a part or a whole. In the preceding example, only a part was transformed, the consequent. By contrast,

(5)   Either Fred did not pass or Patty and Debby both passed

transforms the whole of (1) by virtue of the equivalence

$$p \supset q \overset{\text{df}}{=} {\sim}p \vee q.$$

Something else also happened in going from (1) to (2). We didn't just change the logical forms of the whole or parts; we also changed some words. 'Passed' gave way to 'did not fail' by virtue of the definition

$$x \text{ passed} \overset{\text{df}}{=} x \text{ did not fail.}$$

The same definition would permit us to render (5) as

Either Fred failed or Patty and Debby both passed.

---

* The notorious exception is substituting equals in quoted statements. Smith says the words "Mary and Sam are both redheaded." What she says is equivalent to "Sam and Mary are both redheaded," but it is not accurate to report that Smith said the latter words. The latter is a paraphrase, not a quotation, and Smith might not care for the way you paraphrase her. Perhaps she believes in mentioning women first. If so, she would never make the latter statement, although she would make one that is equivalent to it.

To avoid exceptions like this one, we should perhaps phrase our rule more strictly: equals may be substituted for equals except when they occur within quotations. Sometimes they can be substituted in those cases, too, but not always.

Similar transformations in logical form and phrasing yield all the following, which are so many variations on (1):

> It is false that Fred passed and that Debby and Patty did not both pass.
> If Patty and Debby did not both pass, then Fred did not pass.
> If Fred passed, then it is false that either Debby or Patty failed.
> Either Fred failed or Debby and Patty both passed.
> Either Fred failed or it is false that either Debby or Patty failed.
> It is false that Fred passed and that Debby and Patty did not both pass.
> It is false that Fred passed and that either Debby or Patty failed.

We could show by means of a series of substitutions that if any one of these variations is true, they must all be true. Start again with (1) and consider

(6)   It is false that Fred passed and that either Debby or Patty failed.

To make the argument easier to follow, we first abbreviate (1) as

$$F \supset (D \& P).$$

Then, recognizing that failed $\overset{df}{=}$ did not pass, we abbreviate (6) as

$$\sim [F \& (\sim D \vee \sim P)].$$

Now we can show how to transform (1) into (6), as follows:

1. $F \supset (D \& P)$

∴2. $F \supset \sim (\sim D \vee \sim P)$ De Morgan equivalence

∴3. $\sim [F \& \sim \sim (\sim D \vee \sim P)]$ by '$(p \supset q) \overset{df}{=} \sim (p \& \sim q)$'

∴4. $\sim [F \& (\sim D \vee \sim P)]$ by '$p \overset{df}{=} \sim \sim p$'

Here we have a formal proof that if (1) is true, so must be (6). It is just like the proofs we have been constructing in preceding chapters, except that all the steps are by substitution. The conclusion doesn't just follow from the premise. Since we got the conclusion by substitutions only, it is equivalent to the premise. If this equivalence is not clear, we can make it clear simply by inverting the proof, reversing the substitutions and getting (1) back by a series of transformations on (6).

Substituting in Arguments

Substituting equals for equals not only preserves truth value; it also preserves validity. Suppose we have an argument. We take some statement in that argument—premise or conclusion—and replace it by an equivalent. If the argument was valid to start with, it will remain valid after the transformation. If invalid, it will still be invalid after the replacement. Consider an example:

(7)   If Zeus lost his temper, he threw a thunderbolt; and if he threw a thunderbolt, it wreaked much destruction. So if Zeus lost his temper, much destruction resulted.

That argument is valid, for it has the valid form

(8) $p \supset q, \quad q \supset r, \quad \therefore p \supset r.$

But if (7) is valid, so must be

(9)   If Zeus did not throw a thunderbolt, he did not lose his temper; and if destruction did not result, he did not throw a thunderbolt. So, if there was no destruction, Zeus did not lose his temper.

For (9) results from replacing all the conditionals in (7) by their equivalent contrapositives, to yield an argument of the form

(10) $\sim q \supset \sim p, \quad \sim r \supset \sim q, \quad \therefore \sim r \supset \sim p,$

which must be valid if (8) is valid, being equivalent to it.

Furthermore, if (7) is valid, so must be the far more opaque but equivalent argument

(11)   It is not the case that Zeus lost his temper and threw no thunderbolt, and it is not the case that he threw a thunderbolt and caused no destruction. So it is not the case that Zeus lost his temper and caused no destruction.

For

(12) $\sim(p \,\&\, \sim q), \quad \sim(q \,\&\, \sim r), \quad \therefore \sim(p \,\&\, \sim r)$

is equivalent to (8) by virtue of

(13) $p \supset q \overset{\mathrm{df}}{=} \sim(p \,\&\, \sim q).$

177

Moreover,

(14)   Either Zeus did not lose his temper or he threw a thunderbolt, and
either he did not throw a thunderbolt or there was destruction; so
either Zeus did not lose his temper or there was destruction

comes to the same thing as (7) by virtue of

(15) $p \supset q \overset{\text{df}}{=} \sim p \vee q.$

Knowing that any valid argument remains valid when equals have been
substituted for equals is very useful if you want to show to be valid an
argument that might not at first seem so to others. Consider

(16)   Either Zeus did not lose his temper or he threw a thunderbolt. If
he did not wreak any destruction, he did not throw a thunderbolt.
So, it is false that Zeus lost his temper but did not cause destruction.

Just by reading, it is hard to tell whether this argument is valid, but we can
show it to be valid as follows. First, let us abbreviate the components so
that the form is obvious to the eye:

(17) $\sim Z \vee T, \quad \sim D \supset \sim T, \quad \therefore \sim(Z \,\&\, \sim D).$

Now let us note that (17) can be transformed into

(18) $Z \supset T, \quad \sim D \supset \sim T, \quad \therefore \sim(Z \,\&\, \sim D),$

which can, in its turn, be transformed into

(19) $Z \supset T, \quad T \supset D, \quad \therefore \sim(Z \,\&\, \sim D);$

(19) then turns into an obvious instance of hypothetical syllogism:

(20) $Z \supset T, \quad T \supset D, \quad \therefore Z \supset D.$

Since (20) is obviously valid, (17) must be valid too.

Now, if there is an argument you can see to be valid, you may be able
to show others how it can be transformed by repeated substitutions of
equals for equals into an argument they too can see to be valid. Consider
one more example, the argument

(21)   If we do not retaliate, Harry did not lie. If we do not ignore it,
Susan did not lie. Either Harry or Susan lied. So we shall either
retaliate or ignore it.

If you can see that this argument is valid, you can show others what you
see in the following way. First, abbreviate the argument to expose its
logical structure:

(22) $\sim R \supset \sim H, \quad \sim I \supset \sim S, \quad H \vee S, \quad \therefore R \vee I.$

Then point out that we can replace the first premise by "$H \supset R$" and the second by "$S \supset I$" and thereby get a clear case of constructive dilemma:

(23) $H \supset R,\ S \supset I,\ H \lor S,\ \therefore R \lor I,$

which reads in unabbreviated English:

(24)   If Harry lied, we shall retaliate.   If Susan lied, we shall ignore it.
         Either Harry or Susan lied.   So we shall either retaliate or ignore
         it.

Of course, you may carry out the substitutions in English, if you want,
without benefit of abbreviations.   In fact, that is what you will need to do
if your interlocutor knows no formal logic, but abbreviating and formalizing
will help you to see how to make the substitutions.   If your interlocutor
denies validity to the result or can't follow the substitutions, you might as
well abandon the discussion.   You can't show anything to anybody who
can't see the obvious.

Substitution of equals also preserves invalidity.   So there are also times
when you can rephrase an argument and thereby convince a discussant
that it is invalid.   Suppose he is inclined to subscribe to an argument of
the invalid form

(25) $\sim(p\ \&\sim q),\ q,\ \therefore p.$

You can point out that this is equivalent to the form

(26) $p \supset q,\ q,\ \therefore p,$

the invalidity of which should be obvious.   If the other person can't see
the defect in (26), then produce a counterexample.   If that still doesn't do
the job, find somebody less obtuse to argue with, or somebody less obstinate.

Here is a list of obvious equivalences.   The names given are fairly
standard; you may call the unnamed ones anything you like.

Equivalence	*Name*
$p \supset q \overset{\mathrm{df}}{=} \sim(p\ \&\sim q)$	obversion
$p \supset q \overset{\mathrm{df}}{=} \sim p \lor q$	definition of conditional
$p \supset q \overset{\mathrm{df}}{=} \sim q \supset \sim p$	contraposition
$p \lor q \overset{\mathrm{df}}{=} \sim(\sim p\ \&\sim q)$	De Morgan equivalent
$p \lor q \overset{\mathrm{df}}{=} q \lor p$	conversion of $\lor$
$p\ \&\ q \overset{\mathrm{df}}{=} \sim(\sim p \lor \sim q)$	De Morgan equivalent
$p\ \&\ q \overset{\mathrm{df}}{=} \sim(p \supset \sim q)$	
$p\ \&\ q \overset{\mathrm{df}}{=} q\ \&\ p$	conversion of $\&$
$p \overset{\mathrm{df}}{=} \sim\sim p$	double denial

As before, the definition symbol, $\overset{\mathrm{df}}{=}$, says that you may replace the expression on the left by the expression on the right, or vice versa, without changing the truth value.

All these equivalences are already thoroughly familiar to you, but review them carefully. In the exercises that follow, you will be asked to use them to transform sentences into equivalents.

These equivalences are *formal equivalences*, equivalences of logical form. Remember that you may also use *definitional equivalences* when transforming statements in ordinary English into other statements. That is, you may also substitute in accordance with correct definitions, as we did in the beginning when we replaced 'failed' by 'did not pass'. Just make sure you know which definitions you are depending on, and that they are accurate.

Exercises

A. Each of the following is equivalent by substitution to "If Fred was either drunk or careless, he botched the job." Name the equivalences that justify the substitutions; where there is no name, write the formula. (Hint: Abbreviating will make things easier.)

1. Either Fred was not either drunk or careless or he botched the job.

2. It is false that Fred was drunk or careless but did not botch the job.

3. If Fred wasn't sober and careful, he botched the job.

4. If Fred did not botch the job, he was not either drunk or careless.

5. If it is true that if Fred was not drunk he was careless, then it is true that he botched the job.

B. Each of the following is equivalent by substitution to "If Fred botched the job, he was both drunk and careless." Name the equivalences that justify the substitutions.

1. If Fred was not both drunk and careless, he did not botch the job.

2. If Fred botched the job, he was not either sober or careful.

3. Either Fred did not botch the job or he was both drunk and careless.

4. It is false that Fred botched the job but was not both drunk and careless.

5. It is false that it is false that if Fred botched the job he was both drunk and careless.

180

C. Here are some proofs by substitution of equivalence. Name the equivalence that justifies each step, or write the formula. Where two steps are compressed into one, indicate both.

a. If Fred botched the job, he was either drunk or careless.

∴**1.** Either Fred did not botch the job or he was either drunk or careless.

∴**2.** Either Fred did not botch the job or it is false that he was both sober and careful.

∴**3.** It is false that it is both false that Fred did not botch the job and not false that he was both sober and careful.

∴**4.** It is false that Fred both botched the job and was both sober and careful.

∴**5.** It is false that Fred both botched the job and was neither drunk nor careless.

b. If Fred was both drunk and careless, he botched the job.

∴**1.** It is false that Fred was both drunk and careless but did not botch the job.

∴**2.** Either Fred was not both drunk and careless or it is false that he did not botch the job.

∴**3.** Either Fred was not both drunk and careless or he botched the job.

∴**4.** Either he botched the job or Fred was not both drunk and careless.

∴**5.** Either he botched the job or Fred was either sober or careful.

∴**6.** If he did not botch the job, Fred was either sober or careful.

D. Using the list of equivalences given above, show by a series of substitutions that (a) is equivalent to (b) in each of the following pairs.

1. (a) Either Fred was neither drunk nor careless or he botched the job.

   (b) If Fred was both sober and careful, he botched the job.

2. (a) Either Fred was not both drunk and careless or he botched the job.

   (b) If Fred did not botch the job, he was either sober or careful.

3. (a) If Fred was either drunk or careless, he botched the job.

   (b) If Fred did not botch the job, he was both sober and careful.

4. (a) Fred was either drunk or careless. If he was drunk, he botched the job. If he was careless, he botched the job. So he botched the job.

(b) If Fred was not drunk, he was careless. If he did not botch the job, he was not drunk. Either he was not careless or he botched the job. So he botched the job.

5. (a) If Fred botched the job, he was drunk and careless. He did not botch the job. So he was not drunk and careless.

(b) If Fred was not either sober or careful, he did not botch the job. He did not botch the job. So, if he was drunk, he was careful.

22 / *More Transformation*

The equivalences we used in the preceding chapter were all obvious and familiar. We want here to increase our logical powers by familiarizing ourselves with some that are slightly more complicated but still basic.

Let us look first at *distribution*:

$$p \supset (q \,\&\, r) \stackrel{\text{df}}{=} (p \supset q) \,\&\, (p \supset r).$$

Suppose you know that if you tack in front of a pursuing boat in a sailboat race, you have fouled her and must withdraw. Then you know both that if you tack in front of a pursuing boat you have fouled her and that if you tack in front of a pursuing boat you must withdraw. The converse inference is also valid. For these are just two ways of saying the same thing.

Another form of distribution is

$$p \supset (q \lor r) \stackrel{\text{df}}{=} (p \supset q) \lor (p \supset r).$$

Suppose you know that if you are guilty of a transgression, you must either withdraw or do a "720" (that is, go around twice in a circle). Then you know that it is true either that if you are guilty of a transgression you must withdraw or that if you are guilty of a transgression you must do a 720—the two statements being equivalent to each other.

Two other forms of distribution are

$$p \,\&\, (q \lor r) \stackrel{\text{df}}{=} (p \,\&\, q) \lor (p \,\&\, r)$$

and

$$p \lor (q \,\&\, r) \stackrel{\text{df}}{=} (p \lor q) \,\&\, (p \lor r).$$

183

Suppose you know that the yacht *Gretel* fouled *Hansel* and must either withdraw or do a 720. Then you know that it is true either that *Gretel* fouled *Hansel* and must withdraw or that *Gretel* fouled *Hansel* and must do a 720. The two statements may replace each other, one being true if and only if the other is, false if and only if the other is.

Suppose you know that the yacht *Gretel* was either on starboard tack or was to leeward and had an overlap. Then you know that *Gretel* was either on starboard tack or to leeward and she was either on starboard tack or had an overlap. For, once again, the difference between the two statements is only in phrasing, not in truth conditions.

If you doubt the claim that either form of distribution is an equivalence, test it by means of a truth table. In fact, you should do so anyhow. You will see that no substitution instance of the formula on the left has a truth value different from the simultaneous substitution instance of the formula on the right—not in any one of the preceding four equivalences.

Still another important form of equivalence is *association*:

$$p \vee (q \vee r) \overset{\text{df}}{=} (p \vee q) \vee r.$$

This says that the grouping of alternatives is indifferent. "Either you fouled or you must either withdraw or do a 720" says nothing different from "Either you either fouled or must withdraw or you must do a 720."

There is also a rule of association for conjunction:

$$p \,\&\, (q \,\&\, r) \overset{\text{df}}{=} (p \,\&\, q) \,\&\, r.$$

"You were on the wrong tack and both fouled and must withdraw" is not distinguishable in truth value from "You were on the wrong tack and fouled, and you must withdraw."

Because grouping of conjuncts or alternatives makes no difference logically, we could, if we wished, dispense with parentheses altogether, and just write

$$p \,\&\, q \,\&\, r,$$

and

$$p \vee q \vee r.$$

Grouping is indifferent for conjunction and alternation, but not for conditionals: '$p \supset (q \supset r)$' is not equivalent to '$(p \supset q) \supset r$', and '$p \supset q \supset r$' is hopelessly ambiguous; '$p \supset (q \supset r)$' is equivalent, rather, to '$(p \,\&\, q) \supset r$'. That is,

$$(p \,\&\, q) \supset r \overset{\text{df}}{=} p \supset (q \supset r).$$

Suppose you know that if *Gretel* tacked and collided with *Hansel*, then *Gretel* fouled *Hansel*. You may conclude that if *Gretel* tacked, and if she then collided with *Hansel*, she fouled *Hansel*. Or you may start knowing the latter statement and conclude the former. Both say the same thing and have the same truth value, whatever it is. In doubt? Test the equivalence with a truth table. We shall call it *conditionalization*.

Some other forms of equivalence that have been noted before should also be officially recorded here. First is the *definition of the biconditional*:

$$p \equiv q \overset{\text{df}}{=} (p \supset q) \,\&\, (q \supset p).$$

You know that *Gretel* fouled if and only if she withdrew. Then, you know that *Gretel* fouled if she withdrew and that *Gretel* withdrew if she fouled. Since you also know that '$p \supset q \overset{\text{df}}{=} \sim p \lor q$' and that '$p \supset q \overset{\text{df}}{=} \sim(p \,\&\, \sim q)$,' you can also see that the following are true:

$$p \equiv q \overset{\text{df}}{=} (\sim p \lor q) \,\&\, (\sim q \lor p);$$
$$p \equiv q \overset{\text{df}}{=} \sim(p \,\&\, \sim q) \,\&\, \sim(q \,\&\, \sim p).$$

Seeing all this, you may also recognize the truth of

$$p \equiv q \overset{\text{df}}{=} (p \,\&\, q) \lor (\sim p \,\&\, \sim q),$$

which declares that a biconditional is true if and only if both antecedent and consequent are true or both are false. Once again, you know that *Gretel* fouled if and only if she withdrew. Then you know that either she fouled and withdrew or she did not foul and did not withdraw.

None of the preceding equivalences will give you any trouble, nor will any of the following, but some of them will look a little odd at first. First there is *redundancy*:

$$p \overset{\text{df}}{=} p \,\&\, p.$$

Saying something twice won't make it more true or less false, although some people seem to think so. Nor will alternating a true statement with itself make any difference to its truth value:

$$p \overset{\text{df}}{=} (p \lor p)$$

is a true statement of equivalence.

Since statements equivalent to the same statement are equivalent to each other, the following—odd as they may look at first—are all true:

$$p \lor p \overset{\text{df}}{=} p \,\&\, p;$$
$$\sim \sim p \overset{\text{df}}{=} p \lor p;$$

and

$$\sim \sim p \overset{\mathrm{df}}{=} p \,\&\, p.$$

These last equivalences are strange, however, only because they are rare. You will not often encounter anybody making use of them. Perhaps that is because they are so utterly obvious that no one thinks there is need to take note of them.

Still odder looking, but nevertheless true, is *reductio ad absurdum* (reduction to absurdity):

$$p \supset (q \,\&\, \sim q) \overset{\mathrm{df}}{=} \sim p.$$

To say that 'p' is true only if '$q \,\&\, \sim q$' is true is as much as to say that 'p' is false, and conversely. *Hansel*'s skipper declares, in the heat of the Protest Committee meeting, "If *Gretel* was on starboard, then up is down!" The committee may safely take that remark as just an emphatic way of denying that *Gretel* was on starboard.

The reverse of reductio ad absurdum is *trivialization*:

$$(q \vee \sim q) \supset p \overset{\mathrm{df}}{=} p.$$

Someone says, "*Gretel* was right, whether or not she was on starboard." That claim is equivalent to "*Gretel* was right no matter what." It is just an emphatic affirmation of *Gretel*'s rectitude.

Strange as these last two equivalences may look, they can be very useful. Reductio ad absurdum is handy whenever you want to expose incoherence in the views of others. Those who want both to stop inflation and to eliminate unemployment risk a reduction to absurdity. Lawyers impeach witnesses by exposing the contradictions in their testimony. Mathematicians prove a theorem by assuming it to be false and then showing that the assumption leads to a contradiction. And so on. An interesting use of trivialization is Descartes's famous proof of his own existence. He started with the indubitable fact that he believed in his own existence. That belief was either true or false. If it was true, he existed by virtue of its truth. If false, he existed by virtue of having a false belief. So, Descartes concluded, "Heads I win and tails I win."

The equivalences listed and illustrated above may all be used in the same way as the equivalences listed previously: you may substitute any statement or statement form for one equivalent to it; you may replace what is on the left of the equivalence symbol, $\overset{\mathrm{df}}{=}$, by what is on the right, or vice versa.

That you may do so should increase enormously your ability to prove things, at least to all who can see these equivalences.*

Here is a list of the equivalences given in this chapter:

Equivalence	Name
$p \supset (q \,\&\, r) \overset{\text{df}}{=} (p \supset q) \,\&\, (p \supset r)$	distribution
$p \supset (q \vee r) \overset{\text{df}}{=} (p \supset q) \vee (p \supset r)$	distribution
$p \,\&\, (q \vee r) \overset{\text{df}}{=} (p \,\&\, q) \vee (p \,\&\, r)$	distribution
$p \vee (q \,\&\, r) \overset{\text{df}}{=} (p \vee q) \,\&\, (p \vee r)$	distribution
$p \vee (q \vee r) \overset{\text{df}}{=} (p \vee q) \vee r$	association
$p \,\&\, (q \,\&\, r) \overset{\text{df}}{=} (p \,\&\, q) \,\&\, r$	association
$(p \,\&\, q) \supset r \overset{\text{df}}{=} p \supset (q \supset r)$	conditionalization
$p \equiv q \overset{\text{df}}{=} (p \supset q) \,\&\, (q \supset p)$	definition of the biconditional
$p \equiv q \overset{\text{df}}{=} (p \,\&\, q) \vee (\sim p \,\&\, \sim q)$	definition of the biconditional
$p \overset{\text{df}}{=} p \,\&\, p$	redundancy
$p \overset{\text{df}}{=} p \vee p$	redundancy
$p \supset (q \,\&\, \sim q) \overset{\text{df}}{=} \sim p$	reduction to absurdity
$(p \vee \sim p) \supset q \overset{\text{df}}{=} q$	trivialization

Exercises

A. Name, or write the formulas for, all the equivalences involved in going from (a) to (b) in each of the following.

   1. (a) If Smith lied, then she is either a fool or dishonest.

   (b) It is either true that if Smith lied she is a fool or true that if Smith lied she is dishonest.

---

* Another important use of transformation is to get a statement into a form that may be more convenient for some special purpose, say, for introducing it into the data bank of a computer programmed to accept statements only when they are written in a prescribed form, or for designing the circuitry of a computer.

2. (a) Smith lied if and only if she is a fool and dishonest.

   (b) Either Smith lied and is a fool and dishonest or Smith did not lie and is not a fool and dishonest.

3. (a) If Smith lied, then heaven isn't heaven.

   (b) Smith didn't lie.

4. (a) If Smith is a fool and dishonest, then she lied.

   (b) If Smith is a fool, then if she lied she is dishonest.

5. (a) Smith is a fool, but she isn't dishonest and she didn't lie.

   (b) Smith is a fool and foolish, but she isn't dishonest and she didn't lie.

6. (a) Smith is a fool. If she is a fool, she lied and is dishonest. So she lied and is dishonest.

   (b) Smith is a fool. If she is a fool, she lied; and if she is a fool, she is dishonest. So she lied and is dishonest.

7. (a) Smith is a fool and foolish. So Smith is a fool.

   (b) Smith is a fool. So Smith is a fool.

8. (a) Smith is a fool. So Smith is a fool.

   (b) Smith is either a fool or foolish. So she is a fool and foolish.

9. (a) Either Smith is a fool or Smith is both dishonest and a liar.

   (b) Either Smith is a fool and dishonest or she is a fool and a liar.

10. (a) Either Smith is a fool or Smith is either dishonest or a liar.

    (b) Either Smith is either a fool or dishonest or Smith is a liar.

11. (a) If Smith is a fool, she is dishonest; and if Smith is a liar, she is dishonest. Smith is a fool. So Smith is either dishonest or a liar.

    (b) If Smith is a fool and a liar, she is dishonest. Smith is a fool. So Smith is either dishonest or a liar.

B. Using the equivalences listed in this chapter and the last, show how to transform (a) into (b).

1. (a) $(F \& L) \supset (D \& C)$

   (b) $[\sim(F \& L) \lor C] \& \sim[\sim(\sim L \lor \sim F) \& \sim D]$

2. (a) $[(F \& L) \& D] \lor C$

   (b) $(C \lor F) \& (C \lor L) \& (C \lor D)$

3. (a) $F \equiv D$

(b) $(\sim F \vee D) \,\&\, \sim(D \,\&\, \sim F)$

4. (a) $(F \,\&\, G) \,\&\, H$

(b) $\sim[H \supset (\sim F \vee \sim G)]$

23 / *Conditional and Complex Proofs*

You have learned several rules of inference and several equivalences. Here I want to teach you one more rule of inference and then how to combine all the rules and equivalences in complex proofs.

Conditional Proof

The new rule of inference is slightly more complicated, but it is a powerful and useful rule. It is called *conditional proof* and amounts to assuming some statement, 'p', to be true, deducing some consequence, 'q', and declaring that such a deduction shows that if 'p' is true, then so is 'q'. (1) provides an illustration.

(1)
$$
\begin{array}{ll}
? \; 1. \; S & \text{assumption} \\
\therefore 2. \; S \lor R & \text{from 1 by addition of an alternative} \\
\therefore 3. \; S \supset (S \lor R) & \text{from 1 and 2 by conditional proof}
\end{array}
$$

In (1) "S" abbreviates the assumption "The table is square." We put a question mark in front of this assumption to indicate that it is being assumed, not being asserted as a fact. We don't know whether it is true or not; we are just pretending that it is true for the sake of the argument; and so we flag it accordingly. On the basis of the assumed premise that the table is square we show in line 2 that the table is either square or round ("*R*" abbreviates "The table is round"). Then, in line 3, we *discharge* our assumption: we remind ourselves that line 2 was based on the assumption in line 1. We have not shown "*S* ∨ *R*" to be unconditionally true; we have shown it to be conditionally true, depending on the assumption "*S*." That is, we have shown that the conditional statement "*S* ⊃ (*S* ∨ *R*)" is unconditionally true.

(2) offers another illustration, this time with two assumptions.

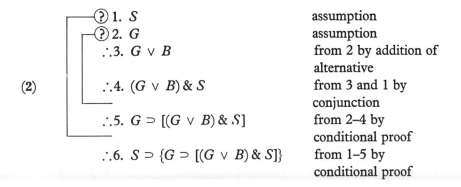

(2)

⑦ 1. *S*		assumption
⑦ 2. *G*		assumption
∴3. *G* ∨ *B*		from 2 by addition of alternative
∴4. (*G* ∨ *B*) & *S*		from 3 and 1 by conjunction
∴5. *G* ⊃ [(*G* ∨ *B*) & *S*]		from 2–4 by conditional proof
∴6. *S* ⊃ {*G* ⊃ [(*G* ∨ *B*) & *S*]}		from 1–5 by conditional proof

In (2) "*S*" again abbreviates "The table is square," "*G*" abbreviates "The table is green," and "*B*" abbreviates "The table is broken down." Line 1 makes assumption "*S*." Line 2 makes assumption "*G*." Line 3 deduces the consequence "*G* ∨ *B*." Line 4 deduces the consequence "(*G* ∨ *B*) & *S*." Line 5 then points out that 4 has been proved not categorically but conditionally on the assumption of line 2. Then line 6 points out that 5 is conditioned on the assumption of line 1.

Conditional arguments are invalid if the assumptions made at the beginning are not eventually discharged. Look at the invalid argument of (3).

(3)

Fallacious ∴2. *S* ∨ *R*   from 1 by addition of alternative

⑦ 1. *S*   assumption

The final line of (3), a shortened version of (1), wrongly asserts "*S* ∨ *R*," as if it had been proved categorically true. It hasn't. What has been proved is that "*S* ∨ *R*" is true if the assumption "*S*" is true. In other words, what has been proved is the conditional statement "*S* ⊃ (*S* ∨ *R*)"; but our invalid proof does not reflect this fact.

191

One other fallacy that you must avoid is illustrated by (4).

(4)

	1. S	premise
(?)	2. G	assumption
	∴3. $G \lor S$	addition of alternation
	∴4. $G \supset (G \lor S)$	from 2 and 3 by conditional proof
Fallacious	∴5. $(G \lor S) \lor R$	from 3 by addition of alternation

Step 5 of this "proof" goes back to pick up step 3, which was proved on the assumption "G." To use 3 in this way, as if it had been unconditionally proved, is an error. Every line between an assumption and its discharge is conditional on the assumption. So no line succeeding discharge of the assumption can invoke such line in its justification.

Conditional proof is handiest when you want to prove conditional statements. Just assume the antecedent of the conditional and show that the consequent follows. (5) is the proof of the conditional '$p \supset (q \supset p)$'.

(5)

(?)	1. p	assumption
(?)	2. q	assumption
	∴3. p	from 1 by repetition
	∴4. $q \supset p$	from 2 and 3 by conditional proof
	∴5. $p \supset (q \supset p)$	from 1–4 by conditional proof

Notice that the last line of (5) is a tautology. This should not be surprising: if line 4 is deducible from line 1, that can only be because line 1 implies line 4, which is the case if and only if the conditional formed from 1 as antecedent and 4 as consequent is a tautology. Indeed, that implications exist only if the corresponding conditionals are tautologies is the basis of conditional proof.

Notice, too, that the last line of the preceding proof is deduced from no premises. So the proof is not merely valid but sound. If there are no premises, there is no way they can be false. As we noticed before, tautologies are true no matter what the facts are. Therefore, they follow from any premises and from none.

Assumptions and premises may be combined in the same proof, as is illustrated in (6).

$$
\begin{array}{lll}
& \text{1. } S & \text{premise} \\
& \text{(?) 2. } G & \text{assumption} \\
\textbf{(6)} & \therefore 3. \ G \lor B & \text{from 2 by addition of} \\
& & \text{alternation} \\
& \therefore 4. \ (G \lor B) \& S & \text{from 1 and 3 by conjunction} \\
& \therefore 5. \ G \supset [(G \lor B) \& S] & \text{from 2–4 by conditional proof}
\end{array}
$$

In this proof, we are given that "S" is true, and we assume that "G" is true as well. Taken together, this assumption and premise, if true, justify claiming that the conditional statement in line 5 is true. Since all assumptions are discharged, the proof is valid. No further steps are needed.

Combining Rules of Transit and Equivalences

Conditional proof completes our list of rules of inference. These rules fall into two groups. First, there are *rules of transit*, which permit us to go from premises to conclusions, but not always from conclusions to premises. Here is a list:

Rules of Transit

$p, \ q, \ \therefore p \& q$	conjoining
$p, \ q, \ \therefore q \& p$	conjoining
$p \& q, \ \therefore p$	separating
$p \& q, \ \therefore q$	separating
$p, \ \therefore p \lor q$	adding
$p \lor q, \ \sim p, \ \therefore q$	disjunctive syllogism
$p \lor q, \ \sim q, \ \therefore p$	disjunctive syllogism
$p \supset q, \ \sim q, \ \therefore \sim p$	modus tollens
$p \supset q, \ p, \ \therefore q$	modus ponens
$p \supset q, \ q \supset r, \ \therefore p \supset r$	hypothetical syllogism
$p \lor q, \ p \supset r, \ q \supset s, \ \therefore r \lor s$	constructive dilemma
$p \supset r, \ q \supset s, \ \sim r \lor \sim s, \therefore \sim p \lor \sim q$	destructive dilemma
$\left(p, \ \overset{\text{(?)}}{\big\vert} \ \therefore q\right), \ \therefore p \supset q$	conditional proof

In addition to such asymmetrical rules of transit , we have also learned equivalences that justify transforming one statement into another and back again. They are collected together here:

Equivalences

$$p \supset q \overset{df}{=} \sim(p \,\&\, \sim q) \qquad \text{obversion}$$

$$p \supset q \overset{df}{=} \sim p \vee q \qquad \text{definition of conditional}$$

$$p \supset q \overset{df}{=} \sim q \supset \sim p \qquad \text{contraposition}$$

$$p \vee q \overset{df}{=} \sim(\sim p \,\&\, \sim q) \qquad \text{De Morgan equivalent}$$

$$p \,\&\, q \overset{df}{=} \sim(\sim p \vee \sim q) \qquad \text{De Morgan equivalent}$$

$$p \,\&\, q \overset{df}{=} q \,\&\, p \qquad \text{conversion}$$

$$p \vee q \overset{df}{=} q \vee p \qquad \text{conversion}$$

$$p \supset (q \,\&\, r) \overset{df}{=} (p \supset q) \,\&\, (p \supset r) \qquad \text{distribution}$$

$$p \supset (q \vee r) \overset{df}{=} (p \supset q) \vee (p \supset r) \qquad \text{distribution}$$

$$p \,\&\, (q \vee r) \overset{df}{=} (p \,\&\, q) \vee (p \,\&\, r) \qquad \text{distribution}$$

$$p \vee (q \,\&\, r) \overset{df}{=} (p \vee q) \,\&\, (p \vee r) \qquad \text{distribution}$$

$$p \vee (q \vee r) \overset{df}{=} (p \vee q) \vee r \qquad \text{association}$$

$$p \,\&\, (q \,\&\, r) \overset{df}{=} (p \,\&\, q) \,\&\, r \qquad \text{association}$$

$$(p \,\&\, q) \supset r \overset{df}{=} p \supset (q \supset r) \qquad \text{conditionalization}$$

$$p \equiv q \overset{df}{=} (p \supset q) \,\&\, (q \supset p) \qquad \text{definition of biconditional}$$

$$p \equiv q \overset{df}{=} (p \,\&\, q) \vee (\sim p \,\&\, \sim q) \qquad \text{definition of biconditional}$$

$$p \overset{df}{=} \sim \sim p \qquad \text{double denial}$$

$$p \overset{df}{=} p \,\&\, p \qquad \text{redundancy}$$

$$p \overset{df}{=} p \vee p \qquad \text{redundancy}$$

$$\sim p \overset{df}{=} p \supset (q \,\&\, \sim q) \qquad \text{reduction to absurdity}$$

$$q \overset{df}{=} (p \vee \sim p) \supset q \qquad \text{trivialization}$$

As (7), a schematization of St. Anselm's famous ontological argument for the existence of God, shows, we may combine inference by rules of transit with inference by transformation. "G" abbreviates "God exists," and "P" abbreviates "God is perfect."

$$
\begin{array}{lll}
 & 1.\ P & \text{premise} \\
 & 2.\ \sim G \supset \sim P & \text{premise} \\
(?)\ & 3.\ \sim G & \text{assumption} \\
 & \therefore 4.\ \sim P & \text{from 3 and 2 by modus ponens} \\
 & \therefore 5.\ P \,\&\, \sim P & \text{from 1 and 4 by conjunction} \\
 & \therefore 6.\ \sim G \supset (P \,\&\, \sim P) & \text{from 3–5 by conditional proof} \\
 & \therefore 7.\ \sim \sim G & \text{from 6 by reductio ad absurdum} \\
 & \therefore 8.\ G & \text{from 7 by double denial}
\end{array}
$$

(7)

In unabbreviated English, (7) says: "For the sake of the argument, assume that God does not exist. If he doesn't, he is imperfect. God is, however, perfect. So, if the assumption is true, then God is both perfect and imperfect, which is impossible. The assumption must be false. So God exists." This argument is perfectly valid. Of course, it may not be sound. Whether it is sound depends on whether the two premises are true—on whether God is perfect and on whether perfection implies existence.

Exercises

A. Here are some proofs. Consulting the list of equivalences and rules given above, give the full justification for each step.

a.

$$
\begin{array}{lll}
 & 1.\ F \supset G & \text{premise} \\
 & 2.\ F \supset \sim G & \text{premise} \\
 & \therefore 3.\ (F \supset G) \,\&\, (F \supset \sim G) & \\
 & \therefore 4.\ F \supset (G \,\&\, \sim G) & \\
 & \therefore 5.\ \sim F &
\end{array}
$$

b.

$$
\begin{array}{lll}
(?)\ & 1.\ F & \text{assumption} \\
(?)\ & 2.\ \sim F & \text{assumption} \\
 & \therefore 3.\ F \vee G & \\
 & \therefore 4.\ G & \\
 & \therefore 5.\ \sim F \supset G & \\
 & \therefore 6.\ F \supset (\sim F \supset G) & \\
 & \therefore 7.\ (F \,\&\, \sim F) \supset G & \\
 & \therefore 8.\ \sim G \supset \sim (F \,\&\, \sim F) & \\
 & \therefore 9.\ \sim G \supset (\sim F \vee \sim \sim F) & \\
 & \therefore 10.\ \sim G \supset (\sim F \vee F) & \\
 & \therefore 11.\ \sim G \supset (F \vee \sim F) & \\
 & \therefore 12.\ \sim \sim G \vee (F \vee \sim F) & \\
 & \therefore 13.\ G \vee (F \vee \sim F) & \\
 & \therefore 14.\ (G \vee F) \vee \sim F & \\
 & \therefore 15.\ \sim F \vee (G \vee F) & \\
 & \therefore 16.\ F \supset (G \vee F) &
\end{array}
$$

∴17. $(F \vee F) \supset (G \vee F)$

∴18. $\sim(G \vee F) \supset \sim(F \vee F)$

c.
      ⑦1. $F \vee G$ assumption

      ⑦2. $H \vee \mathcal{J}$ assumption

      ∴3. $F \vee G$

      ∴4. $(H \vee \mathcal{J}) \supset (F \vee G)$

∴5. $(F \vee G) \supset [(H \vee \mathcal{J}) \supset (F \vee G)]$

∴6. $[(F \vee G) \& (H \vee \mathcal{J})] \supset (F \vee G)$

∴7. $\{[(F \vee G) \& (H \vee \mathcal{J})] \supset (F \vee G)\} \vee I$

d.
    1. $F \supset G$ premise

    2. $\sim(G \& \sim H)$ premise

    3. $\sim H \vee I$ premise

∴4. $G \supset H$

∴5. $H \supset I$

∴6. $G \supset I$

∴7. $F \supset I$

e.
    1. $F \equiv G$ premise

    2. $\sim F$ premise

∴3. $(F \supset G) \& (G \supset F)$

∴4. $G \supset F$

∴5. $\sim G$

∴6. $\sim G \& \sim F$

∴7. $\sim(\sim \sim G \vee \sim \sim F)$

∴8. $\sim(G \vee F)$

B. Using only the rules of transit and equivalences listed in this chapter, prove the following arguments valid by showing how to get from premises to conclusion.

1. $(F \& G) \supset H, \quad \therefore F \supset (G \supset H)$

2. $G \supset F, \quad G \supset H, \quad \therefore G \supset (F \& H)$

3. $F \& G, \quad \therefore H \supset (F \& G)$

4. $H \& I, \quad \therefore H \vee I$

5. $F, \quad \sim F, \quad \therefore G$

6. $F \supset (G \vee H), \quad \therefore (F \supset G) \vee (F \supset H)$

7. $G, \quad \therefore F \vee \sim F$

8. $G, \quad G \supset F, \quad \therefore \sim F \supset \mathcal{J}$

9. $G \vee F, \quad G \vee H, \quad \therefore \sim H \supset (\sim F \supset G)$

10. $G \supset H, \quad G, \quad \sim H, \therefore F$

24 / Enthymemes

Imagine that somebody has advanced the following argument:

(1)   George is a man. So George is mortal.

Is that a valid argument? Most of us would say so. Yet, it has the form

$$p, \quad \therefore q,$$

which is not valid. Supposing, then, that the conclusion does follow, why does it follow?

There are two possibilities. One is that "George is a man" means "George is mortal, etc." If so, the form of the argument would be

$$p \& \ldots, \quad \therefore p,$$

which is valid. That is, the conclusion may follow from the premises by definition of 'man', as

George is a bachelor; so George is unmarried

follows by definition of 'bachelor'.

The other, more likely, possibility is that the argument is an *enthymeme*, a shortened version of a much longer argument that, when fully stated, reads

(2)   George is a man, and if a man, then mortal. So George is mortal.

If so, the thing to do is to supply the unstated, or *suppressed premise*,

If George is a man, he is mortal,

and recognize that the argument is valid because it has the valid form

$$p \& (p \supset q), \quad \therefore q.$$

In ordinary discourse enthymemes occur frequently. People don't normally spell their arguments out; more often they leave what they take for granted unstated, as being too obvious or well known to mention. Doing so may increase the rhetorical effectiveness of the argument by making it shorter and punchier and by enlisting the active participation of the listener, who must supply the missing link and who thereby becomes a party to the argument.

Enthymemes like (1) leave a premise unstated. Others, like

(3)   George is a man, and if a man, then mortal,

leave a conclusion,

So George is mortal,

to be supplied.

Before you can evaluate an enthymeme, you must try to decide what has been taken for granted or what is implied. You must guess at the speaker's intentions, trying to divine what the speaker has left concealed. That can be a tricky business. Suppose you are having a conversation with someone who argues:

George is a man. So he is superior to Mary.

You will, not unnaturally, be inclined to think the speaker is assuming

All men are superior to all women.

If so, you will be surprised when it turns out that Mary is the speaker's cat and that the speaker is only assuming the superiority of men to cats. You will have made a mistake even if Mary is a woman but the speaker, knowing Mary to be a very inferior woman, is only assuming

All men are superior to Mary.

Such are the hazards of guessing at intentions.

Similar risks attend attempts to divine the intended implications of someone's premises. The speaker says:

Jesus was a man. Men are mortal.

You, naturally, take the speaker as intending to conclude

Jesus was mortal.

As it happens, however, the speaker believes Jesus to be immortal, because a god.

The problem in interpreting enthymemes is that you must operate under constraints that are frequently in conflict. You want to be charitable, but you also want to be accurate. Charity demands that you give the speaker the benefit of the logical doubt, that you understand the argument in whatever way makes it most plausible and least vulnerable to refutation. Accuracy demands that you understand the argument, whether plausible or implausible, as the speaker meant it. Suppose a premise was left out. Then you will wish, in the interests of fairness, to avoid attributing to the speaker assumptions that are obviously false or from which the conclusion won't follow. On the other hand, the speaker may in fact believe things that are false or may be advancing an argument that isn't valid. There is no way you can fail to be wrong in such a case. If you make the argument sound plausible, it won't be what the speaker intended. If you guess at what was intended, the argument won't sound plausible.

There is really no satisfactory solution to this problem. Perhaps the best rule of thumb is to start out, if you can, by giving the speaker the benefit of the logical doubt, assuming him innocent of error until he has proved otherwise. Of course, that won't always be possible. Suppose another speaker says,

> Only a crook would steal the money, and Al is a crook.

It is hard to see how we can avoid supposing she intends to advance the conclusion

> Al stole the money

and therefore to make an invalid argument of the form

$$p \supset q, \quad q, \quad \therefore p.$$

Similarly, suppose the speaker says,

> If Smith is a woman and Jones is a man, Smith is smarter than Jones.

It will be difficult to see how we can avoid attributing to her the plainly false assumption that all women are smarter than all men.

Often we have a choice between accusing the speaker of advancing fallacious arguments and chastising her for making false assumptions, without being able to decide which is her offense against logic. Suppose Sue says:

> It is good for me. So it is good for others.

Either she is questionably assuming that what is good for her is good for others, or the conclusion just can't be made to follow.

Enthymemes are even more difficult to evaluate when we are hard-pressed to imagine what is being assumed or implied. Consider the following argument, reported in a June 6, 1977, story in *Newsweek* about the debate over a proposed ordinance against homosexual marriage:

> I don't know what the Bible says about gay people, but I do know that Jesus said go out and have children. I believe in the word of God. So I went out and had ten. Could a gay couple follow the word of God like that?

It is clear here that the speaker makes several assumptions. For one thing, she assumes clearly that the Bible is the word of God and that Jesus is God or his spokesman. She also seems to be assuming that God wants us to have as many children as possible. It is not at all clear, however, what conclusion she intends by this argument. If her point is that the ordinance against homosexual marriages should be defeated, it is hard to see how that conclusion follows from her premises. If her point is just that there is no way a homosexual couple could have children, that conclusion certainly follows, but who would dispute it? Perhaps her point is that those who fail to have children are going against the will of God; but if so, it is not clear how many children she thinks God wants one to have. And does she also intend to defend an ordinance against all childless marriages, including marriages between sterile persons or persons too old to have children? Until we know, it is impossible to say what this argument proves, if anything, or what it fails to prove.

We might be in a better position to interpret the argument if we knew more about the context in which it was advanced, or if the woman who used it were at hand. *Newsweek* merely tells us that she was replying to an argument that, since the only strictures in the Bible against homosexuality are in the Old Testament, they aren't binding on Christians—an argument that is itself an enthymeme with the suppressed premise

> Only strictures in the New Testament are binding on Christians.

Unhappily, that clarification really doesn't help us to decide exactly what thesis the woman thought she was advancing. Perhaps she, herself, didn't know; perhaps she was just expressing a vague feeling that homosexual marriages are somehow or other against the word of God.

Of course, it is not always so hard to guess at the speaker's intentions. Contrast the preceding argument with the following, reported in the same article. The argument was made in reply to the remark "Gays have a choice."

> Why in the world would anyone choose the anguish, heartbreak and discrimination of being gay?

Here there is no doubt what conclusion is intended. It is "Gays don't choose to be gay." Nor is there much doubt what premises are assumed. They are "No one chooses anxiety, etc., and homosexuality means anxiety, etc." This is not to say that the latter argument is sound, just that it is a good deal clearer. Clear arguments are often clearly unsound. The trouble with unclear arguments is not that they are clearly unsound but that they are not clearly sound or unsound. We don't know what to make of them.

When there is difficulty about interpreting an enthymeme or any other argument, all anyone can do is say, "I don't know what is being argued here. It could be A, or it could be B or even C. If it is A, then the conclusion follows but the premise is false. If it is B, the premise is true but the conclusion doesn't follow. And so on." That is to say, the best thing to do is to offer several alternative interpretations and criticize each one separately. A logic book can instruct you in dealing with an enthymeme once you have supplied the missing links, but not in supplying the missing links.

Exercises

A. Supply the unstated premises or conclusions. Where several answers are possible, state as many as you can.

1. God is the supreme being. So he must exist.

2. If the universe exists, it must have a cause. So God exists.

3. Everything is caused. So there is no free will.

4. He didn't do it of his own free will. So he is not responsible.

5. God made everything. So nothing is evil.

6. Most people believe in God. So God must exist.

7. Jesus was not homosexual. So nobody else should be.

8. Everybody believes in something. So everybody believes in God.

9. The Old Testament says, "Honor thy father." So you should.

10. The Old Testament says the sun once stood still. The astronomers say the sun doesn't move. So they must be wrong.

11. If Jesus was God, he wasn't mortal. If he was a man, he was mortal.

12. If God were compassionate, he wouldn't let us suffer.

13. Some behavior is uncoerced. So people sometimes do things of their own free wills.

14. People like to feel that there is some higher power than themselves. So there is.

15. It makes me happy to believe God exists.

16. If p, then q. So q.

17. If p, then q, but not q.

18. Either p or q, but not p.

19. $(p \supset q) \,\&\, (q \supset r), \quad \therefore r.$

20. $[(p \supset q) \,\&\, (r \supset s)] \,\&\, \sim(s \vee q).$

25 / *Schematizing Arguments*

Simple Arguments

We have been discussing the evaluation of arguments, but before an argument can be evaluated it must be analyzed, and that is higher hurdling. What makes it so is that arguments don't usually come in neat, little packages. When they do, they are easy enough to contend with. We all can see easily that a highly schematized and artificially simple argument, like "If one is a communist, one is an atheist; so, if one is an atheist, one must be a communist," is invalid, being an instance of the fallacy of converting a conditional. It is much harder to see the fallacy in the following, more typical tirade of several years back: "These communistic, atheistic perverts are a dangerous lot of people who are out to take over the world and destroy capitalism, godliness, and morality. Khrushchev said they intend to bury us. Everybody knows that the State Department is full of them, and the universities too. You have only to look over here at the faculty of State U to see that it is loaded up with subversive and godless deviates. Look at Professor Whosits. My son told me that she said belief in the divine savior is a myth. That is the sort of blasphemy you would expect from an atheist. Obviously, the woman is a communist. Why it makes my blood boil to know that we are paying the salaries of people who corrupt the mind and hearts of our unsuspecting and innocent young people!" Nevertheless, buried somewhere in this emotional and rambling discourse is the same fallacy as that in the nicely schematized argument above.

The conclusion of an argument is easy to spot when it comes at the end and is clearly labelled as such. Thus, the conclusions were obvious in the examples we have heretofore used to illustrate principles of logic, just as the conclusion is easy to spot in the following example:

(1)   John is in bed, and he only goes to bed when ill. So he must be ill.

Here the conclusion comes last and is introduced by the familiar *conclusion label* 'so'. The list of familiar conclusion labels includes 'therefore', 'hence', 'consequently', 'in conclusion', and 'thus'. These words all occur in a fairly reliable pattern:

    p. Therefore q;
    p. So q;
    p. Hence q;
    p. Consequently q;

and so on. In every case, the premise is p, the conclusion q; in every case the premise comes first, the conclusion last.

Conclusions, however, are not always located at the ends of arguments, and they are not always labelled. They are just as likely to be located at the beginnings and to be unlabelled. Consider, for example, the argument

(2)   John must be ill. For he is in bed and he only goes to bed when he is ill.

Here the conclusion is the first sentence, not the last, and the premise is labelled but not the conclusion. The *premise label* used here is the word 'for'. Other familiar premise introductions are the words 'since' and 'because'. The premise is usually the statement that immediately follows one of these words. Thus, in

    Since p, q,
    q, since p,
    q, for p,
    q because p,

the premise is in each case p, the conclusion q.

Well-written paragraphs, essays, and books will usually locate the conclusion either at the beginning or at the end and sometimes in both places. Frequently, too, either conclusions or premises will be identified clearly. But not all arguments are well written, and some writers do not try to save their readers work. Besides, there are labels for conclusions and premises less familiar than those we have just noted. Consider the following argument, which is slightly more difficult to analyze, if still comparatively easy:

> I observe that the notion of duty cannot be resolved into that of interest, or what is most for our happiness. Every man may be satisfied of this who attends to his own conceptions, and the language of mankind shows it. When I say This is my interest, I mean one thing; when I say It is my duty, I mean another.
>
> *Sir Thomas Reid*

Reid here points a finger at his conclusion by saying, "Every man may be satisfied of this," which refers back to the preceding sentence. The expression "the language of mankind shows it" refers forward to the premise. Hence, the argument, restructured and abbreviated, is

> We mean one thing by the word 'duty' and another by the word 'interest'. So duty is one thing and interest is another.

Thus schematized and reduced to its essentials, the argument will be much easier to evaluate. Now if we ask whether the conclusion follows and whether the premise is true, we will know precisely what we are talking about.

The absence of even unfamiliar conclusion or premise labels makes arguments harder to analyze. Consider, for example, the still short and simple syllogism

> I believe Caleb is sincere. Anybody who attends church that regularly must be sincere.

Which is the premise, the first statement, or the second? Is Caleb's sincerity being inferred from the generalization "Churchgoers are sincere," or is a generalization being based on the case of Caleb? The argument doesn't give us much of a clue. If we decide that its thesis is Caleb's sincerity, we will do so only because that part of the argument makes more sense as a conclusion than as a premise. The first sentence will follow from the second, but not the other way around. Since we see it that way, we may assume that the speaker probably does, too.

We follow the same principle in interpreting the following argument, also devoid of helpful labels:

> Teachers are sometimes told that belonging to an organization affiliated with organized labor is unprofessional, but this idea should be rejected. It comes from organizations dominated by state and city superintendents of schools, where "professionalism" is usually equated with acceptance by teachers of their traditional low status in the organizational hierarchy.
>
> *American Federation of Teachers*

205

The conclusion of this passage is stated in the first sentence, which says that we should reject the idea that unionism is unprofessional. The reason for rejecting this idea is given in the second sentence, which says that the idea depends on a false definition of the word 'professional'. How can I tell? From the fact that thus construed the passage has both point and plausibility; thus interpreted, it makes sense, and no alternative and equally sensible interpretation is forthcoming.

The criterion invoked in analyzing the two preceding examples was our old friend, the principle of charity: interpret what others say in the way that makes it most reasonable. The AFT has every reason to refute a charge of "unprofessionalism"; that it is doing so here therefore makes sense. The principle of charity can lead us wrong, but when it is thus reinforced by all other relevant information about the speaker and the context of the argument, it is quite reliable.

Long or Complex Arguments

In spite of any difficulties they may have presented, the preceding arguments have all been comparatively easy to analyze and schematize because they have been reasonably short, but the difficulties of analysis increase with the length of the argument, and there is no law confining arguments to the length of a few sentences. Often, they are book length. Here is an argument of paragraph length:

Nothing in the world—indeed nothing even beyond the world—can possibly be conceived which could be called good without qualification except a *good will*. Intelligence, wit, judgement, and the other talents of the mind, however they may be named, or courage, resoluteness, and perseverance as qualities of temperament, are doubtless in many respects good and desirable. But they can become extremely bad and harmful if the will, which is to make use of these gifts of nature and which in its special constitution is called character, is not good. It is the same with the gifts of fortune. Power, riches, honor, even health, general well-being, and the contentment with one's condition which is called happiness, make for pride and even arrogance if there is not a good will to correct their influence on the mind and on its principles of action so as to make it universally conformable to its end. It need hardly be mentioned that the sight of a being adorned with no feature of a pure and good will, yet enjoying uninterrupted prosperity, can never give pleasure to a rational impartial observer. Thus the good will seems to constitute the indispensable condition even of worthiness to be happy.

> Immanuel Kant, Foundations of the Metaphysics of Morals, *trans. Lewis White Beck, ed. Robert Paul Wolff (New York: Bobbs-Merrill Co., 1969), pp. 11–12 (used by permission).*

It may take you a couple of seconds to see that the conclusion is the first sentence, that the good will is the only unqualified and unconditioned good thing in the world. The only other candidate is the last sentence, which says that happiness is not good without a good will; but although this is a conclusion from the statement preceding it, it is not the main conclusion of the passage. It is just a conclusion reached along the way in an attempt to establish the main conclusion, which was stated in the beginning. How can I be so sure, seeing that the first statement is not labelled as the conclusion, whereas the last seems to be ? Because the rest of the passage has no point unless the first sentence is its point. If you wanted to go about proving that a good will was the only good thing, you would do it just as has Kant, by eliminating all the other alternatives systematically, showing that they are either not good or not good without good will. So that is what he has done.

Length adds to complexity. When the argument is a long chain, with one conclusion leading to another, deciding which of the labelled or unlabelled conclusions is the main conclusion of the argument can be a task. Really long examples can't be given here because they would take up too much room and because their very complexity would preclude their being good illustrations, but if you want an example, read and try to pick out the main conclusions of a work like David Hume's *Dialogues on Natural Religion* or Charles Darwin's *Evolution of the Species.*

Something of the complexity an argument can have is, however, illustrated by our earlier-mentioned discourse about Professor Whosits. Let us look at it again. First, we notice that the main point of this piece of purple prose is to get something done about Professor Whosits, perhaps to get her fired. This conclusion is not stated, but one gathers from the final remarks that it is the message; and it would be the natural conclusion to draw. Having picked out the main conclusion, we can work backward, noticing that the premises for that conclusion are (1) that Whosits must be a communist and (2) that something ought to be done about the

Figure 25.1
Diagram of Argument

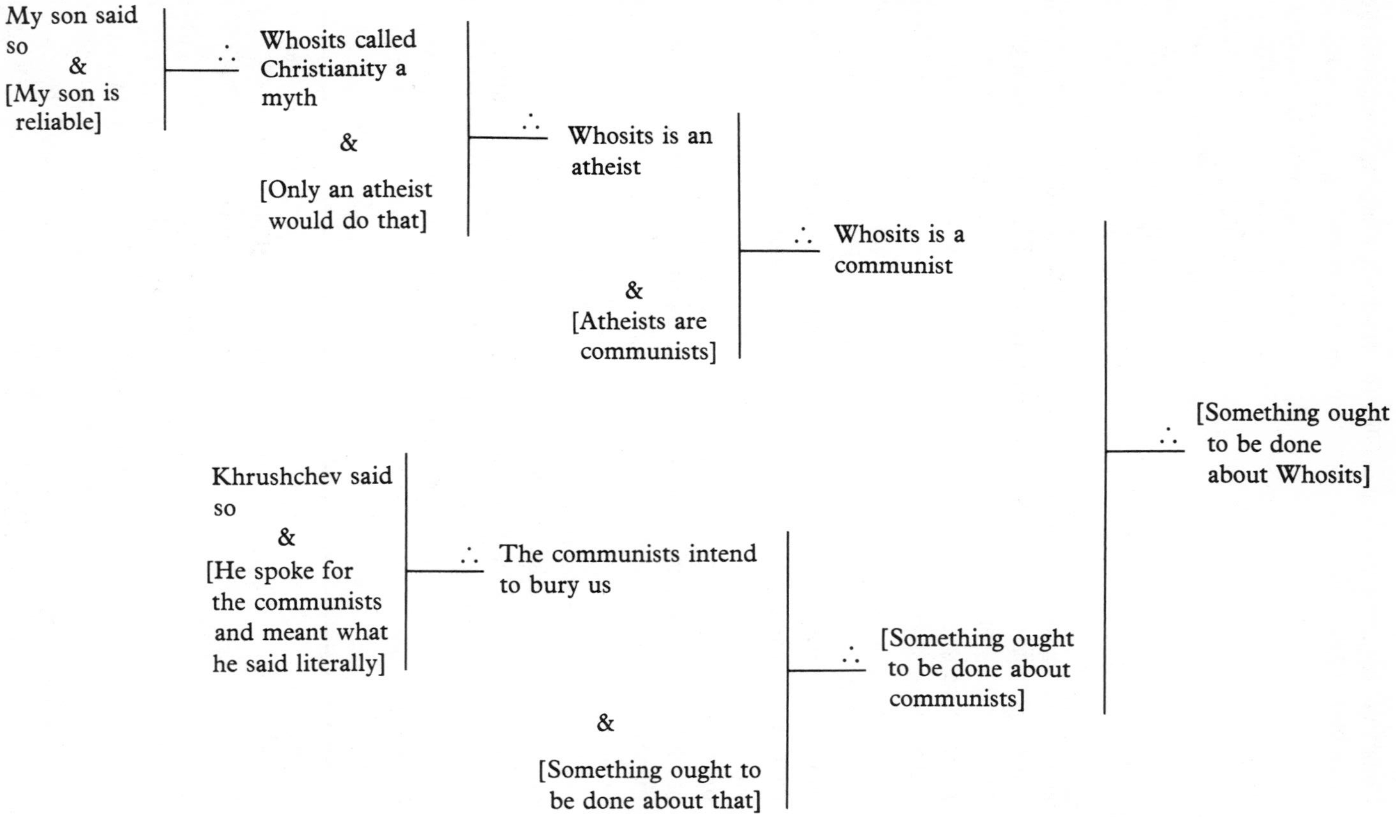

Something ought
to be done
about Whosits]

∴

[Something ought
to be done about
communists]

∴

Whosits is a
communist

∴

The communists intend
to bury us

∴

Whosits is an
atheist

∴

&
[Atheists are
communists]

Khrushchev said

so

&

[He spoke for
the communists
and meant what
he said literally]

&

[Something ought to
be done about that]

Whosits called
Christianity a
myth

&

[Only an atheist
would do that]

My son said

so

&

[My son is
reliable]

communists. Now we need to reconstruct the arguments for each of these premises. That Whosits is a communist is inferred from the proposition that she is an atheist. (So we know the speaker either believes falsely that all atheists are communists or believes truly that all communists are atheists and infers invalidly that therefore Whosits is a communist because an atheist.) The proof advanced that Whosits is an atheist is that she called christianity a "myth," which assumes that all who do so are atheists. The claim that Whosits made this statement is based on the report of the speaker's son and therefore assumes that the son is a reliable witness. The other premise for our final conclusion, premise (2), is based on the proposition that communists intend to bury us and on the assumption that we ought to do something about those who intend to bury us. That communists intend to bury us is inferred from the fact that Khrushchev said as much and presumably meant what he said. The rest of the passage is irrelevant.

The argument, with its unstated premises and conclusion in brackets, is presented as a diagram in figure 25.1. The argument is a reasonably complicated piece of business, but once we have thus analyzed and schematized it, we can see easily that it is unsound. It is full of all kinds of false or questionable assumptions. To see the errors, we need just look at each of the several arguments in this branching chain of arguments, using the tools we have already learned and those we shall learn later.

Exercises

A. In the manner illustrated in this chapter, analyze and schematize all of the ensuing quotations that contain arguments.

1. The phlogiston theory in its day was, we must first realize, a long step forward. In the sixteenth and seventeenth centuries those who were interested in making some sense out of what we now call chemistry were wandering in a bewildering forest. From the alchemists and the practical men, particularly the metal makers, they had acquired a mass of apparently unrelated facts and strange ideas about "elements." . . . How were all these facts, inherited from the Middle ages and before, to be fitted together? By the introduction of a principle called phlogiston, closely related to Aristotle's old element, fire—closely related, yet the relationship was never clear.

James B. Conant, On
Understanding Science (*New
York: New American Library of
World Literature, 1957), p. 85*

2. Although it is difficult to find a flat-earth believer, in or out of Zion, who is not a fundamentalist, it would be a mistake to suppose that all eccentric views about the earth's shape have their origin in religious superstition. The best example in recent centuries of a nonreligious theory is the hollow earth doctrine of Captain John Cleves Symmes, of the U.S. Infantry. After distinguishing himself for bravery in the War of 1812, Symmes retired from the Army and spent the rest of his life trying to convince the nation that the earth was made up of five concentric spheres, with openings several thousand miles in diameter at the poles.

Martin Gardner, Fads and Fallacies in the Name of Science (*New York: Dover Publications, 1957*), *p. 19*

3. Necessarily, the liberal reforms run counter to much that the law now tolerates or protects. This is inevitable because the law now tolerates and protects many practices which make it impossible for men to live successfully in the economy of the division of labor. But liberalism, unlike collectivism, is not a reaction against the industrial revolution. It is the philosophy of that industrial revolution. The purpose of liberal reform is to accommodate the social order to the new economy; that end can be achieved only by continual and far reaching reform of the social order. So, however much they may resemble each other superficially, the difference between the two philosophies is radical and irreconcilable.

Walter Lippmann, The Good Society (*New York: Gosset and Dunlop, 1943*), *p. 237*

4. The courage to take meaninglessness into itself presupposes a relation to the ground of being which we have called "absolute faith." It is without a *special* content, yet it is not without content. The content of absolute faith is the "God above God." Absolute faith and its consequence, the courage that takes the radical doubt, the doubt about God, into itself, transcends the theistic idea of God.

Paul Tillich, The Courage to Be (*New Haven: Yale University Press, 1952*), *p. 182*

5. I have chosen these branches of the law merely as conspicuous illustrations of the application by the courts of the method of sociology. But the truth is that there is no branch where the method is not fruitful. Even when it does not seem to dominate, it is always in reserve. It is

the arbiter between other methods, determining in the last analysis the choice of each, weighing their competing claims, setting bounds to their pretensions, balancing and moderating and harmonizing them.

Benjamin N. Cardozo, The Nature of the Judicial Process (*New Haven: Yale University Press, 1967*), *p. 98*

6. The problem is to free men, not from control, but from certain kinds of control, and it can be solved only if our analysis takes all consequences into account. How people feel about control, before or after the literature of freedom has worked on their feelings does not lead to useful distinctions.

B. F. Skinner, Beyond Freedom and Dignity (*New York: Bantam Books, 1972*), *p. 38*

7. If the anthropomorphous apes be admitted to form a natural sub-group, then as man agrees with them, not only in all those characters which he possesses in common with the whole Catarhine group, but in other peculiar characters, such as the absence of a tail and of callosities, and in general appearance, we may infer that some ancient member of the anthropomorphous sub-group gave birth to man. It is not probable that, through the law of analogous variation, a member of one of the other lower sub-groups should have given rise to a man-like creature, resembling the higher anthropomorphous apes in so many respects.

Charles Darwin, The Origin of the Species and the Descent of Man (*New York: Modern Library, n.d.*), *p. 519*

8. What attitude then should the physiologist adopt ? Perhaps he should first of all study the methods of this science of psychology, and only afterwards hope to study the physiological mechanism of the [cerebral] hemispheres ? This involves a serious difficulty. It is logical that in its analysis of the various activities of living matter physiology should base itself on the more advanced and more exact sciences—physics and chemistry. But if we attempt an approach from this science of psychology to the problem confronting us we shall be building our superstructure on a science which has no claim to exactness as compared even with physiology.

In fact it is still open to discussion whether psychology is a natural science, or whether it can be regarded as a science at all.

I. P. Pavlov, Conditioned Reflexes, *trans. and ed. G. V. Anrep (New York: Dover Publications, 1960), p. 3*

9. Your article of June 30, 1977 showed a total absence of insight or understanding regarding the environment you attempt to describe. Your need to attach labels to people relying solely upon visual data is strangling your brain and stunting your growth. You notice the brand of beer people are drinking and indicate that to you these people are less than a can of beer—that "they are not noticeably anything." Such arrogance and insensitivity is disgusting.

Letter to editor of a student paper

10. It is equally evident, that the members of each department should be as little dependent as possible on those of the others, for the emoluments annexed to their offices. Were the executive magistrate, or the judges not independent of the legislature in this particular, their independence in every other would be merely nominal.

James Madison, The Federalist, *no. 51, ll. 9–15*

11. It is certain, and evident to our senses, that in the world some things are in motion. Now whatever is moved is moved by another, for nothing can be moved except it is in potentiality to that towards which it is moved; whereas a thing moves inasmuch as it is in act. For motion is nothing else than the reduction of something from potentiality to actuality. But nothing can be reduced from potentiality to actuality, except by something in a state of actuality. Thus that which is actually hot, as fire, makes wood, which is potentially hot, to be actually hot, and thereby moves and changes it. Now it is not possible that the same thing should be at once in actuality and potentiality in the same respect, but only in different respects. For what is actually hot cannot be simultaneously potentially cold. It is therefore impossible that in the same respect and in the same way a thing should be both mover and moved, i.e. that it should move itself. Therefore, whatever is moved must be moved by another. If that by which it is moved be itself moved, then this also must needs be moved by another, and that by another again. But this cannot go on to infinity, because then there would be no first mover, and, consequently no other mover, seeing that subsequent movers move only inasmuch as they are moved by the first mover; as the staff moves only because it is moved by the hand. Therefore it is necessary to arrive at a first mover, moved by no other; and this everyone understands to be God.

St. Thomas Acquinas, Introduction to St. Thomas Acquinas, *ed. Anton C. Pegis (New York: Modern Library, 1948), p. 25 (used by permission)*

UNIT IV

Quantification

26 / Plural Statements

Many statements with a plural subject can be thought of as compounds of singular statements. For example, given a list of the three chairs in this room (C_1, C_2, C_3), we could construe the *universal statement*

(1) All the chairs in this room are worn out

as a way of saying

(2) C_1 is worn out & C_2 is worn out & C_3 is worn out.

Likewise, the *particular statement*

(3) Some of the chairs in this room are worn out

can be thought of as saying

(4) C_1 is worn out $\lor$ C_2 is worn out $\lor$ C_3 is worn out.

Hence, universal statements come out to be conjunctions and particular statements disjunctions of singular statements. Statements about all or several things in a group come out to be compounds of statements about each thing in the group.

We shall see later that this way of looking at plural statements has serious limitations, but if we are talking about small groups of objects whose members are all known to us, it has very great advantages.

Universal Statements

Let us begin with universal statements, statements about all the members of our group. An occurrence of the words 'all', 'every', 'any', or 'each' usually marks a sentence as universal. Hence,

> All the chairs in this room are worn out,
> Every chair in this room is worn out,
> Any chair in this room is worn out,

and

> Each chair in this room is worn out

all state what we express by (2).

There are, however, exceptions. After 'if', 'any' means 'some'. Hence,

> If any chair is worn out, I'll be surprised

does not say

> If all chairs are worn out, I'll be surprised.

Rather, it says

> If some chairs are worn out, I'll be surprised.

Sometimes, too, the word 'all' is used to designate the totality of things in a group, not to say something about each thing separately. For example,

(5)   All the furniture in this room weighs ten tons

does not mean

> This piece of furniture weighs ten tons & that piece weighs ten tons & ...,

through a list of the pieces of furniture in the room. Rather, it means that the total weight of the pieces of furniture, when they have all been put together to form one unit, is ten tons. The verb indicates that (5) is singular, not universal. As the scholastic logicians of the Middle Ages used to say, (5) refers to the furniture *collectively*, not *distributively*.

Neglect of this distinction can lead to the fallacies of division and composition. The fallacy of *composition* consists in confusing a statement about each member of the group with one about the whole group. Some people commit this fallacy when they argue that the universe has a cause and a beginning because everything in it does. As Bertrand Russell pointed out, that is like saying that everybody has a mother and concluding that there is one person who is everybody's mother. The fallacy of *division* occurs when someone confuses a statement about the whole group with one about the elements.   A woman once wrote to our local newspaper urging that our state withdraw from the United Nations.   She seemed to think that the fact that the United States is a member of the United Nations means that the individual states are members.

An interesting blurring of the distinction between singular and plural occurs in the ambiguous but highly idiomatic sentence

(6)   This chair is all worn out,

which may be used to mean

This chair is worn out beyond use,

a singular statement, or may be used as elliptical for

All the parts of this chair are worn out,

a universal statement.

The terms 'all', 'every', 'any', and 'each' are not the only terms that are universal in scope.   Others like 'invariably' and 'always' are universal but usually have primary reference to time.   Thus, in spite of the simple subject,

This chair is always in the wrong place

is a universal statement, being equivalent to

At all times, this chair is in the wrong place.

On occasion, however, the terms 'always' and 'invariably' seem to have nothing to do with time.   Consider, for example,

Horses are always mammals,

which just means that all horses are mammals.

With exceptions such as those just canvassed, an occurrence of the words 'all', 'every', 'any', and 'each' signals a universal statement; but don't conclude that their absence means the statement is not universal. Sometimes these words are tacit, as in

The chairs in this room are worn out,

which, presumably, means that all the chairs are worn out.

Also universal in scope is the term 'only', but

(7)   Only people are women

does not mean

(8)   All people are women.

219

Rather, it means the converse,

All women are people.

If you have a hard time keeping this distinction straight, it is perhaps because you confuse (7) with

The only people are women

or

Women are the only people,

which do mean (8).

Universality may also be intended by statements that, at first sight, look as if they were singular. Statements with an abstract singular subject, statements like

(9)   Man has a free will,

are usually about each member of some group, as (9) is a remark about each member of the human species, being equivalent to

Each man has a free will.

Of course, abstract terms don't always designate a plural subject. Often they are genuine singular terms, as in

Man evolved from the apes,

which certainly does not mean

Each man evolved from the apes.

Rather, it means that the species evolved from the apes. So you can't refute the theory of evolution, as I once heard one woman attempt to do, by saying, "You have never seen an amoeba or an ape evolve into a man."

Not only is a term that is singular in form often used to denote a plural subject, but sometimes a term that is plural in form is used to denote a single subject, as, for example, in

(10)   Men are plentiful.

That certainly is not to be construed as meaning

This man is plentiful & that man is plentiful & . . .

(10) means, rather, that the species contains a large number of men.

Deciding whether the subject of a statement is singular or plural becomes very difficult when the remark is a statement about an average, as in

Human beings average about $5\frac{1}{2}$ feet in height.

220

That certainly isn't true of each human being. It must be taken, rather, as a remark about the species. It means "Add the heights of all human beings and divide by the number of human beings. The result is the average height."

So far we have looked only at universal affirmative statements. Universal negatives are just like them except that the conjuncts are not affirmed but denied. Thus, the universal negative statement

> None of the chairs in this room is worn out

just says

> $\sim C_1$ is worn out & $\sim C_2$ is worn out & . . .

Other ways to say the same thing are

> All the chairs in this room are still good,
> Every chair in this room is other than worn out,
> Pick any chair in the room: it is not worn out,

and so on.

Particular Statements

Let us now turn to particular statements.

Particular statements may be definite or indefinite. Such statements as

> Exactly one of the chairs in this room is worn out,
> Exactly two of the chairs in this room are worn out,

or

> Exactly three of the chairs in this room are worn out

are *definite* about the number of chairs that are worn out, if not about their identity. On the other hand,

> At least one of the chairs in this room is worn out,
> Some of the chairs in this room are worn out,
> Several of the chairs in this room are worn out,
> A few of the chairs in this room are worn out,
> Many of the chairs in this room are worn out,

are all *indefinite*.

Some of the latter statements are also ambiguous. Consider (3) again. Does it mean

(11)   At least one of the chairs in this room is worn out

or

(12)   At least two of the chairs in this room are worn out?

The answer is: sometimes one; sometimes the other. If (3) means (11), we can analyze it as (4) and regard it as true in case exactly one chair is worn out and false only if no one of the three is worn out. That analysis won't do, however, if (3) means (12), which is false if exactly one chair is worn out.

Some people also understand (3) to be false if all the chairs are worn out, but they are confusing (3) with

Some, but not all, of the chairs in this room are worn out.

No doubt a person who tries to sell you the chairs by saying, "Some are worn out," knowing perfectly well that they are all worn out, hopes to mislead you into thinking that some are not worn out. But that is not what he says, and what he does say is true. On discovering that all the chairs are worn out, you may accuse him of not telling you the whole truth, but you may not accuse him of telling you a lie. He is guilty of sharp practice, but no court in the land would convict him of fraud. If you are misled, avoid similar disappointment in the future by learning to distinguish what a person actually says from what you might be inclined to read into it.

Definite particulars are harder to analyze than indefinite. They, too, are alternations, but they are alternations of conjunctions. Consider the definite particular

(13)   Exactly one chair in this room is worn out.

(4) won't suffice as an analysis of (13), (4) being true but (13) false if two or three chairs are worn out. The analysis must therefore be somewhat more complicated. It must make clear that the first chair is worn out but not the other two, or the second is worn out but not the other two, or the third is worn out but not the other two. That is, it must say

(14)   (C_1 is worn out & $\sim C_2$ is worn out & $\sim C_3$ is worn out) ∨ ($\sim C_1$ is worn out & C_2 is worn out & $\sim C_3$ is worn out) ∨ ($\sim C_1$ is worn out & $\sim C_2$ is worn out & C_3 is worn out),

which will be somewhat easier to read if abbreviated as

(15)   (C_1 & $\sim C_2$ & $\sim C_3$) ∨ ($\sim C_1$ & C_2 & $\sim C_3$) ∨ ($\sim C_1$ & $\sim C_2$ & C_3).

The analysis of

(16)   Exactly two chairs in this room are worn out

is similar. When we have three chairs, (16) says

$$(C_1 \mathbin{\&} C_2 \mathbin{\&} \sim C_3) \vee (C_1 \mathbin{\&} \sim C_2 \mathbin{\&} C_3) \vee (\sim C_1 \mathbin{\&} C_2 \mathbin{\&} C_3).$$

When there are three chairs,

(17)   At least two chairs in this room are worn out

is equivalent to

> Either exactly three chairs in this room are worn out or exactly two are worn out,

which analyzes as

$$(C_1 \mathbin{\&} C_2 \mathbin{\&} C_3) \vee (C_1 \mathbin{\&} C_2 \mathbin{\&} \sim C_3) \vee (C_1 \mathbin{\&} \sim C_2 \mathbin{\&} C_3) \vee$$
$$(\sim C_1 \mathbin{\&} C_2 \mathbin{\&} C_3).$$

Analysis is easier if you keep in mind that it is just a matter of working out the various permutations and therefore not different in kind from the procedure by which you construct a truth table. Look at the following truth table. Line 1 represents the case in which all three chairs are worn out. Line 8 represents the case in which none of the three chairs is worn out. Lines 4, 6, and 7 represent the three ways that exactly one chair could be worn out. Lines 2, 3, and 5 represent the three ways in which exactly two chairs could be worn out. Lines 2, 3, 5, and 1 represent the four ways in which two or more could be worn out. Lines 2–8 represent the seven ways in which no more than two could be worn out. And so on.

Line	C_1	C_2	C_3
1	T	T	T
2	T	T	F
3	T	F	T
4	T	F	F
5	F	T	T
6	F	T	F
7	F	F	T
8	F	F	F

To expand this sort of analysis to cover cases where larger numbers are involved, we just need to remember the method for finding the various combinations and permutations of truth values of a statement with four or

223

more components. With this method we can define very exactly any statement about any given number of any group of definite size.

As there were universal negative statements, so there are particular negatives. They may be analyzed as alternations of denials. Thus,

At least one of the chairs is not worn out

says

$$\sim C_1 \lor \sim C_2 \lor \ldots$$

Exercises

A. Which of the following statements are plural? Which singular?

1. The elephant is an interesting animal.

2. The elephant is an interesting species.

3. The elephant is large.

4. The elephant has a good memory.

5. Elephants are common.

6. The elephant our zoo has is all grey.

7. Elephants are always heavy.

8. The elephant has been on earth for millions of years.

9. The elephant lives for an average forty years.

10. Elephants live for an average of forty years.

B. Given a list of all elephants, $E_1, \ldots, E_n$, show how you would go about rewriting each universal statement in the list in (A) as a conjunction of singular statements.

C. Which of the following are equivalent to "All elephants are large"?

1. The only elephants that exist are large.

2. Only elephants are large.

3. Elephants are the only large things.

4. Elephants are all large.

5. Elephants are invariably large.

6. Every elephant is large.

7. The elephant is always large.

8. Large size is a universal trait of elephants.

9. Only the elephants there are are large.

10. Only large things are elephants.

D. Classify the following as (a) the fallacy of division, (b) the fallacy of composition, or (c) neither.

1. All men are mortal. So this man will die.

2. All men are mortal. So the species is sure to die out.

3. Man is mortal. So this man will die.

4. The human being is mortal. So this man will die.

5. The human species will not survive. So this man will not survive.

6. Man is mortal. So the species will die out.

E. Suppose there are four chairs, $C_1, \ldots, C_4$. In the abbreviated style of the text, analyze the following.

1. Exactly two chairs are worn out.

2. At most two chairs are worn out.

3. At least two chairs are worn out.

4. All but one chair are worn out.

5. Several of the chairs are worn out.

6. Most of the chairs are worn out.

7. Some of the chairs are worn out.

8. None of the chairs is worn out.

9. All of the chairs are worn out.

10. Exactly three chairs are worn out.

F. Suppose exactly one chair is worn out. Which of the items in (E) are false?

Figure 27.2
Square of Implication

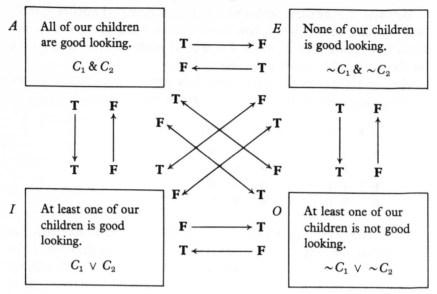

and the truth of I, and that the falsity of A implies the truth of O but does not imply the falsity or the truth of E or I.

We would get the same results if we had more children than two, although the truth tables would get rather tedious. We would also get the same results if we changed the subject. It would make no difference if A were "All horses are green," E were "At least one horse is green," I were "No horses are green," and O were "At least one horse is not green." The same logical relations would maintain. The principles would be the same; just the names would have changed. Hence, our squares of opposition and implication may be taken as paradigms. They will guarantee reliable inferences whatever we may be discussing, whether children or chinks in armor.

Exceptions

These squares are not reliable, however, if we happen to be talking about fewer objects than two. Suppose we had just one child. Then there would be no important difference between "All my children are good looking" and "At least one of my children is good looking." Similarly, "None of my children are good looking" would then be equivalent to "At least one of my children is not good looking." The paradigms would also be changed if we had no children. Usually, however, we do not speak in the plural when exactly one thing, or none, is involved. If I have one child, or none, I normally do not say, "All my children are good looking," or "At least one of my children is good looking." Normally plural statements presuppose a plurality of objects.

Exercises

A. I have exactly three horses, at least one of which is a palomino. Indicate below the truth values of all those statements whose truth values can be determined, given this information alone. Use the square of implication or a truth table. Don't just guess.

1. All my horses are palominos.

2. It is false that all my horses are palominos.

3. None of my horses are palominos.

4. It is false that none of my horses are palominos.

5. At least one of my horses is not a palomino.

6. At least one of my horses is a palomino.

7. It is false that some of my horses are not palominos.

8. It is false that some of my horses are palominos.

9. All my horses are not palominos.

10. None of my horses are not palominos.

B. Given only that none of my horses is a paint, follow the procedure of (A) for each of the following.

1. At least one of my horses is a paint.

2. It is false that all my horses are paints.

3. All my horses are paints.

4. At least one of my horses is not a paint.

5. At least one of my horses is a palomino.

C. Given only that it is false that at least one of my horses is not a paint, redo (B).

D. Pick out the statements that are inconsistent with "At least one of my horses is a palomino."

    1. All my horses are palominos.

    2. All my horses are not palominos.

    3. None of my horses are palominos.

    4. At least one of my horses is not a palomino.

    5. It is false that at least one of my horses is a palomino.

E. Pick out all the statements that contradict "None of my horses are paints." Then pick out all the statements equivalent to it.

    1. All my horses are paints.

    2. All my horses are not paints.

    3. At least one of my horses is a paint.

    4. It is false that none of my horses are paints.

    5. It is false that at least one of my horses is a paint.

F. Pick out all the statements implied by "It is false that at least one of my horses is a paint."

    1. At least one of my horses is not a paint.

    2. None of my horses are paints.

    3. It is false that all my horses are paints.

    4. All my horses are paints.

    5. It is true that none of my horses are paints.

G. Which numbered statements in (F) imply the given statement?

28 / Existence and Universes of Discourse

Existence

In preceding exercises we said that, given a list $F_1, F_2, \ldots, F_n$ of things that are F,

(1)   All F are G

can be construed as saying

(2) F_1 is G & F_2 is G & $\ldots$

What if there is nothing to list? What if we are talking about things that don't exist? In that case it is obvious we can't make a list of them and say something about each one. There is nothing to list and nothing to say anything about.

To see the problem, consider the statement

(3)   All pterodactyls are reptiles.

(3) is true, but since there are no pterodactyls, it can hardly be analyzed as saying

(4) P_1 is a reptile & P_2 is a reptile & $\ldots$,

through a list of pterodactyls. How, then, are we to analyze statements like (3)?

A solution that most logicians have found satisfactory is to treat (3) as saying

(5)   If anything is a pterodactyl, it is a reptile.

The analysis of (5) doesn't require a list of nonexistent pterodactyls. It only requires a list of existing things, $T_1 \ldots$; (5) can be analyzed as

(6) $(T_1$ is a pterodactyl $\supset T_1$ is a reptile$)$ & $(T_2$ is a pterodactyl $\supset T_2$ is a reptile$)$ & $\ldots$

(6) says "If thing$_1$ is a pterodactyl, it is a reptile; and if thing$_2$ is a pterodactyl, it is a reptile; and $\ldots$," and (6) is true even if nothing is a pterodactyl.

Thus, statements that may otherwise seem to be categorical remarks about nonexisting things are to be reconstrued as conditional statements about existing things. There being no pterodactyls for statement (3) to be about, it cannot be, as it seems to be, a statement about pterodactyls. It is, rather, a statement about everything there is. It is about this book, and that pencil, and so on. It says that if this book is a pterodactyl, it is a reptile, and that if that pencil is a pterodactyl, it is a reptile, too, and so on. Of course, the book and the pencil are not pterodactyls. Nothing is. That is the whole point: neither (5) nor (3) says that there are any pterodactyls.

Having thus construed (3) as a generalized conditional, you may notice that you can construe

(7) All horses are mammals

in the same way. (7) amounts to the declaration

(8) If anything is a horse, it is a mammal,

which may be analyzed as

(9) $(T_1$ is a horse $\supset T_1$ is a mammal$)$ & $\ldots$,

through a list of things. That is, (7) says "If this book is a horse, it is a mammal; and if Dobbin is a horse, he is a mammal $\ldots$"

Notice that (9) does not say that there are any horses. Neither does (7). If we want to say that there are some horses, we must not assert merely (9) or (7). We must add an *existence clause*. We must say,

(10) Something is a horse,

an analysis of which is

(11) T_1 is a horse $\vee \ldots$

(11) says that I am a horse, or Dobbin is, or $\ldots$; it says that one or another of the things that there are is a horse.

In general, "All F are G" does not say that anything is an F. Without the addition of an existence clause, "All F are G" says merely

(12)   If anything is an F, it is a G,

the analysis of which has the form

(13) $(T_1$ is an $F \supset T_1$ is a $G) \& \ldots,$

which, to save space, we shall abbreviate as

(14) $(F_1 \supset G_1) \& \ldots$

When we add an existence clause, (12) gives way to

(15)   If anything is an F, then it is a G, and something is an F,

which may be analyzed as

(16) $[(F_1 \supset G_1) \& \ldots] \& (F_1 \vee \ldots).$

This says that if thing$_1$ is an F, it is also a G, and so on through the list of things; then it adds that either thing$_1$ or some other thing in the list is an F.

The point is this: when we don't know whether there is anything that is F, and don't know whether the speaker knows, we must not read a remark of the form (1) as declaring that anything is an F. We must read it as declaring merely that if anything is an F, that thing is also a G.

What goes for the universal affirmative statement (1) also applies to the universal negative statement

(17)   No F are G.

This is to be read as declaring that nothing that is F is also G but not as declaring that anything is F. Suppose, for example, that I say

(18)   No unicorns have two horns.

(18) is true, but if I meant that something is a unicorn, it would be false. I don't. I just mean that if anything is a unicorn, it does not have two horns. So, we should analyze (18) as

(19) $(T_1$ is a unicorn $\supset \sim T_1$ has two horns$) \& \ldots$

This says, quite truly, "If this book is a unicorn, it does not have two horns; and if this pencil is a unicorn, it does not have two horns; and so on."

In general, we should read statements of form (17) as saying

(20) $(F_1 \supset \sim G_1) \& \ldots$

If we wish to say that there are some F, we must do so explicitly. (17) does not say that anything is an F. So, if we think that something is an F and wish to say so, we must add an existence clause. We must say,

(21) $[(F_1 \supset \sim G_1) \& \ldots] \& (F_1 \lor \ldots),$

which reads, "If anything is an F, it is not a G; and something is an F."
   Particular statements are different. Consider

(22)   Some F is G

and

(23)   Some F is not G.

Unlike their universal counterparts, (22) and (23) assert the existence of
some F. (22) means

   Something that is F is also G.

That is, it means

   There is something that is F, and it is also G.

Likewise, (23) means

   There is something that is F, and it is not also G.

If so, (22) and (23) may be analyzed respectively as

(24) $(F_1 \& G_1) \lor \ldots$

and

(25) $(F_1 \& \sim G_1) \lor \ldots$

(24) says that thing$_1$ is both F and G, or that thing$_2$ is, and so on; (25) says
that thing$_1$ is F but not G, or thing$_2$ is, and so on.
   Notice the ampersands: notice that they are not horseshoes. Notice,
that is to say, that we do not analyze (22) and (23) as

(26) $(F_1 \supset G_1) \lor \ldots$

and

(27) $(F_1 \supset \sim G_1) \lor \ldots.$

(26) won't do as an analysis of (22) because (22) doesn't say merely, "If
something is an F, it is also a G," without adding that something is an F;
(22) says that something is an F and adds that the thing is also a G. So
we write (22) as (24) rather than (26), with an ampersand rather than a
horseshoe. We write (23) as (25) rather than (27) for the same reason.

It might seem to you that the other choice would be better when we are talking about nonexisting things. For example, you might suppose it best to read

(28)   Some unicorn is not two-horned

as meaning

(29)   If something is a unicorn, it is not two-horned,

(29) being true and (28) false. This reading would be a good idea except for one thing: people don't seem to use the word 'some' in this way. When they use it, it seems to have existential import. Anybody who says (28) seems to believe, wrongly, that something is a unicorn, and that one of the things that is a unicorn is not two-horned. So we are constrained to read "Some F are G," but not "All F are G," as asserting that something is an F. That distinction confuses some people, but don't let it confuse you.

The main cause of confusion about existence may be our habit of talking about fictional, mythical, and imaginary beings as if they existed. Suppose we are telling the story of Snow White and the seven dwarfs. We name these dwarfs and say something about each of them: Sneezy is always sneezing, and so on. Hence we talk about them as if they really existed. We say "One is sleepy; the others are not." Of course, the dwarfs don't exist. Don't object, "They exist in fiction." What exists merely in fiction doesn't exist. It is true that there are seven dwarfs in the story, but the dwarfs in the story are not dwarfs, and they don't exist. How, then, can we name them and talk about them? We can't. You can't name or talk about what doesn't exist. What we are doing is pretending to name and talk about seven dwarfs. What actually exists in fiction is not seven dwarfs, Dopey, Sleepy, and so on, but seven names 'Dopey', 'Sleepy', and so on—or, rather, what exists are seven pretend names, seven names that we are pretending to be names of dwarfs about which we are pretending to say things that we are pretending to be true. But the pretend dwarfs don't exist, and the pretend statements aren't true. In fact, they aren't dwarfs, or statements. When we are telling a story, we are not saying anything true or false about anything. We are pretending to say things that we are pretending to be true.

To be sure, there is nothing wrong with pretense. The confusion begins when we take pretense literally or talk about things that do exist in the same tone of voice we use to discuss things that don't. It is very tempting to construe "In perfect vacuums, bodies accelerate at thirty-two feet per second squared" as being a remark about perfect vacuums. So construed, however, it would be false. The statement is true only if construed as meaning "If anything is a perfect vacuum, bodies accelerate in it at thirty-two feet per second squared." Pretenses are all right when we are telling tales. When we are doing physics, our logic must be more exact.

Differences Existence Makes

Recognizing the need to discuss nonexisting things in serious contexts thus forces us to abandon our old analyses in favor of new ones. This change has important consequences. Since "All F are G" does not mean that something is F, but "Some F are G" does, the former does not imply the latter. When nothing is F, the former will be true, the latter false. For example, "All unicorns have one horn" is true, but "There is something that is a unicorn and has one horn" is false. In our notation, the reason for this distinction is clear:

(14) $(F_1 \supset G_1) \& \ldots,$

our rendition of "All F are G," does not imply

(24) $(F_1 \& G_1) \lor \ldots,$

our analysis of "Some F are G."

Furthermore, when we are not assuming that something is F, "All F are G" is consistent with "No F are G." The two statements are not contraries. When nothing is F, they are both true. Since there are no unicorns, it is true that if anything is a unicorn it is one-horned and also true that nothing is a unicorn and one-horned. To see this, recall that

(14) $(F_1 \supset G_1) \& \ldots$

was our analysis of "All F are G" and that

(20) $(F_1 \supset \sim G_1) \& \ldots$

was our analysis of "No F are G," and notice that both are true when nothing is F.

In short, logic must be different when we are not given that the things we are talking about exist. The differences are reflected in the revised square of opposition and implication given in figure 28.1. Unlike figures 27.1 and 27.2, figure 28.1 does not assume that anything is an F.

Figure 28.1
Revised Square of Opposition and Implication

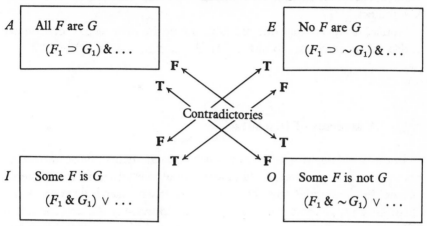

A All F are G

$(F_1 \supset G_1)$ & ...

E No F are G

$(F_1 \supset \sim G_1)$ & ...

F   T

T   F

Contradictories

F   T

T   F

I Some F is G

$(F_1$ & $G_1)$ ∨ ...

O Some F is not G

$(F_1$ & $\sim G_1)$ ∨ ...

Notice that this square shows far fewer inferences to be valid than did the earlier one. You may no longer infer the truth of I or the falsity of E, given the truth of A. You may no longer infer the truth of O, given the truth of E, or the falsity of E, given that of O. And so on. The reason is

Figure 28.2
Resurrected Square of Implication and Opposition (with existence clauses made explicit)

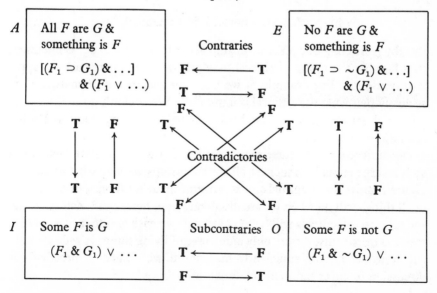

A All F are G &
something is F

$[(F_1 \supset G_1)$ & ...]
& $(F_1$ ∨ ...)

Contraries

F ⟵ T

T ⟶ F

E No F are G &
something is F

$[(F_1 \supset \sim G_1)$ & ...]
& $(F_1$ ∨ ...)

T   F   T   T   T   F

Contradictories

T   F   T   T   T   F

F   F

I Some F is G

$(F_1$ & $G_1)$ ∨ ...

Subcontraries O Some F is not G

$(F_1$ & $\sim G_1)$ ∨ ...

T ⟵ F

F ⟶ T

239

simply that we are now assuming less information than before. Before, we assumed that something is F. When we no longer make that assumption, less follows.

Notice, however, that our old table would be resurrected intact if we added existence clauses to our universal statements, as in figure 28.2.

Universes of Discourse

In the preceding discussion, we construed statements that seemed to be about nonexisting things as statements about everything in the universe. We needn't have gone that far. We could, if we wished, have construed them as remarks about some more limited *universe of discourse*, and it is often convenient to do so. For example, instead of construing the remark

All horses are mammals

as

If anything is a horse, it is a mammal,

we could construe it as

If any animal is a horse, it is a mammal

or as

If any living thing is a horse, it is a mammal,

thereby restricting our remarks to animals or to living things. Sometimes, thus limiting the group of objects to which we wish our remarks to apply is very useful. For example, if we limit our remarks to animals, we can say truly that what isn't mortal is immortal. We couldn't do so if we were talking about all things. This book, not being a living thing, is neither mortal nor immortal.

Our universe of discourse may be as large or as small as we please, just so it is large enough to include all the subgroups we may wish to discuss. Hence a universe of animals, or a universe of living things, or a universe of all things will do when we are discussing both horses and mammals, but the universe of animals will be too narrow if we wish also to discuss orange trees. For that discussion, only a universe of living things is wide enough, and it would not be sufficiently inclusive if we wished to broaden our discussion to cover inorganic materials as well.

Resort to explicit universes of discourse also has another advantage: it facilitates investigation of logical relationships that would have been out of reach before. Let me illustrate. Suppose we want to compare

(30)   At least one of the people in this room is intelligent

with its converse

(31)   At least one of the intelligent beings in this room is a person.

These are equivalent, but they might not seem so if you think of (30) as saying

(32) P_1 is intelligent $\vee$ P_2 is intelligent $\vee$ ...,

while thinking of (31) as

(33) I_1 is a person $\vee$ I_2 is a person $\vee$ ...

Being about different subjects, (30) and (31) will not be comparable. But think of them as both saying something about all things on a common list, and (30) will come to

(34)   (T_1 is a person in this room & intelligent) $\vee$ (T_2 is a person in this room & intelligent) $\vee$ ...,

whereas (31) comes to

(35)   (T_1 is intelligent & a person in this room) $\vee$ (T_2 is intelligent & a person in this room) $\vee$ ...

The disjuncts of (35) are obviously equivalent to those of (34). Thus, thinking of (30) and (31) as having a common universe of discourse, as statements about the same group of objects, makes their equivalence clear.

Some more comparisons that could not have been made before but are easy to make now are tabulated below. You see from these tables that "All F are G" is not equivalent to its converse but is equivalent to its obverse and contrapositive; and so on.

Table of Converses ★

All F are G	$\overset{\mathrm{df}}{\neq}$ All G are F
$(F_1 \supset G_1)$ & ...	$(G_1 \supset F_1)$ & ...
Some F is G	$\overset{\mathrm{df}}{=}$ Some G is F
$(F_1 \& G_1) \vee$ ...	$(G_1 \& F_1) \vee$ ...

★ '$\overset{\mathrm{df}}{\neq}$' means 'is not equivalent to'.

No F are G $\overset{\mathrm{df}}{=}$ No G are F

$(F_1 \supset \sim G_1)\,\&\ldots$ $\qquad (G_1 \supset \sim F_1)\,\&\ldots$

Some F is not G $\overset{\mathrm{df}}{\neq}$ Some G is not F

$(F_1\,\&\sim G_1) \vee \ldots$ $\qquad (G_1\,\&\sim F_1) \vee \ldots$

Table of Contrapositives

All F are G $\overset{\mathrm{df}}{=}$ All non-G are non-F

$(F_1 \supset G_1)\,\&\ldots$ $\qquad (\sim G_1 \supset \sim F_1)\,\&\ldots$

Some F is G $\overset{\mathrm{df}}{\neq}$ Some non-G is non-F

$(F_1\,\& G_1) \vee \ldots$ $\qquad (\sim G_1\,\&\sim F_1) \vee \ldots$

No F are G $\overset{\mathrm{df}}{\neq}$ No non-G are non-F

$(F_1 \supset \sim G_1)\,\&\ldots$ $\qquad (\sim G_1 \supset F_1)\,\&\ldots$

Some F is not G $\overset{\mathrm{df}}{=}$ Some non-G is non-F

$(F_1\,\&\sim G_1) \vee \ldots$ $\qquad (\sim G_1\,\&\sim F_1) \vee \ldots$

Table of Obverses

All F are G $\overset{\mathrm{df}}{=}$ No F are non-G

$(F_1 \supset G_1)\,\&\ldots$ $\qquad (F_1 \supset \sim\sim G_1)\,\&\ldots$

Some F is G $\overset{\mathrm{df}}{=}$ Some F is not non-G

$(F_1\,\& G_1) \vee \ldots$ $\qquad (F_1\,\&\sim\sim G_1) \vee \ldots$

No F are G $\overset{\mathrm{df}}{=}$ All F are non-G

$(F_1 \supset \sim G_1)\,\&\ldots$ $\qquad (F_1 \supset \sim G_1)\,\&\ldots$

Some F is not G $\overset{\mathrm{df}}{=}$ Some F is non-G

$(F_1\,\&\sim G_1) \vee \ldots$ $\qquad (F_1\,\&\sim G_1) \vee \ldots$

You can easily verify all these equivalences and nonequivalences by using truth tables.

Exercises

A. Analyze the following, using things $T_1 \ldots$ as your universe of discourse.

1. Precocious children are tiresome.

2. At least one man has fourteen children.

3. All men with fourteen children have brave or foolish wives.

4. Something made a noise.

242

5. Everything makes noise.

6. Everything that makes noise is tiresome.

7. Children all make noise.

8. No children are tiresome.

9. Some tiresome thing is a child.

10. Some child is a tiresome thing.

B. (a) Which of the following are implied by, (b) which imply, (c) which are consistent with, and (d) which contradict "All satyrs have the heads of men and the bodies of horses"? Use the tables of implication, opposition, and equivalence.

1. Not all satyrs have the heads of men and the bodies of horses.

2. There are no satyrs that have the heads of men and the bodies of horses.

3. Some satyr has the head of a man and the body of a horse.

4. Some satyr does not have the head of a man or the body of a horse.

5. All things with the bodies of horses and the heads of men are satyrs.

6. All things that do not have bodies of horses and the heads of men are non-satyrs.

7. No satyrs lack the head of a man or the body of a horse.

8. All satyrs have the heads of men.

9. There are satyrs.

10. There aren't any satyrs.

C. Given just the information that it is false that all men are mortal, and letting your universe of discourse be living things, decide which of the following are false, which true, and which undecidable on your information.

1. Some man is immortal.

2. Some immortal is a man.

3. No men are mortal.

4. All immortals are non-men.

5. No men are immortal.

6. Every man is not mortal.

7. It is false that some man is mortal.

8. It is false that some man is immortal.

9. Immortality is a trait of no man.

10. Manhood rules out immortality.

29 / *Predicates, Pronouns, and Quantifiers*

Open Sentences

We made sense of talk about groups of nonexisting things by construing it as talk about existing things, but that solution only calls attention to another problem. Treating plural statements as compounds of singular statements is practical when small and definite numbers of things are in question, but it becomes cumbersome when we are discussing large groups, and it will not work at all when those groups have indefinitely large membership. We can easily make a list of the chairs in this room, but how could we list the people in China, or the grains of sand in Arabia, much less all the things in the world? Such cases require more subtle methods, and we shall here find it better to focus our attention on the predicates than on the subjects of our sentences.

Consider the singular statement

(**1**)   Chicago is a beautiful city.

Let us remove the name 'Chicago' and leave a blank:

(**2**)   _____ is a beautiful city.

Unlike (1), this sentence is no longer about anything; it is a sentence without a subject; only the *predicate*, what was said about the subject, remains.* Unlike (1), this sentence has no truth value, although it would become true or false if a name were put in the blank. For example, if you

---

* The predicate includes everything besides the subject.

wrote the name 'Paris' in the blank it would be true. If you wrote 'The Mojave Desert', it would be false.

We shall call such subject-hungry sentences *open sentences*. Where a closed sentence has a name, an open sentence has a blank. A closed sentence is true or false; an open sentence is not. Open sentences are not statements but statements-in-waiting, predicates waiting to be said about something.

In ordinary English we write such open sentences, not by putting a blank, but by putting a pronoun where a name was before, as

(3)   It is a beautiful city.

Out of all context, (3) is neither true nor false, but it becomes true or false depending on what name the pronoun 'it' replaces. If 'it' refers to Paris, (3) is true; if to the Mojave Desert, (3) is false. As the grammar books tell you, a pronoun may replace the name of a person, place, or thing—any person, place, or thing. The reference of a name is constant if it is not ambiguous, but a pronoun has variable reference. 'George Washington' refers to the first president. The pronoun 'it' refers to anything you please.

We may, then, think of an open sentence as a combination of a predicate with a pronoun. The pronoun marks a place for a name and, customarily, refers back to what was formerly named, or otherwise identified, in the same context. (If we have just been talking about George Washington, then 'he' refers to George Washington. If it doesn't, we have changed the subject.)

Rather than use a blank or a pronoun, we shall here write open sentences after the fashion

(4)   *x* is a beautiful city,

marking the blank in (2) with a small letter from the end of the alphabet. Such a letter is called a *variable* because, like a pronoun, its reference varies from context to context. Why not just use pronouns to mark the blanks, as in English? Well, because we might want to say

It is a beautiful city but it is an ugly one

about two previously mentioned but unnamed cities, *x* and *y*, thus:

x is a beautiful city but *y* is an ugly one.

This usage avoids such circumlocutions as 'the former' and 'the latter'.

Open sentences, predicates with blanks or letters or pronouns as subjects, are the solution to the problem of making a statement about indefinitely many unlisted objects. Suppose we want to say that every city is beautiful but have no list of cities or things. No matter. We can declare,

(5)   Name any thing you like; if it is a city, it is beautiful,

or

(6)   Mention any x you like; if x is a city, x is beautiful,

or

(7)   Put any name you wish in the blank; if _____ is a city, then _____ is beautiful.

Using an open sentence like (5), (6), or (7) is like endorsing a blank check with the understanding that the banker will cash the check if and only if the recipient fills in the right amount.

Particular statements and singular statements may be understood in similar terms. For example, the particular statement,

(8)   Something is a beautiful city

is a declaration that the open sentence (2) is true of at least one thing in our universe of discourse, while the singular statement (1) is a declaration that (2) is true of Chicago. Of course, neither (5) nor (8), nor (1) is an open sentence. All three are statements, closed sentences with a truth value. An open sentence like (2) is not about anything, but (5) is about everything, (1) is about Chicago, and (8) is about some unidentified thing. Statements are thus distinguished from open sentences by having referents, by being about something.

As you may have noticed, open sentences may, like statements, be simple or compound. For example, the open sentence (4) is a predicate compression of,

(9) x is a city and x is beautiful,

which is a compound of the simple sentences

(10) x is a city

and

(11) x is beautiful.

Also complex is

(12) x is a city $\supset$ x is beautiful,

which says that x is a city only if it is beautiful.

Quantifiers

As you may also have noticed, open sentences, whether simple or complex, may be true or false of any number, definite or indefinite, of things. One can assert or deny a predicate of one, two, three . . . or all of any given group of things. Thus, one can say:

> All cities are beautiful;
> No cities are beautiful;
> At least one city is beautiful;
> Exactly nine cities are beautiful;
> Some cities are beautiful;

and so on. We shall, however, limit ourselves to just two sorts of statements, statements to the effect that at least one thing has a certain predicate and statements to the effect that everything has a certain predicate. (As it turns out, this is not as great a limitation as it seems; for all the others can be defined using these two.)

The following all assert that the open sentence (11) is true of everything.

> Everything is beautiful;
> All things are beautiful;
> Whatever it might be, it is beautiful;
> Mention anything you please: it is beautiful;
> Beauty belongs to all things;
> Beauty is ubiquitous;

and so on. As usual, there are many ways in English of saying much the same thing, but also as usual, logical analysis is facilitated by reducing them all to one standard way of saying something. We shall express all of the above by saying

$$(\forall x)\ x \text{ is beautiful,}$$

which may be read

(**13**)   For anything x, x is beautiful.

To assert that at least one thing is beautiful, we shall write

(**14**) $(\exists x)\ x$ is beautiful,

which may be read

(15)   There is at least one thing x such that x is beautiful

and is a suitable rendition for

> Something is beautiful;
> At least one thing is beautiful;
> Beauty is the possession of at least one object;
> There is a beautiful thing;
> Beauty exists;

and so on.

The principle is the same when our predicates are complex, as in

(16) $(\exists x)$ (x is a city & x is beautiful),

which says that something is both a city and beautiful, that some city is beautiful, and that some beautiful thing is a city. Similarly,

(17) $(\forall x)$ (x is a city $\supset$ x is beautiful),

says that everything you can mention is beautiful if a city, that all cities are beautiful, that a thing is a city only if it is beautiful, and that the predicate 'x is a city $\supset$ x is beautiful' is true of everything.

We should also observe that even simple open sentences need not have the form 'x is F'. Two that don't are 'x walks' and 'God made x'. An open sentence can have any form that any other sentence has, it being just a sentence with a variable in place of a name. Since, however, sentences like 'x walks' and 'God made x' can be reparsed as 'x is a walker' and 'x was made by God,' we shall take 'x is F' as a paradigm of any open sentence, and what applies to it will be understood to apply to any other.

Bound and Free Variables

Notice the parentheses in (16) and (17). They make quite a difference. To see how much difference they make, compare (16) with

(18) $(\exists x)$ x is a city & x is beautiful.

Whereas (16) says "Something is both a city and beautiful," (18) says "Something is a city and x is beautiful." Thus, where (16) is a compound statement about something, (18) is a compound of a statement about something with an open sentence about nothing. (18) might as well be written

(19) $(\exists x)$ x is a city & y is beautiful

but

(20) $(\exists x)$ (x is a city & y is beautiful)

would not capture the sense of (16). Indeed, (20) says the very same thing as does (19).

Similarly (17) is very different from

(21) $(\forall x)$ x is a city $\supset$ x is beautiful.

Where (17) declares "Every city is beautiful," (21) declares "Everything is a city and x is beautiful."

The difference between sentences (16) and (17) on the one hand and (18) and (21) on the other is that the variables in the first two are all within the scopes of their *quantifiers*, '$(\forall x)$' and '$(\exists x)$', whereas the last occurrences of the variable in the second pair are not within the scopes of their quantifiers. Hence, in (18) and (21), the 'x' in 'x is beautiful', does not refer back to the same entity as is referred to by 'x' in 'x is a city'. Indeed, it refers to nothing at all. So (21) does not tell us whether the thing that is a city is also beautiful.

We shall make this distinction by saying that all occurrences of the variable in (16) and (17), but not all those in (18) and (21) are *bound*. The last occurrence of the variable in (18) is *free*, and so is the last occurrence of the variable in (21). Bound variables have reference, definite or indefinite; free variables do not. Closed sentences contain only bound variables; open sentences are characterized by containing free variables.

How do we decide whether a variable is bound or free? How do we tell whether it is within the scope of the quantifier? Very easily. Quantifiers reach out to all variables in the nearest complete sentence that follows them. If that sentence happens to be a compound one in parentheses, then the quantifier binds all occurrences of that variable in that compound sentence. So the quantifiers in (16) and (17) bind all occurrences of 'x', whereas the quantifiers in (18) and (21) reach out only to the first occurrence and leave the second untouched.

While we are on the topic, let me add one other word about parentheses and quantifiers:

(22) $(\exists x)$ (x is beautiful)

says the very same thing as (14), which omits the parentheses around the open sentence 'x is beautiful'. Not being needed, as in (16), to make the scope of the quantifier clear, the additional parentheses in (22) are acceptable but superfluous.

Not only are (16) and (18) to be distinguished from each other, but neither is to be confused with

(23) $(\exists x)$ x is a city & $(\exists x)$ x is beautiful,

which says that something is a city and something is beautiful, but does not say that the something that is a city is the same something as the something that is beautiful. (23) could as well be written

(24) $(\exists x)$ x is a city & $(\exists y)$ y is beautiful.

In (16) the predicates 'x is a city' and 'x is beautiful' are conjoined and said to be true of some entity, x. In (18) the statement "$(\exists x)$ x is a city" is conjoined with the open sentence 'x is beautiful'. In (23) the closed sentence "$(\exists x)$ x is a city" is conjoined with the closed sentence "$(\exists x)$ x is beautiful."

Special Cases

Predicates may not only be affirmed of some or all things; they may also be denied of some or all things.

(25) $(\exists x)$ $\sim x$ is a city

says "Something is not a city." Don't confuse this true statement with

(26) $\sim (\exists x)$ x is a city.

(26) denies falsely that a city exists. It says "There does not exist an x such that x is a city" or "Nothing is a city." Likewise, distinguish

(27) $(\forall x)$ $\sim (x$ is a city $\supset x$ is beautiful$)$

from

(28) $\sim (\forall x)$ $(x$ is a city $\supset x$ is beautiful$)$.

(28) denies "Every city is beautiful." By contrast, (27) affirms of everything '$\sim$(it is a city $\supset$ it is beautiful),' which is equivalent to saying that everything is a city and not beautiful.

(27) and (28) are also to be distinguished from

(29) $(\forall x)\, (x$ is a city $\supset\; \sim x$ is beautiful),

which says that every city is other than beautiful, that everything you can mention is a city only if not beautiful.

One additional confusion you should avoid is that between

(30) $(\exists x)\, (x$ is a city $\&\, x$ is beautiful)

and

(31) $(\exists x)\, (x$ is a city $\supset\, x$ is beautiful).

(30) says that something is a beautiful city; (31) does not. (31) says that there is something which is such that if it is a city, it is beautiful. That could be true if there were no beautiful cities, but (30) would be false under those same circumstances. So when you are paraphrasing "Some city is beautiful" you should write (30), not (31).

That direction may be confusing, because you should write "All cities are beautiful" as

(32) $(\forall x)\, (x$ is a city $\supset\, x$ is beautiful),

not as

(33) $(\forall x)\, (x$ is a city $\&\, x$ is beautiful),

which means "Everything is a beautiful city." By contrast, (32) just says "Everything is such that, if it is a city, it is beautiful."

Incidentally, you must be careful about the words 'anything' and 'something'. Compare

(34)   If anything is a city, it is beautiful,

which should be written as (32), with

If anything is a city, something is beautiful,

which should be written

$(\exists x)$ is a city $\supset (\exists x)\, x$ is beautiful.

Similarly, notice that

If anything is a city, anything is beautiful

should be written

$(\exists x)\, x$ is a city $\supset (\forall x)\, x$ is beautiful,

it being a way of saying "If something is a city, everything is beautiful."

So 'anything' is sometimes rendered by '$(\exists x)$' and sometimes by '$(\forall x)$'.

In the same way, 'something' is not always rendered by '$(\exists x)$'. Frequently, '$(\forall x)$' is better. Thus,

> If something is a city, it is beautiful

means the very same thing as (34) and should be written in the same way as (32). To decide which quantifier is appropriate in these cases, you are going to have to think very carefully about what the English original means. That makes the exercise of paraphrasing English statements into quantificational symbolism very valuable in understanding the English statements themselves. Since it is quite clear what the symbolic rendition says, you will be able to manage the paraphrase only if you learn to get perfectly clear what the original English says. Hence, as we have seen before, having exactly defined symbols for our logical notations is not just a mathematical game. It has very practical justification.

Exercises

A. Which of the following are open sentences?

1. She is the love of my life.

2. x is the love of my life.

3. _____ is the love of my life.

4. Lois is the love of my life.

5. Think of Lois: she is the love of my life.

6. Every girl is the love of my life.

7. There is a girl who is the love of my life.

8. $(\forall x)$ x is the love of my life.

9. There is a name which, put in the blank, will make true the following open sentence: _____ is the love of my life.

10. Name any girl you like: she is the love of my life.

11. $(\forall x)$ x is a girl $\supset$ x is the love of my life.

12. $(\exists x)$ x is a girl $\supset$ $(\exists x)$ x is the love of my life.

13. $(\exists x)$ $(x$ is a girl $\&$ x is the love of my life$)$.

14. $\sim(\forall x)$ (x is a girl & x is the love of my life).

15. $(\forall x)$ (x is a girl $\supset y$ is the love of my life).

B. Using the open sentences 'x is green' and 'x is cool', the expressions '$(\forall x)$' and '$(\exists x)$', and the symbols &, $\sim$, and so on, paraphrase the following.

   1. All green things are cool.

   2. If it is green it is cool.

   3. Nothing that is not green is cool.

   4. Something green is not cool.

   5. Everything is green but not everything is cool.

   6. There is at least one green thing and there is at least one cool thing.

   7. There are green things and there are cool things, but there are no things that are both green and cool.

   8. Everything green is cool but not everything cool is green.

   9. Everything green is cool but nothing cool is green.

   10. If something is green, it is cool; but nothing is green.

   11. If there is something that is green, there is something that is cool; but there is nothing that is green.

   12. Green things and non-green things are both cool. (This is tricky. Be careful.)

   13. Everything green is not cool.

   14. If anything is green, it is cool.

   15. If something is not green, nothing is cool.

   16. Things that are both cool and not cool don't exist.

   17. Things both green and cool are myths.

   18. If everything is cool, everything is green.

   19. Things both green and cool exist only in your mind.

   20. Greenness exists; coolness does not.

   21. Chicago is cool. (Hint: let 'c' = 'Chicago')

   22. Chicago is cool but not green.

   23. Chicago is cool but Birmingham is not.

   24. If Birmingham is cool, every city is.

Predicate Transformation

Compare the two statements

(1) $(\exists x)$ (x is colored & x takes up room)

and

(2) $(\exists x)$ (x takes up room & x is colored).

Since

(3) x takes up room & x is colored

is equivalent to its converse,

(4) x is colored & x takes up room,

(1) and (2) are equivalent.   So, for a similar reason, are

(5) $(\forall x)$ (x takes up room $\supset$ x is colored)

and

(6) $(\forall x)$ $\sim$(x takes up room & $\sim x$ is colored).

The point is this: if two equivalent open sentences are both preceded by the same single quantifier,* the resulting quantified statements will be equivalent.   '$(\exists x)$' and '$(\forall x)$' are quantifiers, the first *existential*, the second

---

* This remark is not true of multiply quantified statements in more than one variable, statements of such forms as '$(\forall x)(\exists y)(x$ is $F \equiv y$ is $G)$'.

255

is implied by (9) and by (8). (7) is consistent with neither (8) nor (9), but (10) is consistent with both. (10) is not, however, consistent with (7).

So, the second thing to do, after you have transformed all denials into affirmative statements by means of the list of quantifier equivalences, is to see if either of the pair of statements you are investigating is a tautology or a contradiction. If so, the preceding observations apply. If not, there are four cases to consider.

Case 1. Both statements may be universal; that is, they may both begin with '(∀x)'.

If so, the statements are mutually consistent if and only if the open sentences that follow them are mutually consistent. Thus, for example,

(11)   (∀x) x has weight

is consistent with

(12)   (∀x) x is colored

but not with

(13)   (∀x) ~x has weight.

Furthermore, if both statements are universal, one of the two implies the other if and only if the open sentence following its quantifier implies the open sentence following the other's quantifier. Thus, for example, (11) implies

(14)   (∀x) (x has weight ∨ x is colored),

but the converse does not hold. Since 'x has weight ∨ x is colored' does not imply 'x has weight', (14) does not imply (11).

Case 2. Both statements may be existential; that is, both may begin with '(∃x)'.

If so, they are consistent with each other so long as both their open sentences are self-consistent. Thus, in spite of mutually inconsistent predicates, (6) is consistent with '(∃x) ~x is F'. The only time existentially quantified statements are inconsistent with each other is when one of them is inconsistent with itself.

Furthermore, one of the two existentially quantified statements implies the other if and only if its open sentence implies the open sentence of the other. Thus

(15)   (∃x) (x has mass & x has color)

implies

(16) $(\exists x)$ x has color,

but the converse does not hold.

Case 3. The first statement of a pair may be universal, the second existential.

If so, they are consistent with each other if and only if their open sentences are consistent with each other. Thus

(17) $(\forall x)$ x was made by God

is consistent with

(18) $(\exists x)$ x was made by God

but not with

(19) $(\exists x)$ $\sim x$ was made by God;

for if everything was made by God, something was, and there does not exist anything that was not.

Furthermore, the first statement implies the second if and only if its open sentence implies the open sentence of the second. Thus (17) implies

(20) $(\exists x)$ (x was made by God $\vee$ x was made by the devil)

but not

(21) $(\exists x)$ x was made by the devil.

Case 4. The first statement may be existential, the second universal.

As in the preceding case, the two are consistent with each other if and only if their open sentences are consistent with each other. Thus, there is no way (19) could be true but (17) false; but, because (16) does not imply that something was not made by God, (15) and (16) could both be true.

On the other hand, with one exception, no existential statement, except one that is self-contradictory, implies any universal statement that is not a tautology. So (15) does not imply (14). The exception occurs when our universe has exactly one thing in it, in which case '$(\exists x)$ x is F' says exactly the same thing as '$(\forall x)$ x is F'.*

Given that negatively quantified statements can be turned into affirmatively quantified statements, we have exhausted all the cases. We have discovered that two affirmatively quantified and self-consistent statements are consistent with each other if and only if their self-consistent quantified open sentences are consistent with each other. One implies the other if and

---

* I ignore the inutile case of the null, or empty, universe.

only if (a) both have the same quantifier and one has an open sentence that implies the other, or (b) one has a universal quantifier and an open sentence that implies the other. (One does not imply the other if it is existential and the other is universal or if it has an open sentence that does not imply the other.)

So, to decide whether any two quantified statements are consistent, or whether one implies the other, simply transform both into affirmatively quantified statements and use the test just described. Don't try to memorize this test. Try to understand it, and practice using it. Once it makes sense to you, you won't have to memorize it. It is not as hard as it sounds, but if it seems hard, take heart: in the next chapter, we shall learn how to reason with pictures, which is easier to do.

The Strategy Reformulated

In the meanwhile, maybe we can make our test a little easier to use by reformulating it in a more graphic way.

First, take all denials of quantified statements and transform them into affirmations, using the list of quantifier equivalences. You will end up with the four sorts of pairs shown in figure 31.1.

$$(1) \quad \begin{array}{c} (\forall x)\, I \\ (\forall x)\, II \end{array} \quad \Big| \quad (2) \quad \begin{array}{c} (\exists x)\, I \\ (\exists x)\, II \end{array} \quad \Big| \quad (3) \quad \begin{array}{c} (\forall x)\, I \\ (\exists x)\, II \end{array} \quad \Big| \quad (4) \quad \begin{array}{c} (\exists x)\, I \\ (\forall x)\, II \end{array}$$

Figure 31.1

In this figure the roman numerals represent any open sentences you may choose, either the same open sentences or different ones; for example, '*I*' may represent the open sentence '*x* is colored & *x* has weight' and '*II*' may represent the same open sentence or another one. Now we want to know whether the top statement of the pair implies or is consistent with the bottom.

To decide, we must first look at each of the open sentences, *I* and *II*, to see whether either statement is a self-contradiction or a tautology. If either is a self-contradiction or a tautology, then the normal truth functional tests of consistency and implication apply.

If neither is a self-contradiction or a tautology, then, depending on whether we are considering pairs of type 1, 2, 3, or 4, the following rules apply:

1. '($\forall x$) I' implies '($\forall x$) II' if and only if 'I' implies 'II'.
    '($\forall x$) I' is consistent with '($\forall x$) II' if and only if 'I' is consistent with 'II'.
2. '($\exists x$) I' implies '($\exists x$) II' if and only if 'I' implies 'II'.
    '($\exists x$) I' is consistent with '($\exists x$) II'.
3. '($\forall x$) I' implies '($\exists x$) II' if and only if 'I' implies 'II'.
    '($\forall x$) I' is consistent with '($\exists x$) II' if and only if 'I' is consistent with 'II'.
4. '($\exists x$) I' does not imply '($\forall x$) I' unless there is exactly one thing in the universe of discourse.
    '($\exists x$) I' is consistent with '($\forall x$) I' if and only if 'I' is consistent with 'II'.

Since statements that imply each other are equivalent to each other, this same test will do as a test of equivalence. Statements equivalent to each other's denials are mutually contradictory.

Exercises

A. Decide which of the following are consistent with and which are implied by "All living things have value."

1. Some living things don't have value.

2. Some living things have value.

3. It is false that all living things have value.

4. No living things have value.

5. Some valuable things are alive.

6. All valuable things are alive.

7. It is false that all valuable things are alive.

8. No nonliving things lack value.

9. It is false that valueless things are never alive.

10. At least one valuable thing is not alive.

B. Decide which of the following are consistent with and which are implied by
"Some living things have value."

   1. Some living things do not have value.

   2. Some valuable things are alive.

   3. Some valueless things are not alive.

   4. All living things have value.

   5. Some nonliving things lack value.

   6. No living thing has value.

   7. Every living thing is valueless.

C. Redo both (A) and (B), this time deciding which of the statements are
equivalent to the given statement and which contradict it.

32 / *Picturing Statements*

We have learned how to assess two statements for equivalence by successively transforming both into statements whose equivalence or nonequivalence will be obvious. Some people find it easier to use Venn diagrams.

One-Circle Diagrams

Venn diagrams, named after their inventor, John Venn, are based on the principle that any given predicate is either true or not true of everything in the universe.* Consider the predicate 'x is polka dotted.' Mention anything you like: it is or it isn't polka dotted. Venn represented that fact by means of figure 32.1.

The box represents the whole universe. The circle represents the things in it, if any, that are polka dotted. Outside the circle is everything else. Everything in the universe is either in the circle or outside it, and nothing is in both places.

So far, the diagram does not tell us whether there is anything that is polka dotted or whether there is anything that is not polka dotted. If we want to represent the fact that some things are polka dotted, we put a bar in the circle, as in figure 32.2.

---

* That is to say, the universe of discourse, which may or may not be coextensive with the whole universe.

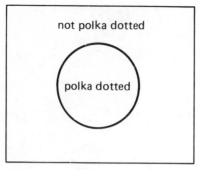

Figure 32.1

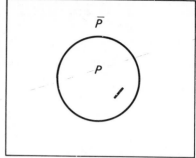

Figure 32.2
(∃x) x is P.

Here we have abbreviated 'polka dotted' to 'P' and its *complement*, 'not polka dotted', to '$\bar{P}$', and we have put a bar in the area labelled 'P' to show that something is polka dotted. Thus, as the legend indicates, we have a graphic way of saying, "There is at least one polka dotted thing."

Notice that we have still said nothing about things that aren't polka dotted. To declare that there are some of those, we put a bar outside the circle, as in figure 32.3.

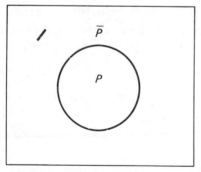

Figure 32.3
(∃x) ~x is P.

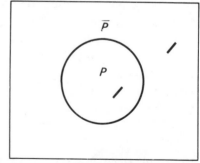

Figure 32.4
(∃x) x is P & (∃x) ~x is P.

Now we have drawn the statement "At least one thing is not polka dotted."

If we want to combine both bits of information, we draw a bar in the circle and another outside (fig. 32.4).

Should we just want to say that there is something in the universe,

268

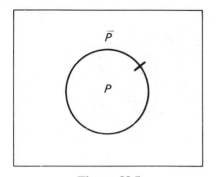

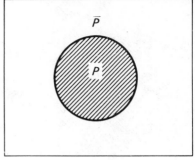

Figure 32.5

$(\exists x)\ (x$ is $P\ \lor\ \sim x$ is $P).$

Figure 32.6

$\sim(\exists x)\ x$ is $P.$

either polka dotted or not, without saying which, we should put a bar on the circumference of the circle (fig. 32.5).

Figure 32.5 does not say that there are any polka dotted things or that there are any things that are not polka dotted. It just says that there are some things that are one or the other.

You now see that a bar in an area means that there is something in it, but don't conclude that the absence of a bar means that there is nothing in the area. Figure 32.1 doesn't say that there is nothing in the universe. It just fails to say that there is something in the universe. It is like a piece of graph paper without a graph drawn on it: there is no information until you draw a graph. Figure 32.1 says nothing; figure 32.2 says something, but only about the circle. Figure 32.3 contains information about the area outside the circle. Figure 32.4 contains information about both areas, and figure 32.5 contains information about the universe but not about either of its two areas. So don't conclude from the absence of a bar that an area is empty.

To say that an area is empty, we shade it out. Suppose we wanted to make the false statement "Nothing is polka dotted." We would then shade out the circle (fig. 32.6).

Shading says the circle is empty, that there is nothing in it. Equivalently, it says that everything that exists is outside the circle, that everything is other than polka dotted. That is, it says

$(\forall x)\ \sim x$ is $P.$

To say that nothing is not polka dotted, or, equivalently, that everything is polka dotted, we shade the area outside the circle (fig. 32.7).

269

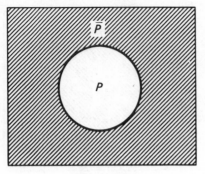 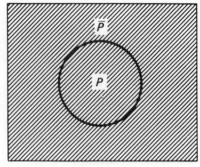

Figure 32.7
~(∃x) ~x is P or (∀x) x is P.

Figure 32.8
~(∃x) (x is P ∨ ~x is P).

If we wanted to say that there was nothing in the universe, we would shade out both areas (fig. 32.8).

Now, just as the absence of a bar did not mean that the area is empty, so the absence of shading does not mean that the area contains something. It means nothing except lack of information; it means that we don't know whether there is anything in the area, that, as yet, nothing has been said about that area.

Obviously, we could combine the assertion that there is something in one area with the denial that there is anything in the other (fig. 32.9).

Figure 32.9 asserts that something is polka dotted and that nothing isn't polka dotted.

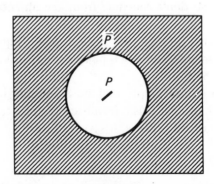

Figure 32.9
(∃x) x is P & ~(∃x) ~x is P.

Multi-Circle Diagrams

Simple, one-circle diagrams are adequate to deal with statements that have simple predicates, but statements with complex predicates, predicates such as "large and polka dotted," require two overlapping circles (fig. 32.10).

In figure 32.10, the universe is divided up into four areas. LP is the area of things, if any, that are both large and polka dotted; $L\bar{P}$ is the area of things that are large but not polka dotted; $\bar{L}P$ is the area of things that are polka dotted but not large; and $\overline{LP}$ is the area of things that are neither.

To say that there is something that is large and polka dotted, we just put a bar in LP (fig. 32.11).

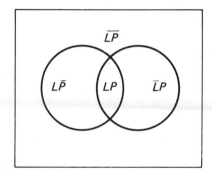

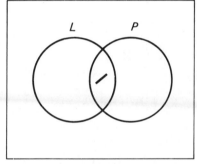

Figure 32.10	Figure 32.11
	$(\exists x)\ (x \text{ is } L\ \&\ P).$

Notice that figure 32.11 does not say "Something is large and something is polka dotted," which is drawn as in figure 32.12.

In figure 32.12 we have two bars. One says that there is something large but does not say whether it is polka dotted. The other says that there is something polka dotted but does not say whether it is large. The diagram thus fails to say whether there is anything that is both large and polka dotted. If what is large were not polka dotted, and what is polka dotted were not large, there would be nothing that is both.

If we want to declare that everything large is polka dotted, which amounts to denying that anything large is not polka dotted, we shade out $L\bar{P}$ (fig. 32.13).

If we want an existence clause, in order to say both that everything there is is polka dotted if large and that there is something large and polka dotted, we draw a bar in LP and shade out $L\bar{P}$ (fig. 32.14).

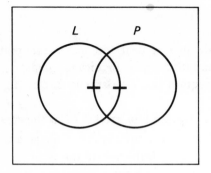

Figure 32.12
($\exists x$) x is L & ($\exists x$) x is P.

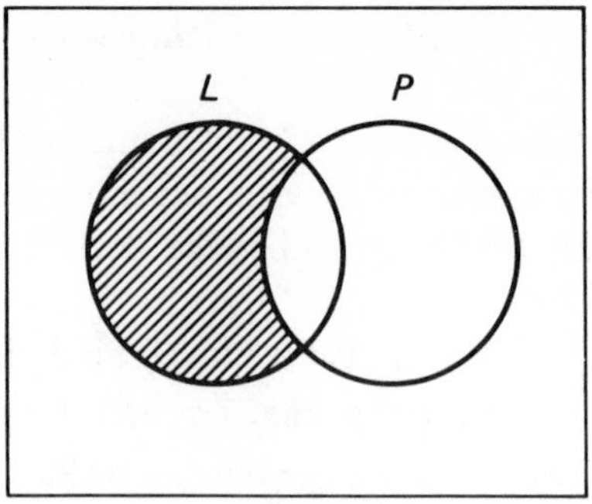

Figure 32.13

If we want to say that something is large, without saying whether it is polka dotted, we draw a bar on the line that divides $L\overline{P}$ from LP (fig. 32.15). It is interesting to note that if we combine the information of figure 32.15 with that of figure 32.13 we again get figure 32.14. That is because figure 32.15 says that there is something in L, while figure 32.13 says that there is nothing in $L\overline{P}$; therefore, what there is must be in the other half of L, namely, LP, which is where figure 32.14 puts it.

Diagrams of statements with three predicates require three overlapping circles and eight different areas. Suppose we wish to consider things that may be large, polka dotted, or stupid. Then we have the diagram given in figure 32.16.

Drawing statements on three-circle diagrams is no different in principle from drawing them on two-circle diagrams. You just have to remember

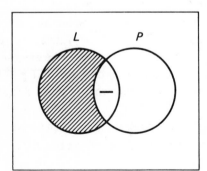

Figure 32.14
($\exists x$) x is L & ~($\exists x$) (x is L & P) or
($\exists x$) x is L & ($\forall x$) (x is $L \supset x$ is P).

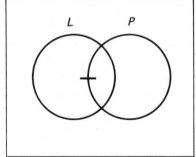

Figure 32.15
($\exists x$) x is L.

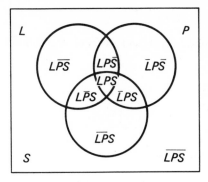

Figure 32.16

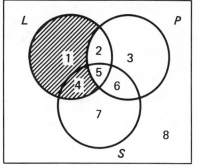

Figure 32.17
All large things are polka dotted.

that, since each area has been halved, you are talking about twice as many areas. Figures 32.17–32.19 illustrate statements on three-circle diagrams.

Notice that in figure 32.17 both areas 1 and 4, the areas outside *P*, are declared empty. Notice that the bar in figure 32.18 crosses the border between 2 and 5, the two halves of the area common to *L* and *P*. Notice, finally, that in figure 32.19 the bar is confined to area 5, 4 having been declared empty; if 4 hadn't been declared empty, the bar would be on the line between 4 and 5.

A four-circle diagram with sixteen areas can be drawn but is difficult, and more predicates than four require different sorts of diagrams; for each new predicate doubles the number of distinct areas needed. (Have you noticed how Venn diagrams are parallel to truth tables? If you haven't, think about the correspondence.)

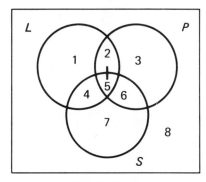

Figure 32.18
Some large things are polka dotted.

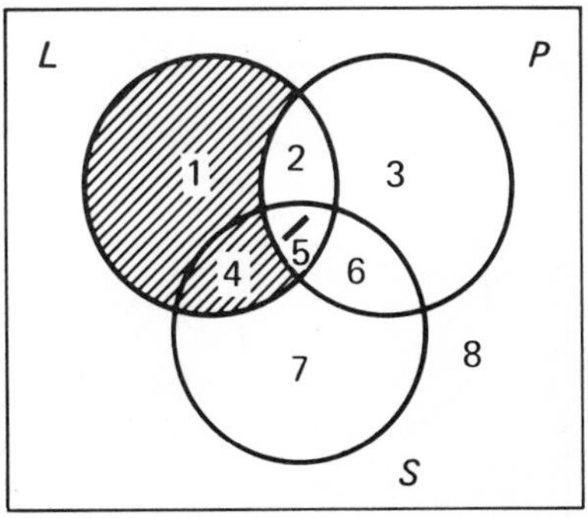

Figure 32.19
All large things are polka dotted and some stupid things are large.

273

Exercises

A. Using Venn diagrams like figure 32.20, diagram each of the following statements.

  1. All that shines is not gold.

  2. Nothing that shines is not gold.

  3. Everything that shines is gold.

  4. Everything that shines is other than gold.

  5. If anything shines, it is gold.

  6. Anything that shines is not gold.

  7. All gold does not shine.

  8. Some gold does not shine and something that does shine is not gold.

  9. Something is neither golden nor shiny.

  10. Something is both golden and shiny.

B. Using diagrams like figure 32.21, draw each of the following statements.

  1. All shiny things are cheap.

  2. All cheap things are shiny.

  3. No gold things are cheap.

  4. Every gold thing is expensive. (Hint: Expensive = not cheap.)

  5. Some gold things are dull. (Hint: Dull = not shiny.)

  6. Some dull things are not golden.

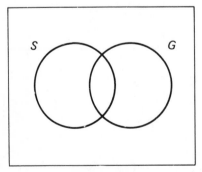

Figure 32.20
S = Shiny, G = Gold.

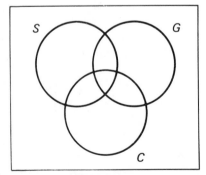

Figure 32.21
S = Shiny, G = Gold, C = Cheap.

7. There are some golden things, but none are cheap.

8. No golden things are cheap but all are shiny.

9. Everything golden is not shiny and everything shiny is not expensive.

10. Some gold things are shiny and some shiny things are cheap.

33 / *Venn Diagram Tests of Implication and Inference*

Tests of Equivalence and Consistency

Venn diagrams can be used to tell whether two statements are equivalent to each other or consistent with each other.

Compare

(1) All polka dotted things are large

and

(2) All large things are polka dotted.

Are they equivalent? To see, we just draw side-by-side pictures of both and see whether we get the same picture (fig. 33.1).

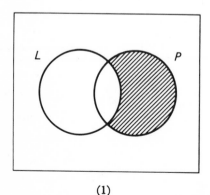

(1)

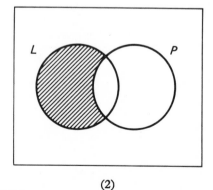

(2)

Figure 33.1

276

We see that the pictures are different. That should help us to see that the statements are not equivalent.

Venn diagrams can also be used as tests of consistency. Compare

(3)   All polka dotted things are large

with

(4)   Some polka dotted thing is not large.

The diagram on the left in figure 33.2 says there is nothing in $\bar{L}P$; the diagram on the right says there is something in $\bar{L}P$. Both can't be true. The statements are inconsistent. Statements, then, are inconsistent if and only if one has a bar where the other is shaded out. (1) and (2), though not equivalent, were at least consistent with each other. Their pictures were different but not in conflict.

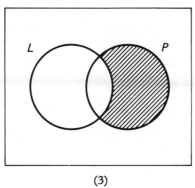 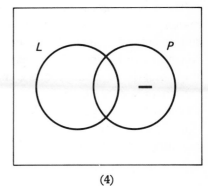

(3)   (4)

Figure 33.2

Tests of Implication

We can also test implications using Venn diagrams. To tell whether a statement 'p' implies another 'q', we draw a picture of 'p' and see whether a picture of 'q' was drawn in the process. Thus, we can see in figure 33.3 that

(5)   There are some large things that are polka dotted and some that are not

implies

(6)   There are some large things that are polka dotted.

277

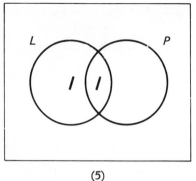

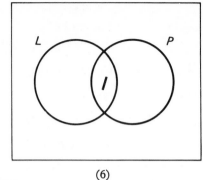

(5)
                 (6)

Figure 33.3

You see that the diagram of (6) on the right in figure 33.3 is part of the diagram of (5) on the left. But the diagram of (5) says more than (6). So (5) implies (6), but (6) does not imply (5).

The Venn diagram method of testing implication is closely related to the method you learned in chapter 31. To make it work, you first have to reduce every statement to a statement asserting or denying that there is something in a given area. Then you simply draw the pictures and make the comparisons. That process is analogous to running a truth table test on the open sentence that follows the quantifier.

Venn diagrams provide reliable tests of implication except in one case. Since the diagram starts out empty—without assuming that there is anything in the universe—it fails to show that

(7)   Everything is F

implies

(8)   Something is F.

(See fig. 33.4.)

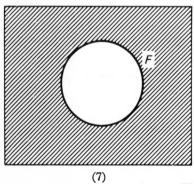

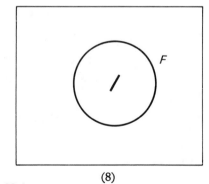

(7)
                 (8)

Figure 33.4

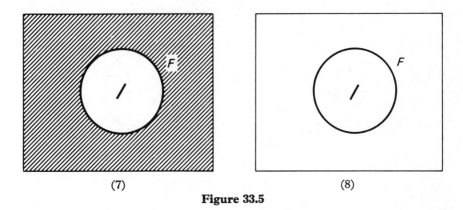

(7)   (8)

Figure 33.5

To fix that difficulty, however, we need only state that there is something in the universe, either F or $\overline{F}$. Then the diagrams could be redrawn as in figure 33.5.

Tests of Inference

If Venn diagrams can be used to test implications, they can also be used as tests of valid inference. The test is simple: draw all the premises, and then inspect the diagram to see whether you have drawn the conclusion. Suppose, for example, that the argument is

All F are G. So all G are F.

To see that this form of argument is invalid, we draw the premise on the left and the conclusion on the right (fig. 33.6).

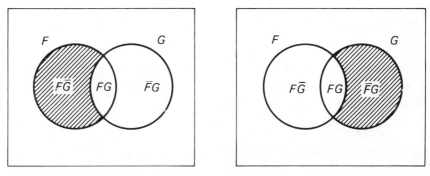

Figure 33.6

279

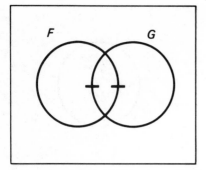 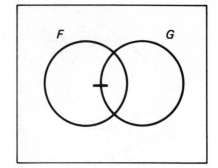

Figure 33.7

The premise says that $F\overline{G}$ is empty. The conclusion says that $\overline{F}G$ is empty. The conclusion is consistent with the premise but does not follow from it. Often you can see this without actually drawing a diagram of the conclusion: just draw the diagram of the premises and then look to see whether, in the course of doing so, you draw the diagram of the conclusion.

The diagrams work in the same way when there are more premises than one. Combine all the information from all the premises into one diagram, and then see whether the conclusion has already been drawn. Consider, for example, the valid argument form

Something is F and something is G. So something is F.

In figure 33.7, the premises are on the left, the conclusion on the right. Clearly, all information contained in the diagram on the right is already contained in that on the left. So the conclusion follows. Of course, the diagram on the left contains more information, but that is all right. It would be objectionable only if our argument were turned around, only if it were

Something is F. So something is F and something is G.

That the diagram of the conclusion says more than the diagram of the premise means that this argument is fallacious.

Of course, you didn't really need diagrams to test any of these inferences. It is already obvious that the valid argument was just a special case of the simplification of a conjunction, just a special case of

$$p \& q, \quad \therefore p,$$

and the invalid argument was just the fallacious converse,

$$p, \quad \therefore p \& q.$$

280

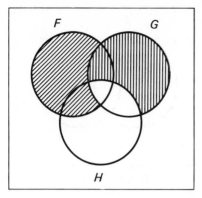 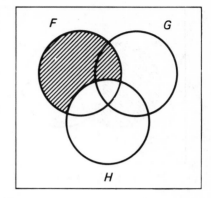

Figure 33.8

Diagrams will, however, be helpful in more complicated cases. For example, consider the following syllogism

All *F* are *G*. All *G* are *H*. So all *F* are *H*.

This syllogism contains three predicates, '*F*', '*G*', and '*H*'. So we need three-circle diagrams. They are presented in figure 33.8, with the combined premises on the left and the conclusion on the right.

You will notice that the two cells of figure 33.8 shaded by the conclusion have already been shaded by the combined premises. So the conclusion follows; the argument is valid. By contrast, the following argument is fallacious, as figure 33.9 shows.

In figure 33.9, the combined premises are on the left, as usual; the conclu-

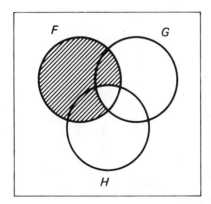 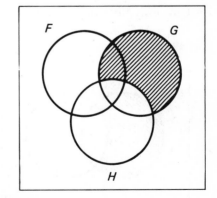

Figure 33.9
All *F* are *G*. All *F* are *H*. So all *G* are *H*.

281

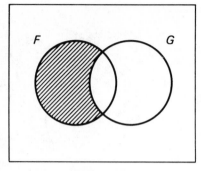

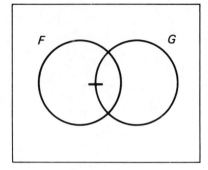

Figure 33.10   **Figure 33.11**

sion on the right. There is an area shaded in the conclusion that is not shaded in the premises (namely, $\overline{F}G\overline{H}$). So the conclusion does not follow.

Using the diagrams to test inferences becomes slightly, but only slightly, trickier when existential statements are involved. Consider the argument

All F are G. There are some F. So there are some G.

For a reason that will become obvious, we diagram the universal premise first (fig. 33.10).

The existential premise would normally be indicated by a bar on the line between $F\overline{G}$ and FG, as in figure 33.11.

Figure 33.11 says there is something either in $F\overline{G}$ or in FG, but figure 33.10 says there is nothing in $F\overline{G}$. So the bar must go in FG. The combined premises are shown in figure 33.12.

The conclusion is shown in figure 33.13.

Obviously, the conclusion follows.

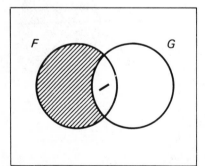

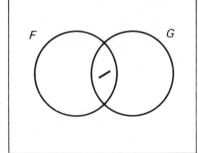

Figure 33.12   **Figure 33.13**

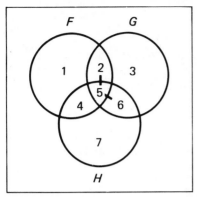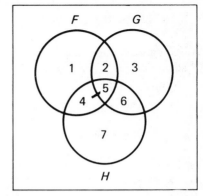

Figure 33.14

An example of an invalid form of inference involving existential statements is

Some *F* is *G* and some *G* is *H*. So some *F* is *H*.

Figure 33.14, premises on the left, conclusion on the right, will convince you that this inference is fallacious.

The premises say there is something in areas 2 or 5 and something in areas 5 or 6. Consistently with that information, there might be nothing in 5 or 4. Hence, the conclusion does not follow from the premises.

With a little practice, you will find that it is very easy to appraise validity using Venn's diagrams. Literally, they are a device for reasoning by means of the eye—or by means of the fingertips, if you are blind but can read braille.

Venn diagrams also have the virtue of being perfectly reliable tests of the validity of that limited class of arguments to which they are applicable.* If you diagram your premises correctly, and then read your diagram correctly, you will get the right answer. You can see why, if you think about it for a minute. Like a truth table, a Venn diagram represents every possible combination of predicates, areas of diagrams corresponding to lines of the truth table. Also like the truth table, there are two possibilities and two only. As a statement either is true or false, so an area either is empty or has something in it. Drawing diagrams of premises is just a matter of recording the information you have. Checking them for the validity of an inference is just seeing whether you have drawn the information the conclusion claims to be implicit in the premises.

---

* Excepting the case already mentioned, which can easily be repaired by supposing that there is something in the universe. Then, if the diagram of the premises leaves just one area not shaded, we will know there must be something in it.

Exercises

A. Using Venn diagrams, decide which of the following are consistent with "All divine beings (if there are any) are immortal." Then decide which imply and which are implied by it. Let your universe be living things.

1. No divine beings are mortal.

2. No mortal beings are divine.

3. All immortal beings are divine.

4. No divine beings are immortal.

5. Something divine is immortal.

6. Something divine is not immortal.

7. Something mortal is not divine.

8. Something immortal is divine.

9. Something is divine.

10. All mortal beings are other than divine.

B. Redo exercise (A), using as your original statement "There are divine beings, and all of them are immortal."

C. In the following, draw Venn diagrams of the premises and declare the argument form valid or invalid.

1. No F are G and no G are H. So no F are H.

2. Only F are G and only G are H. So only F are H.

3. All F are G and some F are H. So some H are F.

4. All F are G but no G are H. So no F are H.

5. All F are G but some G are not H. So some F are not H.

6. The F are all G and the only G are H. So only H are F.

7. Whatever is an F is a G and whatever is an H is a G. So whatever is an F is an H.

8. Whatever is an F is a G and whatever is an H is a G. So whatever is an H is an F.

9. Nothing but F are G and nothing but G are H. So nothing but F are H.

10. Nothing but F are G and nothing but G are H. So nothing but H are F.

11. Nothing is both an *F* and a *G*. Something is an *F*. So something is not a *G*.

12. If it is not a *G*, it is not an *F*. If it is not an *H*, it is not a *G*. So, if it is not an *H*, it is not an *F*.

13. If it is not a *G*, it is not an *F*. If it is not an *H*, it is not a *G*. So if it is not an *F*, it is not an *H*.

14. *F* are *G* but *G* are not *H*. So *F* are not *H*.

15. To be an *F* is to be a *G*, but anything is a *G* only if it is not an *H*. So nothing that is an *F* is also an *H*.

34 / Proofs Involving Quantifiers

Plural Statements as Components

Several chapters back, you learned a long list of valid forms of inference. The rules you learned exploit the logical forms of certain truth functional compounds. For example modus ponens depends on the fact that a conditional of the form '$p \supset q$' is true only if the consequent 'q' is true given that the antecedent 'p' is true. Nothing was said at that time about whether the components, 'p' and 'q' are singular or plural, and nothing needed to be said. For it makes no difference. Modus ponens is as valid when 'p' and 'q' are plural as when they are singular. Hence, the following form of argument,

(1) $(\forall x)$ x is $F \supset (\exists x)$ x is G, $(\forall x)$ x is F, $\therefore (\exists x)$ x is G,

the result of putting '$(\forall x)$ x is F' for 'p' and '$(\exists x)$ x is G' for 'q' in '$p \supset q$, p, $\therefore q$', is valid.

What applies to modus ponens applies to all other valid forms of inference. For example, the following instance of disjunctive syllogism is valid

(2) $(\exists x)$ x is $F \vee (\exists x)$ x is G, $\sim(\exists x)$ x is F, $\therefore (\exists x)$ x is G.

So, it is well to keep in mind that plural statements may be components of larger compounds whose truth values are truth functions of their plural components.

If plural statements deserve special mention, it is because they can have components as well as be components. As you remember, '$(\forall x)$ x is F' is short for the indefinitely extended conjunction 'a is $F \& b$ is $F \& \ldots$,' while '$(\exists x)$ x is F' abbreviates 'a is F ∨ b is F ∨ ....' This means that plural statements have implications as much by virtue of the logical structures embedded in them as by virtue of the logical structures in which they are embedded. The rules we have so far learned only get at the structures external to plural statements. We need special rules of quantificational inference that will enable us to penetrate into their internal structures so as to lay bare the implications therein.

You will understand the preceding remarks better when you reflect that the arguments

(3)   Everything takes up room. So this book does,

and

(4)   This is a logic book. So something is a logic book,

are valid inferences in spite of having the invalid form 'p ∴q'. They are not, however, valid by virtue of this form. The validity of (3) consists in the fact that its premise can be thought of as a conjunction having the conclusion as one of its conjuncts, and the validity of (4) derives from the fact that its conclusion can be analysed as a disjunction having the premise as one of its disjuncts. (4) and (5) dramatize the need for rules of inference that expose the internal structures of plural statements. In what follows, you will be introduced to four such rules.

Rules of Quantificational Inference

The form of inference needed to validate (3) is *choosing an instance*, CI for short.

$(\forall x)$ x is F,   ∴ a is F

CI says that knowing a certain predicate 'is F' to be true of everything justifies concluding that 'is F' is true of any arbitrarily selected object a. For example, given that everything takes up room, I may conclude that this book does. I may also draw the same conclusion regarding any other object I care to mention. If an open sentence is true of everything, it is true of any thing you care to pick.

The rule needed to validate (4) is *existential inference* (EI),

a is F,   ∴$(\exists x)$ x is F.

This rule says that knowing a specific object, a, to be F justifies concluding

35 / Counterexamples to Quantificational Arguments

Refuting an argument whose premises or conclusions are quantified statements is no different in principle from refuting any other argument: just find a counterexample or otherwise show that the conclusion could be false even if the premises are all true.

Consider the invalid form of argument

(1) $(\exists x)\ x$ is $F\ \&\ (\exists x)\ x$ is $G,\ \therefore (\exists x)\ (x$ is $G\ \&\ F)$.

(1) is proved invalid by the following counterexample:

(2)   Something is a woman & something is a man. So something is both a man and a woman.

Similarly,

(3) $(\exists x)\ x$ is $F,\ \therefore (\forall x)\ x$ is F

is proved invalid by

(4)   Something is a woman. So everything is a woman.

When we can't think of a counterexample, there is another way to achieve the same effect. It is based on the familiar fact that existential statements may be analyzed as extended alternations and universal statements as extended conjunctions, and on the consideration that we know how to construct truth tables when these conjunctions or alternations are finite in length. Think once again of argument (1). Given a list $a, b, c \ldots$ of all the things there are, (1) comes to

(5) $(a$ is $F \vee b$ is $F \vee \ldots).\therefore$
        $(a$ is $G \vee b$ is $G \vee \ldots)$
        $\therefore (a$ is $F\ \&\ a$ is $G) \vee (b$ is $F\ \&\ b$ is $G) \vee \ldots$

In this form, no truth table test of validity is possible. As we learned earlier, however, we may, if it suits our convenience, arbitrarily limit our universe of discourse to some finite number of things. Thus, we can limit ourselves to a discussion of just thing *a*, or things *a* and *b*, or things *a*, *b*, and *c*, or so on. That is, we can talk about exactly one thing, or exactly two, or exactly three, and so on, as we please. Truth table tests of validity will be possible in every such case, no matter how many things are under consideration, just so they are of a definite number.

Now, an argument form that is valid is valid. There is no existing, and no imaginable, circumstance under which its premises would turn out true while its conclusion was false. Consequently, an argument that is valid is going to be valid no matter how we restrict our universe; it will be valid in all universes of discourse, however chosen.* And, contrapositively, an argument form invalid in any given universe of discourse is invalid. So if we can find a finite universe of discourse in which a quantificational argument form turns out to be invalid, we shall thereby prove it to be invalid.

To see the utility of these theoretical considerations, think once more of (1), and consider a universe of discourse that has only two things in it, *a* and *b*. Suppose that one or the other of these two things is *F*, as the first premise claims, and that one is *G*, as the second premise claims. It still won't follow that one of them is both *F* and *G*, as the conclusion claims. That is, the following argument is invalid:

(6)   (*a* is *F* ∨ *b* is *F*)
         (*a* is *G* ∨ *b* is *G*)
         ∴ (*a* is *F* & *a* is *G*) ∨ (*b* is *F* & *b* is *G*).

For suppose it true that *a* is *F* but false that *a* is *G* and true that *b* is *G* but false that *b* is *F*. Then the premises will be true and the conclusion false.

In some cases, but not all, we can show an argument invalid by thinking of the universe as consisting of just one thing, *a*. Here is an example:

(7)   Something is *F*. So something is *G*.

If there is just one thing, *a*, (7) is equivalent to

(8)   *a* is *F*. So *a* is *G*,

which is clearly invalid. An actual counterexample to (8) would be

(9)   Fido is a dog. So Fido is a unicorn.

---

* Except the null universe, which we may ignore.

An argument form that can be shown invalid only by considering a universe of discourse of at least three individuals is

$(\exists x)\ x$ is F

$(\exists x)\ x$ is G

$(\exists x)\ x$ is H

$\therefore (\exists x)\ (x$ is $F\ \&\ x$ is $G)\ \vee\ (\exists x)\ (x$ is $F\ \&\ x$ is $H)\ \vee\ (\exists x)$
$(x$ is $G\ \&\ x$ is $H)$.

To see the invalidity, notice that the first two, but not the last, of the argument forms below are valid. Use the short truth table test.

1. a is F

a is G

a is H

$\therefore (a$ is $F\ \&\ a$ is $G)\ \vee\ (a$ is $F\ \&\ a$ is $H)\ \vee\ (a$ is $G\ \&\ a$ is $H)$

2. a is $F\ \vee\ b$ is F

a is $G\ \vee\ b$ is G

a is $H\ \vee\ b$ is H

$\therefore [(a$ is $F\ \&\ a$ is $G)\ \vee\ (b$ is $F\ \&\ b$ is $G)]\ \vee\ [(a$ is $F\ \&\ a$ is $H)$
$\vee\ (b$ is $F\ \&\ b$ is $H)]\ \vee\ [(a$ is $G\ \&\ a$ is $H)\ \vee\ (b$ is $G\ \&\ b$ is $H)]$

3. a is $F\ \vee\ b$ is $F\ \vee\ c$ is F

a is $G\ \vee\ b$ is $G\ \vee\ c$ is G

a is $H\ \vee\ b$ is $H\ \vee\ c$ is H

$\therefore [(a$ is $F\ \&\ a$ is $G)\ \vee\ (b$ is $F\ \&\ b$ is $G)\ \vee\ (c$ is $F\ \&\ c$ is $G)]$
$\vee\ [(a$ is $F\ \&\ a$ is $H)\ \vee\ (b$ is $F\ \&\ b$ is $H)\ \vee\ (c$ is $F\ \&\ c$ is $H)]$
$\vee\ [(a$ is $G\ \&\ a$ is $H)\ \vee\ (b$ is $G\ \&\ b$ is $H)\ \vee\ (c$ is $G\ \&\ c$ is $H)]$

This last argument form has a false conclusion and true premises when a is F but not G or H, b is G but not F or H, and c is H but not G or F. Thus, suppose a is dog Fido, b is horse Dobbin, and c is cat Tabby. Then something is a cat, something is a horse, and something is a dog, but nothing is both a cat and a dog or both a dog and a horse or both a horse and a cat.

There are also argument forms to which counterexamples cannot be found without considering four or more different individuals. So you can never reach a point at which you can safely declare, "There is no counterexample to this argument form." The only thing that will justify such a declaration is a proof that the argument form is valid. In the absence of such a proof, one can only keep looking for a counterexample.

What you have learned in this chapter is this: a quantificational argument form is invalid if some imaginable universe of discourse is such that the premises could be true of things in that universe while the conclusions are false. Put another way, an argument form is invalid if there is a counterexample to it. So, to refute a quantificational argument form we need only imagine some such universe of discourse or think of a counterexample, remembering that failure to find a counterexample or to imagine such a universe does not constitute a proof of validity.

An alternative to our method is to use some such decision procedure for uniform quantificational schemata as that set out in Willard Orman Quine's *Methods of Logic* (3rd ed., New York: Holt, Rinehart and Winston, 1972). Such methods are too complicated to be included in an introductory book such as this one. We have had to content ourselves with partial, and far simpler, decision procedures, and, of course, we have had to omit altogether those portions of quantificational logic for which there is no decision procedure.

Exercises

A. Either produce counterexamples to the following invalid argument forms or think of a universe of discourse in which the premises turn out true and the conclusion false.

1. a is F, $\therefore (\forall x)\ x$ is F

2. $(\exists x)\ x$ is F, $\therefore a$ is F

3. $(\exists x)\ x$ is F & $(\exists x)\ x$ is G, $\therefore (\exists x)\ (x$ is F & x is $G)$

4. $(\exists x)\ x$ is F, $\therefore (\forall x)\ x$ is F

5. $(\forall x)\ (x$ is $F \supset x$ is $G)$, $(\forall x)\ (x$ is $H \supset x$ is $G)$, $\therefore (\forall x)\ (x$ is $F \supset x$ is $H)$

6. $\sim(\forall x)\ x$ is F, $\therefore (\forall x)\ \sim x$ is F

7. $(\exists x)\ x$ is F, $\therefore (\exists x)\ \sim x$ is F

8. $(\exists x)\ (x$ is $F \lor x$ is $G)$, $\therefore (\exists x)\ x$ is F

9. $(\forall x)\ x$ is F, $\therefore (\forall x)\ (x$ is F & x is $G)$

10. $(\forall x)\ x$ is F & $(\exists x)\ x$ is G, $\therefore (\forall x)\ x$ is G & $(\exists x)\ x$ is F

UNIT V

Statistics

36 / Joint Probabilities

Replacing Truth Values by Probabilities

We have been learning ways to analyze compound statements and to tell their truth values from the truth values of their components. Using these methods, we can also determine the probabilities of compound statements, knowing the probabilities of their components.

Suppose someone has flipped a coin. You don't know whether it turned up heads or not, but you know that it did or it didn't.* Letting "H" abbreviate "It turned up heads," you know that $H \vee \sim H$. Put still another way, you know that "H" is either true or false. This is represented by our familiar table:

$$H$$

H
T
F

You know something else: coins come up heads about as often as not; if you toss a coin it will turn up heads about half the time.† Let us represent this information on our truth table, thus:

H
T = 1/2
F = 1/2

---

* We ignore the possibility that the coin will land on its edge.
† This assumes a fair coin.

This defines what it means to say that the *probability* (or *chance*) of a coin landing heads up is 1/2. It means that, on the average, one toss out of two lands heads up. Probability $\overset{\text{df}}{=}$ the ratio of the favorable cases to the total cases. So the probability of heads is

$$\frac{\text{number of heads}}{\text{number of tails}} = \frac{1}{2}$$

So far you have learned nothing you didn't already know, but things get more interesting as they get more complicated. Let us now suppose that two coins have been tossed. What is the probability that both are heads? As we now know, that question comes to this: What is the probability that the first coin is heads and that the second coin is also heads? That is, the question concerns the probability of the conjunction "Coin$_1$ is heads & coin$_2$ is heads." Let us represent this conjunction as "H_1 & H_2." We want to know the probability of "H_1 & H_2."

We can figure this probability in either of two equivalent ways. First we can notice that if the first coin is heads half the times it is tossed, then for half of those times the second coin is heads, too. So both will be heads simultaneously one-fourth of the time, for $1/2 \times 1/2 = 1/4$. Second, we can achieve the same result by looking at our familiar truth table for conjunction:

H_1	H_2	H_1 & H_2
T	T	T
T	F	F
F	T	F
F	F	F

This table shows that four distinctly different things could happen:

$$(H_1 \;\&\; H_2) \quad (H_1 \;\&\; \sim H_2) \quad (\sim H_1 \;\&\; H_2) \quad (\sim H_1 \;\&\; \sim H_2).$$

Each of these things will happen as often as any other, but only one of them is the case in question. So it has the probability 1/4.

Notice that the probability is 1/4, not 1/2, or 1/3. You might be tempted to reason, "Only two things can happen: either both coins will turn up heads, or they won't both turn up heads; there is only one way out of two of getting both heads; the probability must be 1/2." On that line of reasoning, the chances a hundred coins will all turn heads up is the same as that one coin will turn heads up. The trouble with the analysis is that the "one" possibility "they won't both turn up heads" is really three distinct and equally likely possibilities, namely, $(H_1 \;\&\; \sim H_2) \lor (\sim H_1 \;\&\; H_2) \lor (\sim H_1 \;\&\; \sim H_2).$

You might also be tempted to reason: "Both coins can turn heads up, both can turn heads down, or one coin can turn heads up while the other turns heads down. So there are just three possibilities." This analysis overlooks the fact that there are two ways to get one head and one tail, namely, $(H_1 \ \& \sim H_2)$ and $(\sim H_1 \ \& \ H_2)$. The probability of three heads in three tosses is 1/8. We analyze this as the probability of "$H_1 \ \& \ H_2 \ \& \ H_3$." Since "$H_1$" will be true half the time, "H_2" true half the time that "H_1" is true, and "H_3" true half the time that "H_2" is true, the probability is 1/2 × 1/2 × 1/2. Alternatively, we could notice that there are eight possible combinations of heads and tails for three different coins. Then we could notice that only one of those eight combinations is the one we want.

Similarly, the probability of four coins all landing heads up is 1/16. For, given that three coins are heads up only one time out of eight, a fourth coin

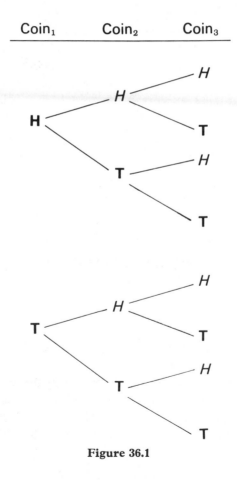

Figure 36.1

will be heads up only half of those times. In general, the probability that n coins will all land heads up is $1/2^n$.

We work out the various combinations in essentially the same way we worked out all possible combinations of truth values for statements, using the branching tree shown in figure 36.1.

Multiplying Probabilities

These examples show that the probability of a conjunction equals the probability of the product of its conjuncts. That is,

$$\text{Prob } (p \,\&\, q) = \text{Prob } p \times \text{Prob } q.$$

So if you know the probability that 'p' is true and also know the probability that 'q' is true, then you just multiply those two probabilities to get the probability that both are true.

Let us see how this principle works when the probabilities of 'p' and 'q' don't equal $1/2$. Instead of a coin, consider dice. A single die has six sides. On one of these six sides, it has a single spot. Now, if the die is rolled, it will either turn up the ace or not—that is, $A \lor \sim A$. But this is not to say that the chances of an ace are $1/2$. The die has five other sides, six altogether. So the chances of an ace (for a fair die) are $1/6$. The truth table with associated probabilities must read

$$
\begin{array}{l}
A \\
\hline
\mathbf{T} = 1/6 \\
\mathbf{F} = 5/6
\end{array}
$$

Now we know the probability of getting an ace on the toss of a single die. What is the probability of getting a deuce on the toss of two dice—an ace on the first die and an ace on the second die ? That is, what is the probability of "$A_1 \,\&\, A_2$" ? The answer is $1/36$. For suppose the first die shows one spot. That will happen one time out of six. The second die will show one spot one-sixth of those times. So the probability of each die showing a single spot simultaneously is $1/6 \times 1/6$.

We could have gotten the same result by noticing that there are thirty-six different things that can happen when you toss two dice: 1 & 1, 1 & 2, 1 & 3, 1 & 4, 1 & 5, 1 & 6, 2 & 1, 2 & 2, 2 & 3, 2 & 4, 2 & 5, 2 & 6, 3 & 1, 3 & 2, 3 & 3, 3 & 4, 3 & 5, 3 & 6, 4 & 1, 4 & 2, 4 & 3, 4 & 4, 4 & 5, 4 & 6, 5 & 1, 5 & 2, 5 & 3, 5 & 4, 5 & 5, 5 & 6, 6 & 1, 6 & 2, 6 & 3, 6 & 4, 6 & 5, and 6 & 6. Only one of these, the first, will satisfy our requirements for a deuce. So the probability of a deuce in the toss of two dice is 1/36.

The principle works no matter what the probabilities of 'p' and 'q'. Suppose it rains one Thursday out of three. Suppose you have spaghetti one Thursday out of five. Then the probability of rain and spaghetti is 1/15. We get this figure by multiplying the probability of rain by the probability of spaghetti, in accordance with the formula 'Prob R & S = Prob R × Prob S'.

Dependent Probabilities

This principle requires only one qualification. Suppose you have spaghetti every fifth Thursday, except when it rains, in which case you never have spaghetti. In that case, the chances of rain and spaghetti are zero, not 1/15. For our rule to work, the two probabilities must be logically independent: one must have no influence on the other. What happens in tossing one die has no influence on what happens in tossing another,* but if we never have spaghetti when it rains, rain has much to do with whether we have spaghetti.

By considering playing cards, we can illustrate how to calculate the joint probability of things whose probabilities are dependent on one another. Suppose you have drawn no cards. Then you draw one. The chances of its being an ace are 4/52. Now suppose you get an ace on the first card. There being one less card and one less ace than before, the chances of getting an ace on the second draw are only 3/51. Hence, the chances of getting four aces in four cards is 4/52 × 3/51 × 2/50 × 1/49.†

So if 'p' increases or decreases the probability of 'q', then to calculate the probability of 'p & q', we must multiply the probability of 'p' by the increased or decreased probability of 'q', given 'p'.

A final point: We have here illustrated how to calculate probabilities on the basis of certain *a priori* assumptions: that coins land heads up as often

---

* It is an error to suppose that a long stretch of tosses without a number coming up makes the likelihood of that number greater on the next toss. That the coin has not come up heads the last four times makes it no more likely to come up heads this time. Supposing otherwise is *The Gambler's Fallacy*.

† If the cards are replaced after each drawing, then each drawing is independent of the others. In that case, the probability of getting four aces in four draws is $(4/52)^4$.

as heads down, that each card in a well-shuffled deck has the same chance
of being dealt first, that one side of the die is as likely to land up as another,
and so on. We make these assumptions because we are more interested
here in the validity of the probability inference than in the truth of the probability premise. It is important to notice, however, that these assumptions
may not be borne out in the particular case. There are, after all, stacked
decks and loaded dice. To find out the actual probabilities in such cases,
one must make observations. Probabilities must be determined empirically,
not settled by making assumptions. By observing a die for some time you
may find that it rolls an ace, not one time out of six, but two times out of
seven. If so, your probability calculations must reflect the fact. The
probability of such a die yielding an ace three times in a row is not $(1/6)^3$
but $(2/7)^3$. The reasoning is, however, the same. We had to find out by
observation that the die was loaded, but once we did so, we calculated the
probability of joint occurrences by multiplying, just as before.

Exercises

1. Suppose Susan and Sam are both sixty-five, and suppose 7/10 men sixty-five years old die before reaching sixty-six, and 6/10 women do the same. What is the probability that both Susan and Sam will die before their next birthdays ?

2. Suppose Susan and Sam are married to each other and that old people tend to die soon after their mates die. How does this condition affect the preceding calculation ?

3. What are your chances of getting no heads in three tosses of a coin ? Of getting no aces in three tosses of a die ?

4. Suppose a gum machine contains five special prizes and forty-five pieces of gum. You have three pennies. What are your chances of getting three prizes ?

5. On the same assumption, what are your chances of getting no prizes ?

6. You have not thrown a deuce all evening. Are the chances of your throwing a deuce next time better, worse, or the same as before ?

7. Calculate the chances of getting the ace of spades five times in a row if (a) you replace the card each time and shuffle, (b) you do not replace the card.

8. What is the probability of throwing a six three times in a row if you are throwing one die at a time ?

9. The Yankees have won the first three games of the World Series. Is the probability they will lose the series (a) 1/16, (b) less, (c) more? Justify your answer.

10. Someone guesses that Smith is a crook, reasoning that, since a guess must be wrong or right, there is a fifty-fifty chance of being right. What is wrong with the reasoning?

37 / Alternative Probabilities

Adding Exclusive Probabilities

We have seen that the probability of a conjunction is the product of the probabilities of its conjuncts. We shall see here that the probability of an alternation is the sum of the probabilities of its alternatives.

Toss a coin. What is the probability it will turn up heads or tails? Well, every case is favorable: if we ignore the inconsequential possibility that it will land on edge, the coin will land up heads or tails every time. So, if probability is the ratio of favorable cases to total cases, the probability of heads or tails is 2/2, or certainty.

Another way to look at the situation is this: the probability of heads or tails is the sum of the probabilities of 1/2 for heads and 1/2 for tails. That is, Prob $H \vee T$ = Prob H + Prob T. To get the probability of an alternation, we add. This procedure works even when the sum is less than 1. Consider an example. What is the probability of getting an ace or a deuce on the toss of a single die? The probability of getting an ace is 1/6, and so is the probability of getting a deuce.* So the probability of getting one or the other is 1/6 + 1/6, which is 2/6. Similarly, the probability of getting an ace or a deuce or a three is 3/6. And so on.

We could get these same results in another way. Notice that each die has six sides. One side has a single dot, another has two dots, and so on. So two sides out of six make true "either an ace or a deuce," three out of six satisfy "an ace, a deuce, or a three," and so on.

One more example. You draw a card from a full deck. The probability

---

* We assume a fair die.

of your getting either an ace or a king is 4/52 + 4/52, there being eight cards out of fifty-two that make true "Ace ∨ King."

So you see that joint probabilities are multiplied but alternatives are added. That can be confusing. You might be tempted to read "the probability of p and q" as "the probability of p plus q." Don't! The word 'and' is not an instruction to add; the word 'or' is. The word 'and' is an instruction to multiply.

Nonexclusive Probabilities

There was a limitation on the rule "Multiply to get joint probability," which was "Multiply independent probabilities to get their joint probability." There is also a restriction on adding alternative probabilities: the alternatives must exclude each other. Let me illustrate.

There is one chance out of two that a coin will turn up heads; there is also one chance out of two that any arbitrarily chosen person is female. It does not follow that if you toss a coin and pick a person, the probability that either the coin will be heads or the person female is 1/2 + 1/2. That says, falsely, there is no way you can get tails and a male; so it must be wrong.

Consider another case. You toss a coin, pick a person, and choose a whole number. There is a 1/2 chance that the coin will be heads, a 1/2 chance that the person will be female, and a 1/2 chance that the number will be even; but there isn't a 3/2 chance that you will get heads, choose a female, or choose an even number. It is not possible to get a result more often than you have chances; the numerator of a probability can't exceed the denominator.

The reason addition doesn't work in these cases is that the alternatives don't exclude each other, as do the alternatives "heads or tails" and "ace or deuce." There is no way you can get heads and tails on the same toss of a single coin, or ace and deuce on the same roll of a single die, but you can get heads on a coin and at the same time pick an even number or a female. So you can't just add alternatives and get the probability of the alternation. The alternatives must exclude each other.

Fortunately, it is easy for those skilled in truth functional analysis to break down recalcitrant cases like the one above into mutually exclusive alternatives that permit addition. Think once again of tossing a coin and picking a person. Let us abbreviate "The coin is heads" as "H" and

"The person is female" as "F." Our familiar truth table for alternation reveals four mutually exclusive alternatives:

H F	$H \vee F$
T T	T
T F	T
F T	T
F T	F

We see that three out of four of these mutually exclusive alternatives satisfy the description "$H \vee F$"; one of four doesn't. That tells us that the probability of getting a female or heads is 3/4.

Notice that we get this result by adding, but not by adding the probabilities of "H" and "F." Instead, we add the probabilities of "$H \& F$," "$H \& \sim F$," and "$\sim H \& F$," each of which has the probability 1/4. Thus, we discover that the probability is 3/4.

In the same way, to get the probability of heads (H), a female (F), or an even number (E), we may draw up a table of all possible combinations, thus:

H F E	$H \vee F \vee E$
T T T	T
T T F	T
T F T	T
T F F	T
F T T	T
F T F	T
F F T	T
F F F	F

This table shows us that there are eight mutually exclusive alternatives, seven of which are favorable and one unfavorable. So the probability wanted is 7/8.

Of course, drawing up such a table can be a bother. So you will be glad to know that there is an easier way to get the same result. The question is: what is the probability of "$H \vee F \vee E$"? If we notice that "$H \vee F \vee E$" excludes only the case "$\sim H \& \sim F \& \sim E$," which has the probability $1/2 \times 1/2 \times 1/2$, we can arrive at the correct result by subtracting this unfavorable possibility from the total for all possibilities, namely, 1. For $1 - 1/8 = 7/8$.

We could have done the same thing in the case where the question was the probability of "$H \lor F$." Only one possibility is unfavorable, namely, "$\sim H \,\&\, \sim F$." That possibility has a probability 1/4. So the probability of all other (favorable) possibilities is $1 - 1/4$, which is 3/4.

This last method of calculation also works, as did the first, when the probabilities of the alternatives are unequal. Suppose three entrees are available and four desserts. I like two of each, but won't get to choose either. What is the probability I will get either a dessert I like or an entree I like? Well, the probability of desired dessert is 2/4, and the probability of favorable entree is 2/3. But the probability of desired dessert or favorable entree is not 14/12. On the contrary, since there is a $1/3 \times 2/4$, or 1/6, chance I won't get either desired dessert or entree, the chances I will get either are only $1 - 1/6$, which is 5/6.

To put the point more briefly, it is better to calculate the chances of nonexclusive alternatives, '$p \lor q$', by calculating the chances of '$\sim (p \lor q)$' that is '$\sim p \,\&\, \sim q$', and then subtracting the result from unity. Where 'p' and 'q' could both be true, the formula is

$$\text{Prob } p \lor q = (1 - \text{Prob } \sim p \,\&\, \sim q).$$

Whichever formula we use, the trick is so to analyze our situation as to be clear what the mutually exclusive alternatives are. Once we have done that, it is just a matter of counting up (that is, adding) the favorable alternatives or subtracting the unfavorable alternatives. Let us look at a couple of more complicated examples to see the importance of truth functional analysis in this connection.

I draw three cards from a well-shuffled deck.* What is the probability that I have three of a kind? This question is equivalent to "What is the probability that I have three aces or three kings or three queens or . . ." All these (thirteen) choices exclude one another. So we can calculate this probability as $13 \times (4/52 \times 3/51 \times 2/50)$.

I take a chance in each of three lotteries, one for a car, another for a motorcycle, and a third for a rifle. The chance of winning the first is 1/1000, the second is 1/500, and the third is 1/300. What are the chances of winning at least two prizes? That means "What are the chances of winning either exactly three prizes or exactly two prizes?" Let "$A \,\&\, M \,\&\, R$" represent three prizes. Winning them all has the probability $1/1000 \times 1/500 \times 1/300$, which comes out to be 1/150,000,000. Now we just need

---

* If the deck isn't well shuffled, the rules don't apply. All our remarks about probability assume randomness.

to calculate the probability of getting exactly two prizes—that is, the probability of getting the automobile and the motorcycle but not the rifle, or of getting the automobile and the rifle but not the motorcycle, or of getting the rifle and the motorcycle but not the automobile. We can represent this probability as "$(A \,\&\, M \,\&\, {\sim} R) \vee (A \,\&\, {\sim} M \,\&\, R) \vee ({\sim} A \,\&\, M \,\&\, R)$" and calculate it as $(1/1000 \times 1/500 \times 299/300) + (1/1000 \times 499/500 \times 1/300) + (999/1000 \times 1/500 \times 1/300)$, which comes out to be 1797/150,000,000. Now all we have to do is add this figure to the figure we got for "$A \,\&\, M \,\&\, R$" to get the probability of winning at least two prizes, which is 1798/150,000,000.

If we wanted to determine the chances of getting at least one of the three prizes, we could do it by calculating the chances of getting all three, exactly two, and exactly one and summing all these sums. A much shorter method, however, would be to compute the chances of getting no prizes and then to subtract this figure from unity. That is, we would ascertain the probability of "${\sim} A \,\&\, {\sim} M \,\&\, {\sim} R$," which is $999/1000 \times 499/500 \times 299/300$. Then the probability of getting at least one prize would be $1 - (999/1000 \times 499/500 \times 299/300)$. I'll leave the final result to you. Once you get the analysis right the arithmetic is easy. Getting the analysis right is the difficult, but essential, part.

Exercises

(You don't need to carry out the arithmetic, but show your analysis.)

A. You throw two dice. What is the chance you will get either a three or an eleven? A six or an eight?

B. You pick a card. What is the chance it will be a face card?

C. The chance of the Smiths getting a divorce is 3/4; the chance of the Joneses getting a divorce is 3/8. Calculate the chance that either the Joneses or the Smiths will get a divorce.

D. You have five cards in your hand, from the same deck of fifty-two cards. What is the probability that all of them will be face cards? What is the probability that at least one of them won't be a face card?

E. Al is thinking of taking a trip, Bertha of going to medical school, and Carl of getting married. The probabilities of these three things are respectively $A = 1/2$, $B = 2/3$, and $C = 3/4$. What is the probability that exactly two of them will happen? What is the probability that one or the other of them will happen?

F. Compute the probability of getting a full house (three of a kind and a pair) by drawing five cards from a well-shuffled deck.

G. Compute the probability of a straight (five cards in a row).

38 / Probabilities Involving Large Numbers

In the preceding two chapters we learned how to calculate the probability of any compound statement, knowing the probabilities of its constituents. In principle, calculation is easy, but in actual practice, it can become very complicated, especially when large numbers are involved. For example, figuring out the probability of two heads in a toss of two coins is easy. We just list the possible combinations:

$Coin_1$	$Coin_2$
H	H
H	T
T	H
T	T

Then we notice that there are four possible combinations and that the probability of each combination is 1/4. But what do we do when there are ten coins? A full list of possible combinations would fill up 1024 lines, and making up such a list would be a very tedious and time-consuming business.

Fortunately, there is a way of discovering how many of each sort of combination are possible without making up such a list: we can use the binomial theorem. The number of permutations of any given combination of 'p' and 'q' is denoted by the appropriate coefficient in the binomial expansion for '$p + q$'.

The Binomial Expansion

Let us review the algebra briefly and then try to explain what this last statement means. You remember from high school algebra that $(p + q)^2 = p^2 + 2pq + q^2$. You also remember that $(p + q)^3 = p^3 + 3p^2q + 3pq^2 + q^3$; that $(p + q)^4 = p^4 + 4p^3q + 6p^2q^2 + 4pq^3 + q^4$; and so on. If you don't, you remember that you can use Pascal's triangle (fig. 38.1) to find the coefficients of all terms in any one of these expansions.★

Pascal's Triangle

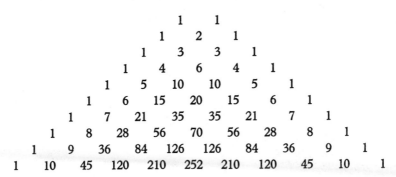

```
          1   1
        1   2   1
      1   3   3   1
    1   4   6   4   1
  1   5   10  10   5   1
1   6   15  20  15   6   1
1   7   21  35  35  21   7   1
1   8   28  56  70  56  28   8   1
1   9   36  84  126 126  84  36   9   1
1  10  45  120 210 252 210 120  45  10   1
```

Figure 38.1

For example, look at the fourth line in the triangle. It reads

1, 4, 6, 4, 1.

This line gives you the *coefficients*† of the terms in the expansion of '$(p + q)^4$':

$$p^4 + 4p^3q + 6p^2q^2 + 4pq^3 + q^4.$$

To find the *exponents*‡ of the terms in an expansion, just start on the left with 'p^n' and go right, subtracting 1 from the exponent of 'p' as you go and adding 1 to the exponent of 'q'. Hence, in the above expansion, you start with 'p^4' on the left, work to 'p^3q^1' on the right, and so on to 'q^4'.

★ To carry out this triangle further, notice that you just add two adjacent numbers to get the number below and between them:

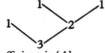

† In the term '$4p^3q$', the coefficient is '4'.
‡ In the term '$4p^3q$' the exponent of 'p' is '3' and that of 'q' is '1'.

This method will help you to find the coefficients and exponents of any expansion of a binomial expression to any power.

Later on we shall have another look at the algebra, but, for now, let us consider its use in calculating probabilities. When we know the probability of 'p', and when the probability of '$p + q$' is 1, we can calculate the probability of any combination of 'p' and 'q' by using the appropriate binomial expansion. Let us first illustrate how to do it and then explain what we did.

Suppose we are interested in the probability of getting three heads and one tail in four tosses of a coin, or in the toss of four coins. We could represent the possibilities as is done in figure 38.2.

$Coin_1$	$Coin_2$	$Coin_3$	$Coin_4$	
H	H	H	H	1
H	H	H	T	
H	H	T	H	
H	T	H	H	4
T	H	H	H	
H	H	T	T	
H	T	H	T	
T	H	H	T	
T	H	T	H	6
T	T	H	H	
H	T	T	H	
H	T	T	T	
T	H	T	T	
T	T	H	T	4
T	T	T	H	
T	T	T	T	1

Figure 38.2

Having worked out the table, we can count up the four ways of getting three heads and one tail. Since each of these permutations* of three heads and one tail has the probability 1/16, the probability of getting exactly three heads in tossing four coins is 4/16. In a similar way, we can ascertain that the probability of getting exactly two heads is 6/16 and that the probability of getting at least two heads is 11/16.

---

* A permutation is a different order. Thus, *HHTT* and *TTHH* are permutations of the same combination of $2H$ with $2T$.

A much quicker way to get the same result is to use the expansion for '$(H + T)^4$', which is

$$H^4 + 4H^3T + 6H^2T^2 + 4HT^3 + T^4.$$

Notice that the coefficient of each term corresponds exactly to the number of permutations in each group in the table in figure 38.2, and that the exponents in each term denote the number of H or T, as the case may be. For example, the term '$4H^3T$' represents the four ways that you can get three heads and one tail in tossing a coin four times, and the term 'H^4' represents the one way you can get four heads in four tosses. Since the probability of heads is 1/2 and so is that of tails, the probability of getting exactly three heads in four tosses is $4(1/2)^3(1/2)$, and the probability of getting 4 heads in four tosses is $(1/2)^4$. The probability of getting at least three heads is just the sum of these two, which is $(1/2)^4 + 4(1/2)^3(1/2)$. That is, the probability is 5/16. Hence the binomial formula, by giving a very brief and perspicuous representation of all the data on the table, makes unnecessary the laborious work of producing the table and counting up all the various permutations of combinations.

The gain of speed in using the binomial formula is most evident with larger numbers. A list of all possible permutations of combinations of heads and tails for tosses of ten coins would contain 1024 items. From it we would have to select and count those of interest. Instead of using that cumbersome procedure, we can use the binomial expansion. Suppose we want to know the probability of getting exactly seven heads in ten tosses of a coin. We just look up the appropriate term in the expansion of '$(H + T)^{10}$', which is

$$H^{10} + 10H^9T + 45H^8T^2 + 120H^7T^3 + 210H^6T^4 + 252H^5T^5$$
$$+ 210H^4T^6 + 120H^3T^7 + 45H^2T^8 + 10HT^9 + T^{10}.$$

The term we want is '$120H^7T^3$', which tells us that there are 120 permutations of seven heads and three tails. Since the probability of each permutation is 1/1024 (that is, $(1/2)^{10}$), it follows that the probability of getting exactly seven heads in ten tosses of a coin is 120/1024.

If we want to know the probability of getting at least seven heads, we add up 1, 10, 45, 120 (the coefficients in the appropriate terms) and get the sum of 176 as the number of favorable cases out of the total possible number of 1024 cases. Thus, we see that the probability of at least seven heads is 176/1024.

If we want to know the probability of getting no more than seven heads, the simplest procedure is to calculate the probability of getting seven heads or fewer (which is 176/1024) and subtract that from 1 (which yields 848/1024).

Now that you know how to use the binomial expansion to calculate probabilities, let us be sure you understand why it works. It is not really very difficult to see. Just recall our two basic rules for calculating probabilities: add alternative probabilities; multiply joint probabilities. That is,

$$\text{Prob } p \,\&\, q = \text{Prob } p \times \text{Prob } q$$
$$\text{Prob } p \vee q = \text{Prob } p + \text{Prob } q$$

The binomial theorem just combines these two rules. Exponents indicate joint probabilities; coefficients indicate alternative ways of getting these joint probabilities. So a term like '$10H^9T$' just indicates that there are ten ways to get the combination of nine heads with a tail. Since each permutation has the probability $(1/2)^9 \times 1/2$, the probability is just 10/1024 of getting exactly nine heads in tossing ten coins.

One final point. We have used the binomial theorem only when $p = 1/2$ and $q = 1/2$, but we could also use it to calculate probabilities when 'p' and 'q' have other values, providing we make sure that $q \equiv \sim p$, so as to satisfy the requirement that alternatives be mutually exclusive. For example, suppose we want to calculate the probability of getting ten aces in tossing ten dice. Let "P" abbreviate "the die is an ace"; let "Q" abbreviate "the die is not an ace." Then "P" has the probability 1/6 and "Q" has the probability 5/6. Thus, the probability of ten aces is $(1/6)^{10}$, and, the probability of nine aces and something other than an ace is $10 \times (1/6)^9 \times (5/6)$. So long as '$p$' and '$q$' are mutually exclusive alternatives, we just plug in the probability of each, whatever it may be, at the appropriate place and proceed with the arithmetic.

For Advanced Students

Those familiar with the factorial method for finding permutations can shorten calculations still further and dispense with Pascal's triangle, by using the following formula for the coefficient of any term '$p^{n-y}q^y$' in the expansion of '$(p + q)^n$' (note: $n! = n \ldots 3 \times 2 \times 1$):

$$\frac{n!}{(n - y)! \, y!}$$

Suppose, for example, that we wish to know how many ways to get nine heads and six tails in fifteen tosses of a coin. The answer will be

$$\frac{15!}{9!\,6!},$$

or

$$\frac{15 \times 14 \times 13 \times 12 \times 11 \times 10}{6 \times 5 \times 4 \times 3 \times 2},$$

which equals 5005.

Hence, the probability wanted is

$$5005(\tfrac{1}{2})^9(\tfrac{1}{2})^6,$$

which equals

$$\frac{5005}{32768}.$$

The preceding formula for the coefficients of terms in any expansion of the binomial theorem is, of course, derived from the following generalized formula, which describes a method for finding both coefficients and exponents in binomial expansions:

$$(p + q)^n = p^n + \frac{n}{1} p^{n-1}q + \frac{n(n-1)}{1 \times 2} p^{n-2}q^2$$

$$+ \frac{n(n-1)(n-2)}{1 \times 2 \times 3} p^{n-3}q^3 + \cdots q^n.$$

This formula and the preceding one look formidable, but if you will take a little trouble to understand what they say, your efforts will pay off manyfold in saved time.

Exercises

(You don't need to carry out the arithmetic. Just write the needed formula.)

A. Construct Pascal's triangle to $n = 12$.

B. Using the result of (A), write the expansion of $(H + T)^7$.

C. Using the result of (B), calculate the probability of getting either four heads or four tails in tossing seven coins.

D. Using the same expansion, calculate the probability of getting at least four heads; no more than two heads.

E. Imagine that twelve men in a home for the aged are sixty-seven years old. Suppose the probability, according to actuarial tables, that a sixty-seven-year-old man will die before he is sixty-eight is .72. Calculate the probability that exactly half of these old men will die before their next birthdays. Calculate the probability that at least half of them will live to enjoy their next birthdays.

F. Compute the probability of getting at least six items right on a ten-item true-false exam just by guessing.

G. Recalculate (F), assuming that each of the ten items offers four choices, one right and three wrong.

H. Redo (F) and (G), assuming twenty-item tests and using the factorial formula. (Skip this one if you can't handle factorials.)

39 / *Reasoning from Samples*

Inconclusive Arguments

In earlier portions of this book I said that arguments are either good or bad, good if the premises are known to be true and there is no way for the conclusion to be false consistently with the premises being true; bad otherwise. We must now recognize that that was an oversimplification, a distinction, not between good and bad arguments but between *conclusive* and *inconclusive* arguments. Inconclusive arguments are not as good as conclusive arguments, which leave no room for doubt as to the truth of their conclusions, but they can nevertheless be very good. It is a question of standards. Because we cannot have more, we must learn to demand less. Certainty is not always available. So we must learn to settle for likelihood instead. We must learn to count arguments as good if their premises are likely to be true and their conclusions are unlikely to be false consistently with the premises being true. And, since likelihood exists in degrees, we must learn to recognize that arguments are not either good or bad, but are more or less good and more or less bad, depending on how likely it is that their premises are true and how unlikely it is that their conclusions are false consistently with their premises. In a word, we must learn statistical reasoning, the logic of inconclusive inference.

Sampling

Fundamental to statistical reasoning is reasoning from samples, drawing generalizations from limited evidence. We want here to come to some

321

understanding of what is involved in doing that and what is required for it to be a reliable form of inference.

A typical statistical problem is to find out something about a large group, our *population*, by examining a select few things, the *sample*, from that group. For example, we want to find out how 100 million voters will cast their ballots in the upcoming election, but we can't ask all 100 million. We must settle for asking a small sample of them. We want, however, to be able to make a generalization about the whole population. We want to predict the outcome of the election. Our generalization will be accurate, however, only if our sample is *representative* of the whole—that is, only if it is like the original population in relevant respects. Suppose, for example, that 50 percent of the population prefer the candidate of party X, the remaining 50 percent prefer other candidates. We shall be able to predict the outcome only if the same proportions are maintained in our sample. So the question is: how can we assure that?

Randomness

The answer to that question is that there is no way to guarantee, but there are ways to increase the likelihood, that a sample will be representative. The most basic of these ways is to sample *randomly*, in such a way as to give every member of the population an equal chance of being chosen. To illustrate what this means, let us change examples for a moment. Our "population" is a jar of beans, 90 white and 10 red. Blindfolded, we pick the smallest possible sample, a single bean. Will it be white or red? That depends on many things. If we pick from the top, and the red beans were put in last, the bean we pick will almost certainly be red, and our sample will be unrepresentative, misleading as to the character of the beans in the jar. A white bean would be more representative, but how are we to make sure we get a white bean? As noted before, we can't make sure, but we can increase our chances by stirring the beans very thoroughly before we pick one. Once we have thoroughly mixed the red beans with the white, the likelihood of getting a white bean is 90 percent, the likelihood of getting a red bean only 10 percent. A white bean is not certain, but given thorough stirring, it is a very good bet. The inference, "90 percent of the beans are white. So the one we pick will be white," is not valid, but the inference "90 percent of the beans are white. Consequently there is a 90 percent chance this randomly selected bean will probably be white" is valid.

Random distribution gives each of the 100 beans 1 chance out of 100 of being chosen. Because there are 90 white beans, the chance that one or the other of them will be chosen is 90/100.

This simple case illustrates the logical basis of all reasoning from samples; it gives the justification of induction: randomness increases the likelihood that a sample is representative of the population. Let us go back to our poll of voters to illustrate this point more fully. We assume, remember, that the population is divided evenly between supporters and opponents of party X. The pollsters don't know this, however, and are trying to find it out. So they take a sample. For simplicity's sake, let it be a small sample of ten persons, chosen randomly so as to give every voter an equal (that is, a one millionth) chance of being chosen. (That, as we shall see later, is quite a trick, and much harder done than said, but assume it done.) Here are the various possibilities: all ten voters declare their preference for party X, or nine do, or eight do, and so on. The most representative sample would be a sample of five voters who declare their preference for X and 5 who declare their opposition to X. Will our pollsters get such a sample? We can't say, but given that they are sampling randomly, we can determine the probability of their getting any one of the samples mentioned, including the representative sample. The calculation is just a matter of using the binomial theorem, as before. Using it, we see that the probability of getting ten expressions of support for X is only 1/1024, the probability of nine expressions of support out of ten is 10/1024, and so on. The probability of an evenly divided sample, five for X and five against, is 252/1024, the greatest probability of any simple sample. Hence, the single most likely sample out of all possible samples is the most representative sample. The next most representative samples are the next most likely to occur and the least representative samples are the least likely to occur. All of this is summed up on the following graph, where 'X' represents supporters and '$\overline{X}$' represents others.

Figure 39.1 shows that the most representative samples are also the samples most likely to occur. True, the sample that is exactly representative is not more likely than are all the other samples put together, but it is more likely than any other sample. So, if we are sampling randomly, there is a very good chance that we are getting a representative sample. Furthermore, if we are content to settle for an approximately representative sample, content, say, to count a four to six division as more or less representative of the population, then we can say that the probability of getting a representative sample is better than half, being 210/1024 + 252/1024 + 210/1024, which comes to 672/1024.

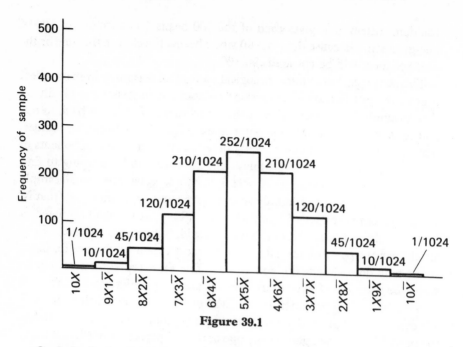

Figure 39.1

Such is the logic behind generalizing from samples. One's reasoning will be good only if one's sample represents the population, which is more likely than not if the sample has been chosen randomly—that is, in such a way as to give every member of the population an equal chance of being chosen. Random sampling means that people are more likely to be selected in numbers proportional to their numbers in the larger population. One's reasoning will be further strengthened if one weakens the conclusion to the claim that the sample will be approximately, but not exactly, representative of the population. In that case, the probability of the conclusion is the sum of the probabilities of the next most representative, and therefore next most likely, samples.

The principles illustrated above hold good no matter what characteristics the population may have. Only the numbers will change. Suppose our population is a species of birds. Of these birds, 1/5 have a certain marking on their heads; 4/5 lack it. A biologist takes a random sample of ten birds. What is the probability he will get a representative sample? That is, what is the probability that exactly two of the ten birds will have the marking? The answer is $45(4/5)^8(1/5)^2$, which is .30. What is the probability that the sample will be approximately representative? That is, what is the probability that between one and three of the birds will have the markings? The answer is $10(4/5)^9(1/5) + 45(4/5)^8(1/5)^2 + 120(4/5)^7(1/5)^3$, which comes to

.77. The probability is, of course, even higher of getting a sample in which fewer birds have the marking than lack it. Indeed, that degree of accuracy is all but certain. All this is summed up in figure 39.2, which, as before, shows the most representative sample to have the highest probability.

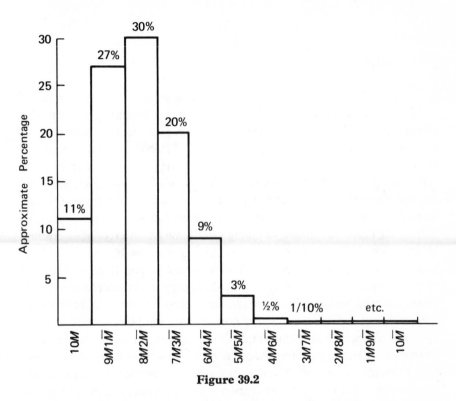

Figure 39.2

Clearly, generalizing from samples is risky business. You can be wrong. Indeed, there is a very good chance you will be. So don't bet too much on the outcome. Calculate the odds and place your bets accordingly. Don't risk everything on the inference that the population will be just like your sample. It probably won't be. Yet, if you have sampled randomly, your sample has a good chance of being exactly representative of your population, and it is highly likely to be approximately representative of your population. So don't say things like "Our sample shows that 48 percent of the population prefer X." Instead, say things like "Our sample shows that, in all probability, between 40 and 60 percent of the population prefer X." That is what statistical scientists do. Recognizing that there is a certain probability that their sample is in error, they will even go so far as to state the probable error.

325

We won't learn to do that here. Our purpose here is just to understand why and under what conditions reasoning from samples is a justifiable way to reason. What we have learned is that, given randomness, a sample is more likely than not to be approximately representative.

Bias

Notice that everything depends on randomness, giving every member of the population an equal chance with every other of becoming a member of the sample. *Biased sampling*, sampling which gives some members more chance than others, has the opposite result. It has a greater chance of resulting in an unrepresentative sample. The famous example is the telephone poll conducted during the Roosevelt-Landon election, when wealthy Republicans, but not the poor Democrats who outnumbered them, had telephones. Not surprisingly, the poll mistakenly predicted a landslide victory for Landon. Biased sampling would also be the error of an attempt to ascertain public support for legalizing marijuana by polling college students, or of forming an opinion of someone's character by observing how he performs under stress. You might get a representative sample when sampling in these biased ways, but if you do, you should attribute it to luck, not to logic. Logic requires random sampling.

Incidentally, by "random samples" we don't mean *haphazard* samples. Offhandedly asking your friends or the people you meet on the street is not taking a random sample. On the contrary, both are very biased sampling procedures. Your friends are a special group, not representative of the general population—and so are the people you are likely to bump into on the street. Sampling randomly takes careful thought and preparation. It can't be done casually.

How can we randomize a sample? The answer is: not easily. Sometimes we do it by putting names in a hat and stirring, sometimes by listing the population in alphabetical order and selecting every nth name. Statisticians often assign people random numbers from tables of random numbers especially constructed for the purpose. Mostly, we just try to avoid biasing the results in any way that we know will make a difference.

When the population is too large to list and randomize, statisticians *stratify* the population: they break it down into smaller groups whose proportions in the total population are known, using divisions known to be relevant to the question; then they sample from those groups. Knowing that union members tend to vote Democratic and that a certain portion of voters are members of unions, political pollsters include that same proportion of union members in their sample, sampling as randomly as they can from union members. When they have their quota of union members, they may sample Chamber of Commerce members, who tend to vote Republican, in proportion to their numbers; and so on. By thus stratifying their sample in ways known to make political differences, pollsters reduce biases that might otherwise vitiate their sample.

Sample Size

You may have noticed that I have so far said nothing about the size of the sample. Size is important, it being hazardous to base anything on too small a sample. Suppose that someone reports that 3/4 of those polled expressed preference for the candidate of party Y. It makes considerable difference whether that 3/4 represents three people out of four or seventy-five out of one hundred. Indeed, there is a big difference between three out of four and nine out of twelve. Assuming that 50 percent of the population prefer the candidate, there is a .31 chance of getting three or more people out of four to say they prefer the candidate. By contrast, if the sample contains twelve people, there is only a .07 chance of getting nine or more who express preference for the candidate. That is still a sizeable chance, but it is less than 1/4 the chance of getting the same proportion in the smaller sample. So size matters: randomness being assured, the larger the size of the sample, the more significant the results. Getting seventy-five out of one hundred people to express preference for the candidate would be even more significant than getting nine out of twelve to do so. For this reason, scientific statisticians usually indicate the sizes of their samples, and dishonest or loose-minded people fail to do so. Beware, therefore, of the advertiser who reports, "80 percent of doctors surveyed expressed a preference for brand X" without telling you that only five doctors were surveyed—beware even more of the advertiser who fails to tell you that he conducted thirty-nine other surveys before he got that desired result.

In spite of its importance, however, the size of a sample is less important than how you take it. Randomness counts more than bigness. Assuming randomness, a sample is the more accurate the larger it is, but even a small sample is likely to be fairly accurate if it is random, and a large sample is more likely to be unrepresentative if it is biased. Besides, the greatest increases in accuracy are produced by initial increases in size. A sample of 50 voters is far more likely to be representative than one of 5, but a sample of 250 voters is not proportionally more likely to be representative than one of 50, and there is even less increase in significance enlarging a sample of 250 to one of 2500. It is like horsepower on a powerboat. Five horsepower moves the boat at three miles per hour; ten horsepower moves it at twelve miles per hour, four times the speed for only twice the horsepower; but twenty horsepower does not move it at forty-eight miles per hour; instead, it only ups the speed to eighteen. When you have reached a certain size, you need an enormous increase in the size of the sample to increase its reliability, as you need an enormous increase in horsepower to increase the speed of a boat already moving at a fast clip. By contrast, eliminating bias by increasing randomness always pays off manyfold. So worry about size, but worry less about whether your sample is large than whether it is random.

In summary, generalizing from samples is legitimate when the sample is random enough and large enough and when we don't make the mistake of claiming that the population is exactly like our sample. Under those conditions, there is a very good chance that the generalization will be right. Nothing is certain, of course, but logic is like life in that respect, and life is a gamble. You will lose in the end, and you may lose in the beginning, but you can stay in the game longer if you calculate your chances carefully and hedge your bets accordingly.

Exercises

A. A test can be thought of as a sample of a student's knowledge. Assume a student who knows nothing and is just guessing on a ten-item true-false test. Calculate the probability of his getting (a) all ten items right, (b) at least seven right, (c) half or more right, (d) eight or more right or eight or more wrong.

B. Do the calculations of (A) over again, assuming that the test is multiple choice and that each of the ten items has three choices.

C. Is a student who gets all ten items right on the exams described in (A) and (B) guessing? Justify your answer. What about a student who gets them all wrong?

D. Explain the likely sources of bias in the following polling methods:

1. an attempt to discover the prevailing attitude towards TV by polling those in line at a movie house;

2. an attempt to predict the outcome of the election between a liberal and a conservative by polling a group of intellectuals;

3. an attempt to discover the proportion of red beans to white in a jar without stirring the beans;

4. an attempt to discover the level of voter satisfaction by asking people to write in expressions of opinion.

E. An election is about to be held. Two polls are conducted. One takes a sample of five persons, one of ten. In each case, 80 percent of the sample say they will vote for party X. For each such poll, calculate the probability of getting that large an expression of preference for X on the assumption that exactly half the population favors X. Assume random sampling.

F. Recalculate the chances in (E) on the assumption that only 1/4 of the population prefer X.

329

40 / Experiments

The Null Hypothesis

In the preceding chapter you learned to apply the calculation of probabilities to reasoning from samples. Here I want to teach you how to apply it to estimating the value of an experiment.

We can begin by noting that a sample can be thought of as an experiment. A professor thinks she has taught a student rather well, but she is not sure. So she conducts an experiment to test her hypothesis: she samples the student's knowledge by administering a ten-item true-false exam, reasoning that the student will score high if he knows the material but not if he is merely guessing. The student scores high. In fact, he gets all ten items right. Does his score confirm the professor's hypothesis? Not quite. Don't commit the fallacy of reasoning: "If the student knows the material, he will score high. He scores high. So he knows the material." What the experiment does is disconfirm the *hypothesis* that the student is merely guessing. If he were doing so, it is highly unlikely that he would have gotten all ten items right. In fact, there is only a 1/1024 chance of his having done so. Consequently, the professor can reason validly: "If he was guessing, he would probably not have scored high.* He scored high. So he was probably not guessing." But there are other ways to score high than by knowing the material—cheating, for one. The professor can regard the hypothesis "The student is guessing" as disconfirmed. She

---

* Don't confuse not scoring high with scoring low. Getting all ten wrong by guessing is as improbable as getting all ten right. To get ten wrong you have to be positively misled.

can reject it as highly unlikely. But that does not mean that she may regard her original hypothesis, "The student knows the material," as confirmed. All she may conclude is that the data are consistent with that hypothesis. Before she may conclude more, she is going to have to rule out other possibilities, say, the possibility that the student was cheating.

Should the student score lower on the exam, the professor would not even be able to reject the "guessing" hypothesis with assurance. Suppose, for example, that the score was seven. Since the probability of getting seven or better right just by guessing is .17, the professor cannot safely reject the possibility that the student was merely guessing. The result of her experiment does not have the same significance; it does not clearly settle any questions. Of course, it is still unlikely that the student is guessing, but if he were guessing, there is a .34 chance he would get seven or better right or seven or better wrong;* and that is a considerable chance, not lightly dismissed. The professor will need another test.

This simple example illustrates the logic of all experimental reasoning. One has a hypothesis, a theory, a belief. One would like to have it confirmed; one would like assurance of its truth. Usually, however, one can't get such a confirmation directly. What one can do directly is disconfirm alternative hypotheses. So that is typically what a good experimenter tries to do. He tries to disconfirm the contradictory of his hypothesis. He tries to disconfirm the *null hypothesis*, hoping thereby indirectly to confirm his hypothesis. An experimenter has the hypothesis that p. If he can conduct an experiment having results inconsistent with '$\sim p$', then he will confirm 'p' indirectly by disconfirming '$\sim p$', the contradictory, or null, hypothesis. Suppose our professor thought the student knew the answers, either by studying or by cheating. That would be the professor's hypothesis. Her null hypothesis would then be "The student doesn't know the answers," which is equivalent to "The student is guessing, answering randomly." By disconfirming the null hypothesis, the professor would confirm the hypothesis. (The logic has the form '$p \lor \sim p; \sim p \supset q; \sim q$. So p'.) Of course, the professor may still not know whether the student got the answers by studying or by cheating. Before she can decide, she will need to eliminate one of the alternatives. She will need, say, to proctor the exam. Only then will she be able to conclude from a high score that the student probably knows the answers.

To get a better idea of the logic involved in experimental reasoning, let us look at some more examples. Imagine that eight randomly chosen

---

* In this case, both possibilities must be considered. Think why.

persons are put on a special diet for a year. Suppose that, during that year, seven of the eight have fewer colds than previously; one has more. We are likely to think that the special diet had something to do with the change. That is our hypothesis. We cannot test this hypothesis directly, but we can test the null hypothesis that the reduced frequency of colds was purely a product of chance, with which the diet had nothing to do. So let us see what the evidence against that hypothesis is. We calculate the chances that no more than one person would have more colds by chance. That turns out to be a very small number, 9/256. Such is the improbability of our null hypothesis being true. Since it is such a small probability, we may reject the null hypothesis. We may regard it as disconfirmed.

Have we confirmed our original hypothesis that the diet made the difference? Not quite. To justify that conclusion we also need to eliminate alternative possibilities. If our subjects had been exposed to fewer infections, or had got more exercise, or had had better medical care, or spent more time in the sun, and so on, then our null hypothesis—that the difference in frequency of colds was a chance occurrence—would still have been disconfirmed, but the hypothesis that the diet was the cause of the difference would not have been confirmed. To repeat: don't commit the fallacy of affirming the consequent. Don't reason: "If the diet made a difference in colds, there is a difference in colds. There is a difference in colds. Therefore the diet made the difference in colds." That doesn't follow. The valid form of reasoning is: "If nothing made a difference, there will be no difference. But there is a difference. Therefore, something made a difference." If one or both of two things could have made that difference, we can't conclude that it was one to the exclusion of the other. To exclude other possible explanations, we need to know that there was no other difference in our subjects except a difference in diet.

The Sign Test

One more example. Imagine you have eleven different brands and types of automobiles, two of each. You have two Ford Pintos, two Cadillac de Villes, and so on. The two cars in each pair are made as much like each other as possible, except for one difference: brand X tires are put on one; brand Y tires on the other. The cars are then driven on a track at sixty

CHAP. 40 / Experiments

miles per hour until their tires are worn out. The results expressed in terms of mileage in thousands are given below:

Pair	Brand X	Brand Y	Sign
1	19	20	+
2	16	17	+
3	18	21	+
4	16	17	+
5	20	23	+
6	21	22	+
7	19	17	−
8	20	20	
9	18	21	+
10	19	21	+
11	20	22	+

Is brand Y longer lasting than brand X? Well, the results of our experiment disconfirm the null hypothesis that the differences in mileage are random, the result of chance. Let us see how. First, we go to the column headed "Sign" and count the plus signs and the minus signs, omitting the case where there was no difference in mileage. (That case is like the coin landing on edge and makes no difference either way). We see that there are nine plus signs out of a total of ten signs. The probability of this happening by pure chance is very small. We can see just how small by asking ourselves, "What is the likelihood that one sign or fewer out of ten would be negative as a result of pure chance?" It is the probability that nine or more coins out of ten would land heads up, which is only 11/1024. The probability that only one sign out of ten would be either plus or minus is just twice this figure.* So we can safely reject the null hypothesis that there is no systematic difference between the tires.

Can we conclude safely that Y is better than X? Only if we know that there is no other difference between the cars besides the difference in tires. If, however, we know them to be perfectly matched, disconfirming the null hypothesis is confirming our hypothesis. In that case, the probability that brand Y is more durable is very high.

Such is the *sign test*, the simplest of experiments. Essentially, it comes to this. Change something. See if that makes a difference, up or down. Make a record. Repeat the experiment several times. Then count the

---

* We compute the probability of the least number of signs because it is simpler than computing the probability of the most signs.

333

pluses and the minuses, ignoring the cases where there was no difference. Then take the least number of signs and, using the binomial theorem calculate the probability that so small a number or fewer of such changes, out of the total number of changes, could be the result of pure chance. If the result is a very small probability, you may reject the null hypothesis as unlikely—just how unlikely being a matter of how small your probability is.* Assuming that there was originally a change in only one thing, you may then regard as being confirmed, the hypothesis that that change made the difference the degree of confirmation being the probability figure.

Experimental Controls

This last assumption is important. Taking steps to assure that it is true is known as using experimental *controls*. There are several ways to gain control over the results of an experiment. Each of our examples illustrates a different way. By proctoring the exam, the professor could eliminate the possibility that the student's high score was the result of cheating. In the diet experiment, alternative variables could be eliminated from consideration by randomly selecting the eight subjects, it being unlikely that a group of randomly selected subjects all have anything else in common—unlikely for example, that eight randomly selected people all got better medical care, or all got more sunshine, and so on. (The larger the randomly selected group, the smaller the likelihood.) Finally, the tire experiment managed control by using matched pairs of subjects, pairs of subjects chosen for their great similarity to each other. Then one of each pair was made different in a certain way. Since it is highly unlikely that there is any unnoticed way in which each member of every pair was unlike the other member, we may largely disregard such a possibility. The more unlikely something is, the more safely we can disregard it.

These are some of the more typical ways in which control is effected. There are others, but we shall not spell them out here. More important here than a catalogue of the various ways of achieving control is understanding the reason for having it; so let us review the reason. We have a belief, a hypothesis, a theory. We would like to see it confirmed. We can't confirm it directly by conducting an experiment whose results are consistent

---

* This improbability is the measure of the *significance* of the experiment, and scientists frequently report it by saying that an experiment is significant to, say, 5 percent, meaning that the probability of error does not exceed .05.

with it. To suppose that we can is to be guilty of affirming the consequent. Perhaps, however, we can confirm it indirectly by disconfirming the null hypothesis that the results of our experiment were the product of chance. So we devise an experiment to try to disconfirm this hypothesis. If our results are unlikely to be true consistently with the null hypothesis, we may reject the null hypothesis, may regard it as disconfirmed. Then, assuming the experiment was well controlled to eliminate all other alternative hypotheses, we may regard our original hypothesis as confirmed. Should our controls be deficient, we can make no judgment about the original hypothesis. Experimental reasoning is thus an intricate weaving together of hypothetical and alternative reasoning with probability calculations. It can become extraordinarily complex, but the basic ideas are rather simple.

There is no way to exaggerate the importance of experimental reasoning or, therefore, the need to understand it. Ours is a technological culture. So it is a scientific culture, a culture dominated by science. Many people decry that fact, but few can deny it is a fact. Well, the essence of science is experimental reasoning. So, to understand science and our scientific culture is to have some understanding of what is involved in experimental reasoning, the heart of the scientific method.

Exercises

A. Imagine biases that would vitiate our tire experiment.

B. A feed advertiser claims that his feed, brand X, increases the butterfat content of milk over brand Y, his chief competitor, "in four cases out of five" and offers as proof records on five cows fed one year on brand Y, then fed the next year on brand X. Here are the data:

Cow	Butterfat content	
	Brand Y	Brand X
1	4%	$4\frac{1}{2}\%$
2	5%	4%
3	$4\frac{1}{2}\%$	5%
4	4%	$4\frac{1}{2}\%$
5	$3\frac{1}{2}\%$	4%

Calculate the probability of getting these results by chance. Then discuss whether the results support the claim.

C. Brand Y counters with an experiment in which cows are paired up according to the butterfat content in their milk. Then one of the pair is fed on brand X, the other on brand Y, with the following results:

Pair of cows	Brand X cow	Brand Y cow
1	4%	$4\frac{1}{2}\%$
2	5%	4%
3	$4\frac{1}{2}\%$	5%
4	4%	$4\frac{1}{2}\%$
5	$3\frac{1}{2}\%$	4%
6	4%	$4\frac{1}{2}\%$
7	$4\frac{1}{2}\%$	5%

Calculate the probability of the null hypothesis. Is this experiment better or worse controlled than that in (B)? Why? Does the experiment give good reason to believe that cows on brand Y produce more butterfat?

D. A certain logic teacher claims that his course raises IQs. In support of this claim he offers the following before and after scores of ten randomly chosen students in his course:

Subject	Before	After
1	109	111
2	105	107
3	103	109
4	110	112
5	122	115
6	135	130
7	130	133
8	140	144
9	129	120
10	119	117

Discuss whether his data support his claim.

E. Smith match races five randomly chosen sailors, with these results:

Sailor	Smith's performance
1	wins
2	loses
3	wins
4	wins
5	wins

Do these data support the conclusion that Smith is a better than average sailor? Discuss.

F. Nine overweight subjects take a diet pill for three months. Their weights, before and after, are shown below. Discuss whether the data confirm the hypothesis that the diet pill works.

Subject	Before	After
1	263	240
2	270	265
3	292	300
4	300	312
5	213	193
6	209	199
7	200	208
8	227	212
9	254	240

Design a better-controlled experiment to test the same question.

41 / *Correlations*

In the preceding chapter, we described simple experiments in which we changed one thing to see if it would result in a change in something else. We didn't ask how much change there was, just whether there was change. Often, however, we want to know not whether changing something makes a difference but whether changing it more makes more difference. For example, we want to know whether putting more fertilizer on the crop produces a greater yield, not whether putting fertilizer on the crop produces a yield. We want to know whether each new increase in the quantity of fertilizer will be accompanied by a corresponding increase in the size of the crop. The methods of reasoning you have learned are applicable to this sort of question. You will just find that it is a little more complicated than the simple sort of experiment considered earlier.

Some Terminology

Let us start by learning a little terminology. A *variable* is anything that can differ in value, anything that there can be more or less of. Thus, the amount of water in a glass is a variable: it can vary from none to a full glass. Similarly, height is a variable: it can vary indefinitely upward from nothing. Temperature is a variable: things can vary from very cold to very hot. And so on. Now two variables will be said to be *positively* (or directly) *correlated* if and only if an increase in the value of one is accompanied by an increase in the value of the other. Therefore, height is positively correlated with weight if taller things are correspondingly heavier. Quantity of fertilizer is positively correlated with crop yield if and only if the size of the crop tends to increase as the quantity of fertilizer increases. Two variables are *negatively* (or inversely) *correlated* if and only if an increase in one is usually accompanied by a decrease in the other. For example, weight is negatively correlated with exercise if and only if increased amounts of exercise usually go along with weight loss. Similarly, longevity is negatively correlated with cigarette smoking because smoking more means that you are likely to die sooner. Variables are neither negatively nor positively correlated—that is, they are uncorrelated—if an increase in one is accompanied equally by increases and decreases in the other. That is, things are uncorrelated if it is a question of chance (a coin toss) whether an increase in one will be accompanied by an increase or decrease in the other.

Figures 41.1–41.3 illustrate a high positive correlation, a high negative correlation, and practically no correlation between variables x and y.

Obviously, negative and positive correlation are matters of degree. There is a perfect degree of correlation if you get an increase or decrease in one variable with every increase in the other. There is less correlation if you get an increase or decrease in one variable only 3/5 of the time that you increase the other variable. Obviously, too, the higher the degree of correlation, the more significant it is. If we get a crop increase every time we increase the fertilizer, that means more than if we get a crop increase only half the time we increase the fertilizer. The question is what degree of correlation is significant and how we calculate it.

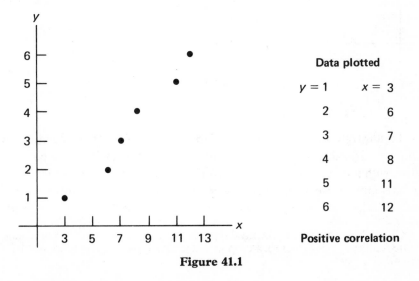

Data plotted

$y = 1$	$x = 3$
2	6
3	7
4	8
5	11
6	12

Positive correlation

Figure 41.1

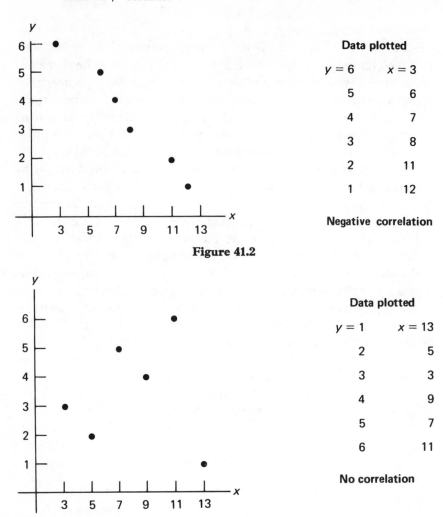

Data plotted

$y = 6$	$x = 3$
5	6
4	7
3	8
2	11
1	12

Negative correlation

Figure 41.2

Data plotted

$y = 1$	$x = 13$
2	5
3	3
4	9
5	7
6	11

No correlation

Figure 41.3

Coefficients of Correlation

To illustrate the process of calculating significance, let us conduct an inquiry. It will go something like this. First, we begin with the hypothesis that, within certain limits,* a new Miracle Manure will yield increasingly greater crops as we use increasingly greater amounts. To test this hypothesis, we select seven plots of land. In all agriculturally relevant respects,

---

* This clause is necessary because there is likely to come a point when adding more fertilizer begins to cause a drop in yield. This is a complexity we will here ignore.

these are as nearly alike as we can make them. They get equal amounts of sun, equal amounts of water, equal amounts of plowing, and so on. The only difference is that we put one ton of MM on plot 1, two tons on plot 2, and so on, adding a ton to each plot. The following table of data shows the results:

MM-tons	Yield-tons	S − L =
1	12	0 − 0 = 0
2	14	1 − 0 = 1
3	16	2 − 0 = 2
4	10	0 − 3 = −3
5	11	1 − 3 = −2
6	13	3 − 2 = 1
7	18	6 − 0 = 6
		13 − 8 = 5

Do these data prove or disprove our theory? Here is how we decide. Our strategy will be to assume the null hypothesis that each increase (or decrease) in yield is purely random, and calculate whether the data are consistent with that hypothesis. The main trick will be to compute the probability that the increases in yield are purely coincidental, not the result of increased doses of MM.

When we first think how to do this, we may be tempted to reason: "There is an increase in plots 2, 3, 5, 6, and 7 but not in plot 4. So there is an increase in five cases out of six. MM must be pretty good cow droppings!" That would be very bad reasoning: there are two fallacies in it. In the first place, the probability of five or more increases out of six happening by chance is 7/64, which would be too high for us to reject the null hypothesis with much confidence. But secondly, and even more seriously, there were not five increases out of six. There were only five out of twenty-one.

How do I figure that? Well, notice to begin with that P_5 yields an increase over P_4 but not over P_3, P_2, or P_1. Similarly, P_6 yields an increase over P_5 and P_1 but not over P_2 or P_3. We want to know whether each successive plot has a larger yield than all the preceding plots, not just whether it has a larger yield than the immediately preceding plot. So we must ask whether P_2 has a bigger yield than P_1, whether P_3 has a bigger yield than P_2 and P_1, whether P_4 has a bigger yield than P_3, P_2, and P_1, and so on. When we have finished comparing a plot with all preceding plots and totalled up the scores, subtracting the number of larger yields on preceding plots from the number of smaller yields on preceding plots, we end up subtracting eight larger yields from thirteen smaller yields, giving us a total of twenty-one comparisons of yield, with a net increase in only five cases. The '5/21' figure was derived accordingly.

The fraction '5/21' is our *coefficient of correlation*. More specifically, it is the coefficient of correlation known as *Tau*. In this case Tau represents the proportion of the net increases of yield over the total number of comparisons of yield. If Tau had been a negative figure, showing a decrease in yield with additions of fertilizer, it would have represented net losses divided by comparisons of yield. Thus, speaking generally, Tau represents the proportion of net changes in the same direction (up or down) to the total number of changes.

Correlation and Causation

To calculate the probability of getting this degree of Tau by chance, we have to compute the probability that there would be thirteen or more increases of yield as against eight or fewer decreases of yield when considering twenty-one increases of fertilizer. Using the binomial theorem again, we calculate that probability as approximately .17.* So there is a 17 percent probability of getting our Tau by pure chance. Since that is a considerable probability, we have no good reason to think that the observed increases in yield were not purely coincidental. For all we know, MM is a waste of money and time. There is no compelling reason to think otherwise. The data are consistent with the hypothesis that MM increases yield, but they are also consistent with the hypothesis that it doesn't. So, if we are wise we shall wait upon more compelling evidence in the form of a higher coefficient of correlation before we conclude that MM makes any significant difference.

That is not to say that we have reason to believe that MM doesn't make a difference. Not having reason to believe something is true is different

---

* Here in detail is our calculation:

$$1 + \frac{21!}{20!\,1!} + \frac{21!}{19!\,2!} + \frac{21!}{18!\,3!} + \frac{21!}{17!\,4!} + \frac{21!}{16!\,5!} + \frac{21!}{15!\,6!} + \frac{21!}{14!\,7!}$$

$$+ \frac{21!}{13!\,8!} = 1 + 203490 + 116280 + 18088 + 20349 + 5985 + 1330$$

$$+ 210 + 21 = 365733.$$

Because $2^{21} = 2097152$, the probability of our *Tau* is $365733/2097152 = .17$.

than having reason to believe it false. The data are consistent both with the hypothesis that the increases in yield were a chance occurrence and with the hypothesis that they were not. The probability of getting five or fewer increases out of twenty-one by chance is less than the probability of getting five or more, but it is still considerable. So, even assuming perfect experimental controls, we can't draw any definite conclusions about the effectiveness of the fertilizer. But, because fertilizer is expensive, that is sufficient for our purposes. If there is no proof of its effectiveness, why use it?

The point would have been quite different if we had used competing brand Super Stuff and got the following results:

SS	Yield	$S - L =$
1	12	$0 - 0 = 0$
2	10	$0 - 1 = -1$
3	14	$2 - 0 = 2$
4	16	$3 - 0 = 3$
5	18	$4 - 0 = 4$
6	20	$5 - 0 = 5$
7	22	$6 - 0 = 6$
		$20 - 1 = 19$

In this case, Tau is 19/21. That is a very high coefficient of correlation. There is practically no chance it could have occurred by accident.* And if our experimental controls are good, SS might indeed be Super Stuff.

Notice that I say "might be," not "is." The reason is that, strictly speaking, a correlation between variables A and B fails to prove that increase in A causes increase in B. Other equally good possibilities are (1) that increases in B cause increases in A or (2) that increases in some third thing, C, cause increases in both A and B. Perhaps the truth is that we put more fertilizer on because the crop increased in yield the last time we did it, not that it increased in yield because we put fertilizer on. Perhaps, without noticing, we got more rain each time we added fertilizer, and the larger crop was due to the rain. Or still more likely, perhaps we tend to care better for crops that we have gone to the trouble and expense of fertilizing, so that we get better crops as a result not of fertilizer but of care. Strictly speaking, coefficients of correlation, like other experimental data,

---

* The probability calculation is $(1 + 21!/20!)(\frac{1}{2})^{21} = 22(\frac{1}{2})^{21} = 22/2097152 = .000001.$

don't so much prove hypotheses as disprove alternative hypotheses. Only this is sure: if the crop increased as fertilizer increased, that can be no accident. Something must have caused something. Our guess is that the fertilizer increased the crop, but that is still a guess, as yet unconfirmed.

The experimental procedure we have illustrated here may be summarized in the following steps:

1. Arrange the data so that increases in one variable are ranked from lowest value down to the highest.
2. Then look at the corresponding changes in the other variable. Going from top to bottom, count how many preceding values on the second variable are higher and how many are lower.
3. Subtract the higher from the lower to get the net number of changes.
4. Divide this number by the sum of all changes, higher and lower. The result will be the coefficient of correlation known as Tau.
5. To calculate the probability of getting a Tau of that size or larger* by chance, use the binomial expanded to the number of your denominator.
6. If the probability is very small, you may reject the null hypothesis and conclude that the correlation is not coincidental, but otherwise not.

Tied Scores

The calculation of Tau and of its probability is a little more complicated when there are tied scores. Look at the following list of data:

V_1	V_2	$S - L =$
2	3	$0 - 0 = 0$
3	5	$1 - 0 = 1$
4	5	$? - ? = ?$
7	5	$? - ? = ?$
9	7	$4 - 0 = 4$
14	9	$5 - 0 = 5$
19	8	$5 - 1 = 4$
20	5	$? - ? = ?$
		$? - ? = ?$

---

* If Tau is negative, less than zero, you will calculate the probability of getting a Tau that small or smaller.

Here there are three measures of '5' on variable V_2. Neither is larger nor smaller than the other two. So what shall we do when we total up the net of larger over smaller scores? Several methods are possible, but the simplest is to calculate Tau twice, first counting each score higher than all preceding tied scores, then counting it lower. Then average the two to get the result.

Applied to the preceding data, this procedure would yield a Tau of .5. Here is the calculation:

V_1	V_2	Calculation$_1$ $S - L =$	Calculation$_2$ $S - L =$
2	3	$0 - 0 = 0$	$0 - 0 = 0$
3	5	$1 - 0 = 1$	$1 - 0 = 1$
4	5	$2 - 0 = 2$	$1 - 1 = 0$
7	5	$3 - 0 = 3$	$1 - 2 = -1$
9	7	$4 - 0 = 4$	$4 - 0 = 4$
14	9	$5 - 0 = 5$	$5 - 0 = 5$
19	8	$5 - 1 = 4$	$5 - 1 = 4$
20	5	$4 - 3 = 1$	$1 - 6 = -5$
Totals		$24 - 4 = 20$	$18 - 10 = 8$

$$\text{Tau} = \frac{20}{28} \qquad \text{Tau} = \frac{8}{28}$$

$$\text{Average Tau} = \frac{14}{28}$$

I leave the calculation of the significance of this Tau to you.

There are other coefficients of correlation besides Tau, and some of them are more useful for certain purposes, but none are so easy to calculate, and their calculation depends on assumptions about measurement that don't need to be made when you are calculating Tau.* So Tau, besides being simpler, has wider applicability. Take the trouble to understand it and you will add an extremely useful tool to the kit of logical tools this book has tried to provide you.

---

* Specifically, they presuppose ratio scales whereas Tau, being a measure of correspondence of rank order, requires only an ordinal scale.

Exercises

(All but the last are imaginary experiments.)

A. Four groups of subjects brushed their teeth zero, two, four, and six times per day. After a year, the average incidence of new cavities for the four groups was three, two, one, and zero. Calculate Tau and the probability of getting it by chance. Did brushing help?

B. The pulse rates of five joggers are on the left; the number of miles they jog per day on the right. Is there a significant correlation? How significant?

Pulse	Jogging miles
65	3
68	2.5
70	2
73	1.5
74	1

C. On the left, four shotguns are ranked according to choke (taper in barrel). On the right is the number of successful shots out of ten. Is there any reason to think the choke helped?

Choke	Successful shots
1	6
2	5
3	7
4	8

D. Figures released by the U.S. Bureau of the Census in 1972 show the following correlation between number of cigarettes smoked per day and percent of women with "chronic conditions."

Chronic conditions	Cigarettes per day
54.5	under 11
59.8	11–20
68.8	21–40
76.9	41 or more

Calculate Tau. Then, assuming these figures to be representative of the population, calculate the significance, or probability, of this Tau. Finally, discuss whether the data justify the warning "Cigarette smoking may be hazardous to your health."

Glossary[*]

adding an alternative, n. Argument of the form '$p \therefore p \vee q$.'

affirming the consequent, n. Fallacious argument of the form '$p \supset q$, $q \therefore p$.'

alternation, n. Statement true if either of its components is true. (Also called **disjunction**).

ambiguous, adj. Having two or more meanings. Can be taken in a way that might be true or in a way that might be false. noun: **ambiguity**.

ampersand, n. Sign of conjunction, &.

amphibolous, adj. Ambiguous by virtue of looseness or insufficiency of grammar. noun: **amphiboly** or **amphibology**.

analyze, v. To break down into components.

antecedent, n. The first component of a conditional statement.

a priori probability, n. Probability assigned before observation.

arbitrarily selected individual, n. Individual selected for a role that any individual could fulfill.

argument, n. An attempt to show that a statement, the conclusion, must be true because certain other statements, the premises, are true.

argument from ignorance, n. Inference depending on what one does not know.

assigning truth values, n. The short method for assessing validity.

---

[*] n = noun, v = verb, adj. = adjective, and adv. = adverb.

347

Assigning truth values to the components so as to make the conclusion false, then checking to see if any of the premises remain true.

association, n. (1) The equivalences '$p \vee (q \vee r) \overset{\text{df}}{=} (p \vee q) \vee r$' and '$p$ & $(q$ & $r) \overset{\text{df}}{=} (p$ & $q)$ & r.' (2) Transformation in accordance with (1).

attributive, adj. As distinct from syncategorematic, descriptive apart from the context in which it is used.

beg the question, v. To argue in a circle; to assume what wants proving.

biased sample, n. Sample that is not random.

biconditional, n. Conjunction of conditional with its converse. Statement of the form 'p if and only if q.'

binomial expansion, n. Result of multiplying out an expression of the form '$(p + q)^n$.'

bound variable, n. Variable in the scope of a quantifier. Hence variable whose reference is determinate.

burden of proof, n. The obligation to prove.

chain argument, n. Argument with conclusions that are themselves premises for further conclusions.

choosing an instance, n. Inference that what is true of everything must be true of any arbitrarily chosen instance.

circular definition, n. A definition that uses the term being defined.

closed sentence, n. Sentence whose variables are all bound.

coefficient, n. The multiple of an expression.

coefficient of correlation, n. Number between $+1$ and -1 indicating the degree of correlation.

collectively, adv. We refer to a group collectively as distinct from distributively, when we speak of it as a group without making reference to its individual members.

component, n. Part of a compound of the same logical order as the compound. For example, a component of a compound sentence is itself a sentence.

composition, n. The fallacy of attributing to the whole what is true of the parts.

compound, adj. Having components.

compression of subjects (or **predicates**), n. The means by which a compound statement is turned into a statement with a compound subject (or predicate).

conditional statement, n. Iffy statement.

conclusion, n. Statement an argument is trying to prove true.

conclusion label, n. Word indicating conclusion.

conclusive, adj. Leaving no doubt.

conditionalization, n. The equivalence '$(p \,\&\, q) \supset r \overset{\text{df}}{=} p \supset (q \supset r)$,' and transformation in accordance with it.

conditional proof, n. Argument of the form $p \,\therefore\, q \,\therefore\, p \supset q$.'

conjoin, v. To assert the conjunction of two statements.

conjunct, n. Component of a conjunction.

conjunction, n. Statement true if and only if all its components are true.

consequent, n. The last component of a conditional statement.

consistent, adj. Could all be true; are all true on some line of the truth table.

constructive dilemma, n. Argument of the form '$p \lor q, p \supset r, q \supset s, \therefore q \lor s$.'

context, n. The circumstances and history of a remark.

contradictory, adj. Having opposite truth values on every line of the truth table.

contraposition, n. The equivalence '$p \supset q \overset{\text{df}}{=} \sim q \supset \sim p$,' or transformation in accordance with it.

contrapositive, n. The contrapositive of '$p \supset q$' is '$\sim q \supset \sim p$.'

contraries, adj. Cannot both be true, but could both be false.

converse, n. The result of converting.

conversion, n. The equivalences '$p \,\&\, q \overset{\text{df}}{=} q \,\&\, p$,' '$p \lor q \overset{\text{df}}{=} q \lor p$,' or transformation in accordance with them. Also, the process of converting.

correlation, n. The relation between two variables that tend to change concomitantly, either in the same direction or in reverse directions.

counterexample, n. (1) An example showing a definition false because it is an instance of the definiens but not the definiendum or vice versa. (2) An example showing an argument form invalid by having the form and true premises but false conclusions.

deduction, n. (1) As opposed to induction, conclusive inference or argument. Valid argument. (2) Inference, or argument. (3) The result of deducing. *deduce*, v. (1) To infer validly. (2) To infer.

definiendum, n. Expression being defined.

definiens, n. Defining expression.

define, v. (1) To say what a word means. (2) To give a word meaning. (3) To give a word more precise meaning.

definition, n. Explanation or assignment of meaning. Statement equating one expression with another.

definitional equivalence, n. As distinct from formal equivalence, equivalence by definition.

DeMorgan equivalence, n. Equivalence of alternation with denial of conjunction of denials or of conjunction with denial of alternation of denials.

denying the antecedent, n. Fallaciously arguing after the manner '$p \supset q, \sim p, \therefore \sim q$.'

destructive dilemma, n. Argument of the form '$p \supset q, r \supset s, \sim q \vee \sim s, \therefore \sim p \vee \sim r$.'

disconfirm, v. To show a hypothesis false.

disjunct, n. Component of a disjunction.

disjunction, n. Statement true if either of its components is true. (Also called **alternation**.)

disjunctive syllogism, n. Argument of the form '$p \vee q, \sim p, \therefore q$.'

distribution, n. The equivalences '$p \supset (q \mathbin{\&} r) \overset{\text{df}}{=} (p \supset q) \mathbin{\&} (p \supset r)$,' '$p \supset (q \vee r) \overset{\text{df}}{=} (p \supset q) \vee (p \supset r)$,' '$p \mathbin{\&} (q \vee r) \overset{\text{df}}{=} (p \mathbin{\&} q) \vee (p \mathbin{\&} r)$,' and '$p \vee (q \mathbin{\&} r) \overset{\text{df}}{=} (p \vee q) \mathbin{\&} (p \vee r)$,' and transformation in accordance with them.

distributively, adv. We speak of a group distributively, as distinct from collectively, when we refer to each of its members.

division, n. The fallacy of attributing to the parts what is true of the whole.

double denial, n. The equivalence '$p \overset{\text{df}}{=} \sim\sim p$,' or transformation in accordance with it.

dummy statement, n. Sentence posing as a statement.

enthymeme, n. Argument with suppressed premise or conclusion.

equivalent, adj. Having the same truth values on every line of the truth table.

equivocate, v. To use one expression in two different ways in the same context. noun: *equivocation*; adjective: *equivocal*.

evidence, n. (1) That which is evident; that which is known without proof. (2) That which is used to prove other things. Hence, the premises of arguments.

exclusive disjunction, n. Disjunction that is false if both components are true.

existence clause, n. Statement that something exists.

existential inference, n. Inference that what is true of one specified thing is true of something or other.

existential quantifier, n. See *particular quantifier*.

experiment, n. Test of a hypothesis.

experimental control, n. Holding some variables constant while allowing others to vary.

exponent, n. The number of times a term is to be multiplied by itself.

extension, n. As distinct from intension, all of the objects denoted by an expression.

factorial, n. The factorial, $n!$, of any number, n, is $1 \times 2 \times 3 \times \ldots \times n$.

fallacy, n. Invalid form of argument. adjective: *fallacious*.

false, adj. Not true.

false dilemma or **false dichotomy**, n. False disjunction.

formal equivalence, n. Equivalence of form.

free variable, n. Variable with undetermined reference; variable not in the scope of a quantifier.

generalizing from an instance, n. Inference that what is true of one thing is true of everything. Valid if the thing is arbitrarily chosen.

going between the horns, n. Denying the disjunctive premise of a dilemma.

good argument, n. Argument that advances knowledge.

grasping a horn, n. Denying one of the conditional premises of a dilemma.

grouping words, n. Words that punctuate.

haphazard sample, n. Sample chosen without regard to how it is chosen.

horseshoe, n. Sign of conditional statement, $\supset$

Humpty Dumptyism, n. Using ordinary words in idiosyncratic ways.

hypothesis, n. Guess at an explanation.

hypothetical syllogism, n. Argument of the form $'p \supset q, q \supset r, \therefore p \supset r.'$

implication, n. That which is implied.

imply, v. To be inconsistent with the denial of. Noun: *implication*.

inconsistent, adj. Not consistent.

induction, n. Nondeductive or inconclusive inference. Generalization.

independent, adj. Consistent with each other and with each other's denial.

infer, v. To conclude that one statement is true believing that another is. Noun: *inference*.

intension, n. As distinct from extension, the characteristics of a thing uppermost in our minds when we use its name.

invalid, adj. Not valid.

joint probability, n. Probability of a conjunction.

knowledge, n. Beliefs that one can prove true, or that are self-evidently true.

lexical definition, n. Statement of how an expression is ordinarily used.

logical constant, n. Everything in a statement form that is not a statement letter: signs like the tilde, ampersand, horseshoe, and wedge. Correspondingly, the parts of a compound sentence besides the component sentences: words like 'not', 'and', etc.

mention, v. To refer to, as distinct from use, an expression.

misplaced middle, n. Fallacious argument of the form $'p \supset q, r \supset q, \therefore p \supset r.'$

modus ponens, n. Argument of the form '$p \supset q, p, \therefore q$.'

modus tollens, n. Argument of the form '$p \supset q, \sim q, \therefore p$.'

naming an unknown, n. The act of arbitrarily assigning a name to one of the unidentified objects of which a given predicate is said to be true. Valid if the name is not already in use.

necessary condition, n. That which must be true for something else to be true.

negative correlation, n. Relation between two variables that tend to change in opposite directions.

nominal definition, n. Supposedly definition of the word, as distinct from definition of the thing; not "real" definition.

null hypothesis, n. Supposition that the events to be explained happened by chance.

obverse, n. The result of obverting.

obversion, n. The equivalence '$p \supset q \overset{\text{df}}{=} \sim (p \,\&\, \sim q)$,' and transformation in accordance with it.

open sentence, n. Sentence with a free variable.

ostensive definition, n. Supposedly definition as the result of pointing at examples.

paraphrase, v. To state differently, or in a different notation.

Pascal's triangle, n. Triangular display of coefficients of terms in expansions of binomials.

particular quantifier, n. (1) The sign '$(\exists x)$.' (2) Any expression doing similar work.

particular statement, n. Statement about some members of the group.

plural statement, n. Statement about more than one object.

population, n. The group from which our sample is selected.

positive correlation, n. Relation between two variables that tend to change in the same direction.

predicate transformation, n. Transformation of a quantified statement by substituting an equivalent open sentence.

premise, n. Statement made by way of arguing that a conclusion is true.

premise label, n. Word indicating premise.

probability, n. The ratio of the favorable to the total number of cases.

proof, n. Good argument.

pseudo dilemma, n. Fallacious dilemmatic form of argument.

quantifier, n. Expression indicating how many of something is being discussed.

quantifier exchange, n. Transformation in accordance with the equivalences, '$(\forall x) \ldots x \ldots \overset{\text{df}}{=} \sim (\exists x) \sim \ldots x \ldots$' and '$(\exists x) \ldots x \ldots \overset{\text{df}}{=} \sim (\forall x) \sim \ldots x \ldots$'

random sample, n. Sample chosen in such a way as to give every member of the population an equal chance of being selected.

real agreement (or *disagreement*), n. Agreement (or disagreement) that is not purely verbal.

real definition, n. Supposedly definition of the thing; not nominal definition.

reductio ad absurdum, n.. Reduction to absurdity. The equivalence '$p \supset (q \ \& \sim q) \overset{\text{df}}{=} \sim p$,' and transformation in accordance with it.

redundancy, n. (1) The equivalences, '$p \overset{\text{df}}{=} p \vee p$' and '$p \overset{\text{df}}{=} p \ \& \ p$.' (2) Transformation in accordance with them.

refute, v. To be invalid, unsound, not good, or false.

representative sample, n. Sample that is sufficiently like the population to insure an accurate generalization.

resolve ambiguity, v. To substitute an unambiguous expression for one that is ambiguous.

rule of transit, n. Rule permitting deduction of one statement from another, but not conversely.

rule of transformation, n. Rule permitting substitution of an equivalent.

salva congruitatae, adv. Saving congruity.

salva veritatae, adv. Saving truth.

sample, n. A portion of the population.

scare quotes, n. Quotation marks used to question the appropriateness of the expression they enclose.

schematize, v. To set out in schematic or diagrammatic form. Noun:

schema; plural: *schemata*.

self-consistent, adj. True in some line of the truth table.

self-contradictory, adj. False in every line of the truth table.

separation, n. Argument of the form 'p & q, $\therefore p$.'

simultaneous substitution instances, n. The results of substituting the same statements for the same letters in different statement forms.

sign of definitional equivalence, n. $\overset{\text{df}}{=}$.

significance, n. Improbability of results occurring by chance.

sign test, n. A count of the number of increases or decreases on one variable that occur upon some change in another, and a calculation of the probability of that number occurring by chance.

singular statement, n. Statement about one thing.

sound, adj. Valid with true premises, and, therefore, true conclusion.

statement, n. Anything that has truth value. Usually a sentence used on a particular occasion to say what is true or false.

statement form, n. Schema (diagram) of statement.

statistics, n. The logic of probable inference. Induction.

stipulation or **stipulative definition**, n. Statement of how one uses, or intends to use, an expression oneself. Also invitation to use an expression in a certain way.

stratify, v. To break the population down into subgroups or strata.

subaltern, n. If 'p' implies 'q' but not conversely, 'q' is a subaltern of 'p', its superaltern.

subcontraries, n. Statements that cannot both be false but can both be true.

substitution instance, n. Result of substituting statements for lower case letters in a statement form.

sufficient condition, n. That which, if true, makes something else true.

superaltern, n. If 'p' implies 'q' but not conversely, 'p' is a superaltern of 'q,' its subaltern.

suppressed, adj. Unstated.

syncategorematic, adj. Not attributive.

tau, n. Coefficient of correlation of rank order.

tautologous, adj. True in every line of the truth table. noun: *tautology*.

tilde, n. Sign of denial. $\sim$.

transformation, n. Substitution of equivalent.

triple bar, n. Sign of biconditional, $\equiv$.

trivialization, n. The equivalence '$(q \text{ v} \sim q) \supset p \overset{\text{df}}{=} p$,' and transformation in accordance with it.

true, adj. (Said of statements, or of what can be stated.) The statement "It is raining" is true if and only if it is raining.

truth conditions, n. The circumstances under which a statement would be true.

truth function, n. Statement whose truth value is completely determined by the truth values of its components.

truth table, n. Tabular display of all possible permutations of combinations of truth values for the components of a compound and for the compound as a function of those components.

truth value, n. Truth or falsity.

uniform substitution, n. Substitution of the same statement for all occurrences of the same letter, and of different statements for different letters.

universal quantifier, n. (1) The sign '$\forall x$.' (2) Any expression doing similar work.

universal statement, n. Statement about everything, or about everything or a certain type.

universe of discourse, n. The group of objects inclusive of all we are discoursing about.

use, v. To utter, inscribe, etc., as distinct from mention, an expression.

use-mention confusion, n. Confusion of using an expression with mentioning one.

vague, adj. Having indeterminate meaning. Not clearly true or clearly false.

valid, adj. Being an argument whose premises imply its conclusion, or the conclusion of such an argument.

variable, n. That which can vary in its reference or value.

Index